Daughters of Dún Iascaigh

Daughters of Dún Iascaigh

A Light on the History of Cahir Women

Edited by

Josephine O'Neill
Karol DeFalco
Mary Caulfield
Breeda Ryan

Edited and Published by Cahir Women's History Group

Published by

Cahir Women's History Group
Cahir, Co. Tipperary

December 2018
ISBN: 978-0-9569861-4-6

Front Cover Illustration: 'Born Seeing' Woodcut by Alice Maher 2014

Back Cover Photo: Eileen McEniry, Mortlestown, Cumann na mBan
(Courtesy of Mary Moloney)

Printed by Lettertec - Carrigtwohill, Co. Cork

lettertec

Dedicated to the women of Cahir
past and present.

Timeline

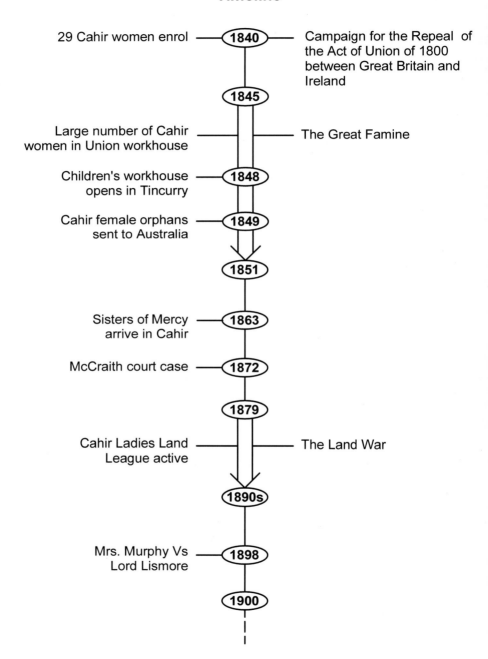

29 Cahir women enrol — **1840** — Campaign for the Repeal of the Act of Union of 1800 between Great Britain and Ireland

1845

Large number of Cahir women in Union workhouse — The Great Famine

Children's workhouse opens in Tincurry — **1848**

Cahir female orphans sent to Australia — **1849**

1851

Sisters of Mercy arrive in Cahir — **1863**

McCraith court case — **1872**

1879

Cahir Ladies Land League active — The Land War

1890s

Mrs. Murphy Vs Lord Lismore — **1898**

1900

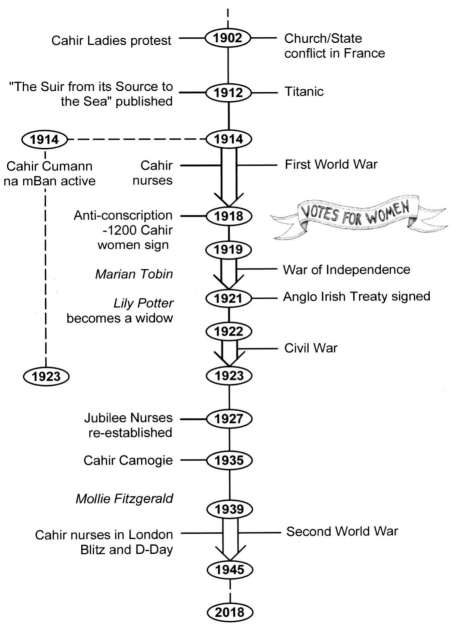

Cahir Ladies protest — **1902** — Church/State conflict in France

"The Suir from its Source to the Sea" published — **1912** — Titanic

1914 - - - - - - - - - **1914**

Cahir Cumann na mBan active — Cahir nurses — First World War

Anti-conscription -1200 Cahir women sign — **1918**

VOTES FOR WOMEN

1919

Marian Tobin — War of Independence

Lily Potter becomes a widow — **1921** — Anglo Irish Treaty signed

1922

Civil War

1923

1923

Jubilee Nurses re-established — **1927**

Cahir Camogie — **1935**

Mollie Fitzgerald — **1939**

Cahir nurses in London Blitz and D-Day — Second World War

1945

2018

Cahir Women's History Group Formed

Layout- Paula Conlan

Here's to strong women

May we know them

May we be them

May we raise them

Amy Rees Anderson

List of Contributors

Mary Caulfield

Mary Byron

Paul Buckley

Karol DeFalco

Edmund O'Riordan

Josephine O'Neill

Ciara Coughlan

Breeda Ryan

Margaret Galvin

Pauline Martin

Annette Condon

Liam Roche

Maurice J. Casey

Jenny Kiely

PJ O'Meara

Sinéad McCoole

Kathleen O'Neill Carroll

Alice Maher

Kevin Sullivan

Mary Beston

Table of Contents

Acknowledgements XII

Women of Cahir XIV

Introduction XVI

Chapters

1. Badamair - Cahir's First Lady 1
2. Dorothea Herbert 3
3. Ladies Who Passed By 7
4. Cáit ó Gharrán a' Bhile - Kate of Garnavilla 11
5. The Legacy of Mary O'Donnell 17
6. Cahir Women and the Great Famine (1) 27
7. Cahir Women and the Great Famine (2) 43
8. Cahir Female Orphan Emigrants 1849 65
9. Cahir Women in the News 1827-1935 71
10. "Don't Start the Revolution Without Me!" 85
11. McCraith vs.Quinn (Quin) 103
12. Author – Artist – Photographer, Laura Mary McCraith 109
13. Women's Role in the Rituals of Death 113
14. Mercy Nuns at the Heart of Cahir 121
15. Mary Dillon's Typical Family 137
16. Our Lady of the Laundry 141
17. From Cahir to the USA 1900-1920 143
18. Women's Occupations a Century Ago 151
19. Cahir Women and the Titanic 171
20. Women Who Spoke Irish in Cahir a Century Ago 175
21. Bridget Ryan - A Nurse of the Great War 181
22. Regret to Inform You 189
23. Cahir Cumann na mBan 193

24. Votes for Women - A Cahir Link 199

25. Marian Tobin and the War of Independence 203

26. Lily Potter - Victim of War 217

27. Mollie Fitzgerald - Irish Republican and Socialist 225

28. Women's Work – Never Done...231

29. Women in Farming..237

30. Reopening Cahir Jubilee Nurse Association in 1927 243

31. Miss Burke and Miss McCoole of Cahir House Hotel 247

32. Sarah Rummel – Cahir Lady of Note..257

33. I was an Upper Housemaid 261

34. Banished Women 265

35. Agnes Sullivan: Show-woman Extraordinaire!...........................269

36. Flying Pigs 277

37. Cahir Woman at Navajo Pow Wow 279

38. The Colonel and the Nurse 281

39. Ellen Conway – Single Mother 285

40. Lillian Grubb Metge - Suffragette 295

Acknowledgements

The editors extend their thanks to all who contributed to the production of *Daughters of Dún Iascaigh – A Light on the History of Cahir Women*. Firstly, we are most grateful to the people who contributed wonderful material about women of Cahir. The time they spent researching, creating, writing and rewriting is greatly appreciated.

We are indebted to Ed O'Riordan. Not only did he contribute chapters, he put in weeks of time, advising, proofreading, editing, and pre-formatting the book. His patience, skill, and constructive involvement throughout this project is not matched.

Alice Maher, a daughter of Dún Iascaigh, donated her artwork, including the image for the cover. We are honoured to have her work included and grateful that she has agreed to launch *Daughters of Dún Iascaigh*.

In addition to writing chapters, Paul Buckley advised other authors, contributed information to their chapters, and proofread. From his vast collection of Cahir memorabilia, he donated many photographs which were used throughout this book.

To the following patrons who supplied necessary funding towards the printing and launch costs, we sincerely thank: Tipperary County Council and the Department of Culture, Heritage and the Gaeltacht; and Cahir Social and Historical Society.

Many others helped in various ways, offering advice, transport, research, typing, photographs, and graphics, etc. We thank you all:

David Walsh, Cahir House Hotel
Jerry Sheehan
Arthur O'Donnell
Councillor Marie Murphy
Colm O'Flaherty
Róisín O'Grady, Heritage Officer, Tipperary County Council
Library staff, Royal Irish Academy, Dawson Street, Dublin
Andrew Haworth, Lettertec, Carrigtwohill, Co. Cork
Shelley O'Reilly, Lettertec, Carrigtwohill, Co. Cork.
Paula Conlon Smith

Michelle O'Loughnane
Catherine Sutcliffe
Sr. Bernadette, Charleville Diocesan Library
Waterford & Lismore Diocesan Library
National Library of Ireland
O'Briens Pharmacy, The Square, Cahir
Mary Guinan Darmody, Local Studies Department, Tipperary Libraries, Thurles
Sharon Fitzgerald, Secretary, St. Mary's Church, Cahir
Margaret O'Grady, Swiss Cottage
Tipperary County Museum, Clonmel
Seamus Martin; Annette Condon; Sr. Eileen Fahey; Liam Roche; Angelina Cooke; Noel Beardmore; Joe Walsh, The Square; Ann Tuohy, Cahir Library; Rosemary Horan; Eilis Condon; Eileen Ryan; Clare O'Reilley; John McCarthy

Women of Cahir

~~~~~~~~~~~

I was recorded in the "Great Book of Lecan"
I brought your children into the world and laid out your dead
I experienced unrequited love
I wrote, painted and inspired song
I kept my out-of-wedlock children
I excelled at sport.
I emigrated
I joined the Whiteboys in a robbery
I ran away with a handsome soldier and was followed
to France
I argued for women's suffrage
I keened at your funerals
I founded convents, schools and hospitals
I spoke Irish
I gave birth to nuns and priests, radicals and revolutionaries
I was regarded as less than the men in my family
I was "churched"
I played camogie
I know that some men saw my worth
I was lost along with my friends on the Titanic
I was the companion of a radical feminist
I toiled on your farms, in your shops and in your homes
I taught in your schools
I was strong because my survival and the survival of my children
depended on me
I nursed in your homes and hospitals
I collected money to repeal the Act of Union
I starved with my children during the Famine

I was sent to the workhouse

I was deserted and sent to institutions

I was deported for prostitution

I asked to be jailed for the Land League

I took landlords to court

I set up and managed businesses

I was a spy

I buried my unbaptised child in unsanctified ground

I took on the French government

I lived in a two-bedroomed house with 14 children, a husband,
a boarder and a lodger

I nursed in two World Wars

I received a telegram informing me of the death of my soldier son

I grew herbs by Cahir riverbank to use for healing

I carried gelignite for the IRA

I had a special female friend and we pretended . . .

I played "God Save Ireland" on my piano while the Black and Tans
ransacked my home

I conducted séances

I collected my husband's body from the IRA under cover of darkness

I opposed conscription alongside hundreds of local women

I performed in a travelling circus

I was the first white woman to attend a Navajo Pow Wow

I stood on the Square in the middle of the night, waiting to be
collected and taken to a mother and baby home

I was sent to a Magdalene laundry

I watched my children taken from me

I was a woman from Cahir.

Introduction

Cahir
Women's History
Group

7 December 2018

Dear Friends,

In early 2017, a small group was formed in the rural town of Cahir (*Cathair Dún Iascaigh*), County Tipperary, with no purpose other than to discuss, and possibly put to rights, the fact that Cahir, in similar fashion to most other Irish towns, identified its past, for the most part, with the history of the menfolk of the town and district. That valuable recording of history was laudable and competently done; but it did seem, from the group's perspective, that women had been neglected in that historical narrative. We had seen glimpses of their presence behind the lives of men, behind the words in chapters of Cahir history, hinted at in archives, recalled to some extent in folklore, and occasionally mentioned in public records.

The group planned to collect, if possible, the histories of ordinary women of Cahir, to collate their stories and perhaps put them in an archive for future researchers. However, it soon became obvious, as material was collected and as volunteers offered chapters and photographs, that hiding the material away in another archive was not the way forward. Archiving the material would not do justice to the women whose stories we were uncovering. The decision was made then to publish the material in December 2018 to coincide with the centenary commemorations of the first election in which women were allowed to vote in Ireland. *Daughters of Dún Iascaigh* was born.

As women's history is so significantly under-recorded, we have attempted to bear witness to previously untold stories. Our contributors come from diverse backgrounds and each one brings knowledge of their topic that is rewarding to read. The editors did not stifle the contributors' creativity by imposing stringent rules and styles, and the chapters are all the richer for that. This is by no means a complete history of the women of Cahir, and we hope that others will go on to fill in the gaps left by us and uncover more. The book does not delve into post-1940 material and we encourage daughters and sons of Cahir to record their own family stories from their parents and grandparents, elderly neighbours and friends.

Travelling through the alleyways of the history of Cahir, we met women who told tales of suffering, violence, anger and silence but also of courage, resilience and survival. We have been humbled, inspired and moved to tears.

These, then, are the stories of those Cahir women, compiled to mark the centenary of the first election in which some women were allowed to vote. It is time for women to leave the margins and footnotes of Cahir history. These are ordinary Irish women. They are extraordinary.

We are eternally grateful to them,

Josephine O'Neill   Karol De Falco

Mary Caulfield   Breeda Ryan

Section from *Great Book of Lecan* which mentions Badamair and Cahir. MS. 23 P 2, f.237v
(Courtesy of the Royal Irish Academy)
Bai banchara oc Find in iarthar Fhemin ar bru tShuire i Cathair Duine Iascaid.
Badamair a hainm. Is ar do gairthear Raith Badamrach

Badamair - Cahir's First Lady
By Mary Caulfield

The ancient name from which the town and parish of Cahir is derived was Cathair Dhúna Iasca, meaning the Cathair (stone fort) of the Dún (fortress or enclosed stronghold) of the Iasca (fish). This is evident from passages in the *Great Book of Lecan* and in *the Annals of the Four Masters*. The earliest mention of Cahir, in an account of the murder of Badamair, is to be found in the *Great Book of Lecan*. This manuscript was written by the Mac Firbisigh family, from Co. Sligo, in the late 14th century. It contains a reference to Badamair, a 3rd century Cahir woman, and this is the first mention in history, to date, of a Cahir female.

When a country wide valuation of property was carried out in Ireland by the British Parliament in the 1830s and 1840s, the surveyors, as well as mapping areas, also compiled field notes. These notes were sent to the Ordnance Survey Office in Dublin and became known as the Ordnance Survey Letters. They give an account of the local history, antiquities and place names of each parish. In relation to Cahir, the Letters refer to the account in the *Great Book of Lecan* and can be paraphrased as follows:- Badamair was the mistress (banchara - lady friend) of a local chieftain, Finn Mac Radamain, and she supplied him with "food and raiment". This man, Finn, killed the brother-in-law of Cuirreach Life, and in revenge, Cuirreach murdered Badamair and plundered the fort of Cathair. (This fort, Rath Badhamhrach, was occupied by Badamair in the 3rd century and later became the site on which Cahir Castle was built.) Finn then went in pursuit of the murderer across the Suir, over the Nore, over the Gowran, over the Barrow, until he saw him sheltered by others. Finn, after having pronounced an incantation on the top of his spear, hurled it at him over the heads of others, struck and slew Cuirreach and carried his head with him early on the next morning to Comairnaic whence he saw Femin to the west. Here he interred the head of Cuirreach and the place has been ever since called Ceann Cuirrich.[1]

According to the *Ordnance Survey Letters*, Cahir is situated in the west of the ancient territory called Maigh Fhemin. The following excerpt in Middle Irish is from the original manuscript which is to be found in the Royal Irish Academy, Dawson Street, Dublin.

---

1   *Ordnance Survey Letters*, 1840, Tipperary, Vol 1, O'Donovan and O'Curry.
     Typescripts of OS Letters edited by Rev. M. Flanagan 1927 - 1930

Bai banchara oc Find in iarthar Fhemin ar bru tShuire i Cathair Duine Iascaid. Badamair a hainm. Is ar do gairthear Raith Badamrach[2]

Finn had a lady friend in west Femin on the bank of the Suir in Cahir. Badamair was her name. That is what is called Rath Badamrach.

(In Memory of P.J. Duggan, Loughloher, Cahir, who first brought Badamair to my attention.)

2   *Great Book of Lecan*, Royal Irish Academy,MS.23 P2, f.237v

Dorothea Herbert

By Mary Byron

The Retrospections of Dorothea Herbert is the published work containing the diary entries of Dorothea (Dolly) Herbert, which draws the reader into the eighteenth century world of the mainly prosperous and comfortable section of society of South Tipperary.

Dorothea was the eldest child of Rev. Nicholas Herbert and the Hon. Matilda Cuffe. Herbert was placed in the parishes of Carrick, Kilmurry, Kilsheelan and Knockgraffon, Cahir. Here, the Protestant rector's family moved among relatives, clergy, gentry and friends, while living on a good income afforded by these parishes.

Much of the income came from tithes collected from the Catholic

Self Portrait by Dorothea Herbert

community in the area, these tithe collections gave rise to much resentment, and lead to opposition in the form of "Whiteboy" violence. The parish of Knockgraffon gave reason for particular concern and may have been the reason why Nicholas Herbert built a glebe house on the edge of the village now known as New Inn. Nicholas was required to live at the glebe house for the duration of three months each year, thereby giving Dorothea time near Cahir most of her life.

Dorothea does not dwell on political matters but does make reference to agrarian violence, by Whiteboys, arising from Rev. Herbert's "tithe activities". The worst attack took place in 1799 when Richard Shortis, one of Rev. Herbert's tithe proctors, along with his wife were murdered at Knockgraffon parsonage.

My poor nurse's body was like a riddle with shots – her neck and arm broke, and other marks of horrid violence - poor Shortis seem'd to have been killed with a hatchet...

– Then they broke all the furniture, and as far as they could, pulled down the house, leaving lighted straw to set it on fire.

Dorothea does not dwell on the cause of such an atrocity, or the reason for continuing hostility in the area.

Place in Society

In *Retrospections*, Dorothea gives us a glimpse of social occasions and dances, and a look at the rules of the time. Place in society was clearly emphasised by an incident over the church pew at Knockgraffon in 1789. Mrs. Herbert had been given the head pew by Mr. Roe, the church warden. One Sunday, Mrs. Robbins, whose father was Lord Massey, entered the church with a group of gentlemen and demanded she be given the head pew. Grudgingly, Mrs. Robbins entered another pew, but the matter did not end there. "After church there was a horsewhipping bout amongst the gentlemen". Andrew Roe of Rockwell sided with Otway Herbert in defence of Mrs. Herbert, while Mrs. Robbins rushed to Rockwell to make "a most bitter complaint". There, Mrs, Robbins maintained that as she was a peer's daughter, that she claimed privilege of seating in the church. "Miss Roe sneered at such a claim" and proceeded to show her in "Lodges Peerage" that "Lord Desart was a much older peer than Lord Massey". Mrs. Herbert's father was the first Lord Desart. After some weeks a duel was to be fought "between the gentlemen of Rockwell and the gentlemen of Hymenstown", but before this could happen, Mrs. Robbins relented and an apology made. "And from thenceforward Mrs. Robbins left the church to ourselves".

Social Standing

The main aim of young ladies of the time was to marry a man of good social standing and considerable wealth. Much depended upon the young lady's own social background. By 1800, many of Dorothea's friends had married, thereby making her feel all the more keenly, her own lack of progress in that area. It is understandable therefore that she became hopelessly infatuated with the young John Roe, of Rockwell Estate. She found him very attractive, and attentive towards her. She was convinced of his interest in her. Referring to several visits to the Roe's household for tea, she says, "John seemed always to seize the boon with animated pleasure, and seemed to entirely devote himself to me for the length of the entire evening".

As nothing definite developed from this particular evening, Dorothea was to find herself obsessing joyfully about John Roe or obsessing miserably about him. Over the next six years she was to continue to meet him at tea at Rockwell, dinners at other houses or at the Cashel Races. At times he seemed to pay her his utmost attention, while at other times seemed not to notice her.

In 1793, she attended "a most flaming Fête Champetre" at Cahir. "We dined under marquees on the lawn and danced all the evening – but again I droop'd like a blighted flower, for the Roes were not there". She describes how Lady Caher danced an "Irish Jig for us in her stockings to the music of an old blind piper", and Lord Caher himself "did me the honour to dance with me". Her observations allow us to see that at some social events, the Herberts were deemed not quite high enough in the social hierarchy.

Marriage Proposal and Broken Heart

Dorothea Herbert received one proposal of marriage from Rev. John Gwynne, a curate near Castletown, close to Carrick. She passed the love letter and marriage proposal to her parents who were infuriated at such a lowly pastor would dare set his sights on their eldest daughter. The man who previously had been warmly welcomed by the Herberts was now forbidden to cross their threshold. Dorothea felt some regret at his treatment, but would never have considered marriage to a pastor of low position. Her heart was broken forever when John Roe married in 1805. She was never to marry. Her infatuation with John Roe led to very low spirits and damage to her physical and mental health. Her younger sisters married, leaving Dorothea at home to seek refuge more and more in her writings, which illustrate her continued passion for John Roe, her isolation and derangement.

Address to Old Maids

Dr. Frances Finnegan presents the poetry of Dorothea Herbert in a publication by Congrave Press which proves her literary skills. Her dread of being a spinster is obvious in the poem, "An Address to Old Maids by One of the Sisterhood":

> *Just enter'd on that certain State of Life*
> *When I no longer girl, am yet no Wife*
> *I mean the Station of a good Old Maid*
> *When Life's more glittering prospects seem to fade*
> *When all its tinsell'd frothy scenes are fled*
> *And to the World we seem as persons dead.*

Sources:

Retrospections of Dorothea Herbert 1770 – 1800
Foreword by Louis M. Cullen
Pub: Town House, Dublin 1988, 2004
First Published in 1929-30 – Gerald Howe, London

Introspections - The Poetry and Private World of Dorothea Herbert
Author: Frances Finnegan
Pub: Congrave Press, Piltown, Co. Kilkenny 2011

Ladies Who Passed By
By Paul Buckley

Marguerite Power (1789 – 1849)

The Gorgeous Lady Blessington, as one captivated admirer described her, worked from 1807-1809 in Cahir Post Office. Born near Clonmel, she was a daughter of Edmund Power and Ellen Sheehy, small landowners. After a short but difficult marriage, she came to work in Cahir for a time. Thereafter she went to England where in the course of her life she became a noted novelist, journalist and literary hostess. In England, she married an Irishman, Charles John Gardiner, 1st Earl of Blessington, thus giving her the title, Countess of Blessington. To cite some of the experiences in her literary life, on her travels she met in 1823, for the first time, Lord Byron, which led her to penning a work entitled, *Conversations with Lord Byron.* She was long a friend of Charles Dickens, a frequent visitor to her home, and a rich abundance of correspondence between both of them survives. It was at her home Dickens first met Hans Christian Andersen. Benjamin Disraeli, later Prime Minister, in 1834 penned a novel, *Venetia,* whilst staying with Countess Blessington

Mabell Ogilvy (1866 – 1956)

Mabell Frances Elizabeth Ogilvy on her marriage in 1886 to army officer, David Ogilvy, 11th Earl of Airlie, became Countess of Airlie. As to her connection with Cahir, it lies in the fact that in the aftermath of their marriage, as a result of her husband being in the army, she found herself residing for a time in Cahir, the town at the time being the location of a cavalry barracks at Kilcommon. They had six children, of whom the fourth, was her first son. He was born in 1893 on the Mall, where she resided. The press recorded the birth of her son, adding she gave birth on a Tuesday morning to a son and heir, with both mother and son doing well. She subsequently described her time in Cahir as the most perfect years of her marriage. Sadly, her married life was relatively brief, for her husband, on the outbreak of the Second Boer War in South Africa, was killed in action at the Battle of Diamond Hill.

In 1902, she became lady in waiting to the Princess of Wales, later Queen Mary, wife of George V. In 1962, there was a publication of her life entitled *Thatched with Gold: The Memoirs of Mabell Countess of Airlie,* it being a work compiled as a result of her keeping detailed reminiscences and memoirs. On a slightly different note, in the aftermath of her departure from Cahir to Newbridge, John A. Ross, Cork considered it beneficial to his business to advertise the fact that he was furniture remover to Lady Airlie and she found his work most satisfactory.

Rose Barton (1856 – 1929)

Rose Mary Barton, from Rochestown, was an artist, a watercolourist who painted landscape, street scenes, gardens, child portraiture and illustrations of the townscape of Britain and Ireland. Rose was born in Dublin in 1856. Her father was a lawyer from Rochestown, County Tipperary, and her mother's family was from County Galway.

She exhibited with a number of different painting societies, notably the Watercolour Society of Ireland (WCSI), the Royal Academy (RA), the Royal Hibernian Academy (RHA), the Society of Women Artists and the Royal Watercolour Society (RWS). In 1911, she became a full member of the RWS. Her works are to be found in public collections of Irish paintings in both Ireland and Britain, including the National Gallery of Ireland and Dublin City Gallery, The Hugh Lane in Dublin, and the Ulster Museum in Belfast. She began exhibiting her broad-wash watercolours painting with the Watercolour Society of Ireland (WCSI) in 1872. She and her sister Emily visited Brussels in 1875, where they received drawing tuition in drawing and fine art painting under the French artist, Henri Gervex. There, along with her close friend Mildred Anne Butler, she began to study figure painting and figure drawing. In 1879, she joined the local committee of the Irish Fine Art Society. Afterwards she trained at Paul Jacob Naftel's art studio in London. In 1882 she exhibited her picture *Dead Game* at the Royal Hibernian Academy (RHA). In 1884, she exhibited at the Royal Academy (RA). Later, she showed at the Japanese Gallery, the Dudley Gallery and the Grosvenor Gallery in London. In 1893, she became an associate member of the Society of Painters in Water Colours, attaining full membership in 1911.

Her watercolours and townscapes became well known in Dublin and London, helped by her illustrations in books of both cities including *Picturesque Dublin, Old and New* by Francis Farmer and her own book *Familiar London*.

Lena Rice (1866 – 1907)

Helena (Lena) Bertha Grace Rice is to date the only female player from Ireland to ever win a singles title at Wimbledon (1890). Lena and her sister, Annie, often played at Cahir Lawn Tennis Club which, towards the end of the 19th century had four tennis courts. L.B. Rice is recorded as being one of those who presented gifts to Miss Cecil Violet Denny on the occasion of her wedding in 1902. She was born in 1866 and was the second-youngest of eight children of Spring Rice and Anna Gorde. Her family lived in a Georgian building at Marlhill, close to New Inn. Her father passed away when she was a child, in 1868. Lena learned to play tennis with her sister, Anne, in their large garden at Marlhill; and both girls entered the Cahir Lawn Tennis club. Lena's first tournament outside County Tipperary was the Irish Championships held in Dublin in May 1889. She lost to Blanche Bingley Hillyard in the semi-finals. In the doubles competition, she reached the final, partnering Hillyard; and in mixed doubles, she won the title along with Willoughby Hamilton. That same year, Lena played at Wimbledon, reaching the final; she again lost to Hillyard. The following year, 1890, only four players participated in the singles event at Wimbledon, with Lena being Wimbledon champion that year, on 4th July defeating May Jacks. After that success, there is no record of Lena again playing tennis at a tournament. Her mother's death in 1891 may have played a part, preventing her from continuing her tennis career. Lena, who never married, died of tuberculosis, aged forty-one in 1907. On her early death, her remains were interred in a small cemetery adjacent to what was the site of the Church of Ireland, New Inn. She was buried with her parents, her brother Samuel and her sister Agnes.

Edel Quinn (1907 – 1944)

Edel Quinn was born in Castlemagner, County Cork, the eldest child of bank official Charles Quinn and Louisa Burke Browne of County Clare. During her childhood, her father's career brought the family to various towns in Ireland, including Cahir. Though her time in Cahir was relatively brief, it was here in June 1916, that she made her First Holy Communion at Saint Mary's Church. A plaque in the grounds of the church commemorates the event. Later in life, she wished to join the Poor Clares but was prevented by tuberculosis. After spending several months in a sanatorium, her condition did not improve so she decided to become active in the Legion of Mary which she joined in Dublin at age 20. In 1936, with tuberculosis soon to take a fatal hold on her, she became a Legion of Mary Envoy, an active missionary to East and Central Africa, departing in December 1936 for Mombasa. She settled in Nairobi having been told by Bishop Heffernan that this was the most convenient base for her work. By the outbreak of World War II, she was working as far off as Dar es Salaam and Mauritius. In 1941, she was admitted to a sanatorium near Johannesburg. Fighting her illness, in seven and a half years she established hundreds of Legion branches and councils in today's Tanzania, Kenya, Uganda, Malawi, and Mauritius. Fr. McCarthy, later Bishop of Zanzibar, wrote of her:

> *"Miss Quinn is an extraordinary individual; courageous, zealous and optimistic. She wanders around in a dilapidated Ford, having for sole companion an African driver. When she returns home she will be qualified to speak about the Missions and Missionaries, having really more experience than any single Missionary I know."*

She died in Nairobi, Kenya of tuberculosis in May 1944, buried there in the Missionaries' Cemetery. The cause for her beatification was introduced in 1956, and she was declared venerable by Pope John Paul II on December 15, 1994.

Cáit ó Gharrán a' Bhile - Kate of Garnavilla
By Paul Buckley and Mary Caulfield

Cáit Ó Gharrán a' Bhile is the title of a poem about Catherine Nagle or Cáit de Nógla, who once resided at Garnavilla, in a residence along the banks of the Suir. She caught the eye of a visiting poet, Edward Lysaght who penned a poem in her honour.

Garnavilla House, the home of Kate Nagle about whom the poem was composed.
(Image Courtesy Carolyn and Diarmuid Healy)

Garnavilla

Catherine (Kate) born in 1783 was the daughter of Richard Geoghegan Nagle and Mary Ann O'Flaherty. She was one of four children born to the couple, her siblings being Jane, Sarah and John. They resided at Garnavilla, on the outskirts of Cahir. Garnavilla is beautifully situated on the banks of the Suir amid lush meadows and rolling parkland. The name comes from *Garrán a' Bhile*, Grove of the Old Tree, if one is to take the translation of Reverend Patrick Power's translation in *Place-names of the Decies*. Another slight variation of the Irish translation is Garrán, from Garraí, meaning grove, and 'bile'- an old Irish word for a sacred, notable, bell tree, hence, the Grove of the Sacred Tree. Bile becomes Bhile, pronounced 'villa', in the genitive case and is not to be confused with the English word 'villa'. The Bell Tree was often found in medieval church sites, such as at Rochestown, close to Garnavilla, where a Nagle tomb is to be found.

Edward Lysaght

Edward Lysaght (1763-1810), was the son of John Lysaght from East Clare. Though both his parents were Protestant, he attended a Catholic school in Cashel run by Doctor Hare. In 1779, he entered Trinity College (BA), Dublin, thereafter attending Oxford (MA). He subsequently studied law at Middle Temple, London. In 1798 he was called to the English Bar, that same year to the Irish Bar. Edward married but his father in law, whom he believed to be a wealthy Jew, turned out to be a bankrupt Christian. Lysaght found himself in debt. Leaving England, he returned to Ireland and built up a practice as a barrister. He occupied his leisure time by writing poems, described as an excellent lyric poet. *A Volume of Poems by the Late Edward Lysaght Esq.* was published in Dublin in 1811. One such poem was *Cáit Ó Gharrán A Bhile (Kate of Garnavilla).* The poem itself, while not widely known today, featured in secondary school textbooks in the past. The story goes that Lysaght was riding his horse on the avenue leading to the house when he spotted Kate at an upstairs window. Inspired by her beauty he wrote a poem in her honour. Though written in Irish, it has seen numerous variations of its translation into English.

Marriage

Kate married in March 1804 Richard Fitzgerald (1766-1840) of Muckridge House, Youghal. Muckridge was leased from a Mr Hobson, with the *1824 Pigot's Directory* informing us this was the seat of Richard Fitzgerald. They had 12 children. Her husband is buried in the family vault at North Abbey Cemetery, Youghal, Co. Cork. Kate died at Belmont, County Kilkenny in March 1862 and was laid to rest in Barron Memorial Cemetery near Belmont.

The Garnavilla residence was later occupied by the Archer-Butler family. In 1889, there was an auction of the house contents in the aftermath of the death of Miss Helen Butler. Thereafter the Nolan family leased Garnavilla in 1892, and in 1915, Walter Nolan Snr bought out his corporate landlord under the Wyndham Land Act Purchase Scheme. The residence is still in the family.

A modest connection with Kate survives in that a family tomb stands by the walls of the ivy covered ruins of Rochestown church, close to Garnavilla. Upon it are the faded inscriptions of family members including Kate's father. However, in more recent times, another connection with Kate came into being. As a result of a severe winter storm in 2014, trees fell in the Inch Field adjacent to Cahir Castle. Stonemason and sculptor, Philip Quinn, from Holycross, carved from one large trunk, a love seat and fittingly inscribed lines from the poem into the wood:

> *'S milse a póg ná drúcht ar rós;*
> *'Sí Cáit mo stór i nGarrán a' Bhile.*

Sources

Cabinet of Irish Literature, Vol. 2, by Charles A. Read

Changing Times, by Edward Mac Lysaght (MacLysaght claimed kinship with the poet Edward Lysaght, author of the poem.)

Maureen Ahearn, "New Haven", Cahir.

CÁIT Ó ŠARRÁN A' ƁILE

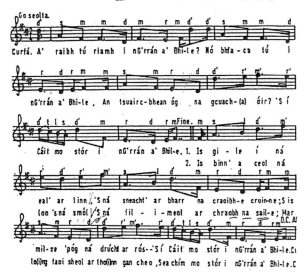

Cáit Ó Gharrán á Bhile

1.
A' raibh tú riamh i nGarrán a' Bhile?
Nó a' bhfaca tú i nGarrán a' Bhile,
An tsuairc-bhean óg na gcuacha óir?
'Sí Cáit mo stór i nGarrán a' Bhile.

2.
Is gile í ná eala ar linn,
'S ná sneachta ar bhárr na craoibhe cruinne,
'S milse a póg ná drúcht ar rós;
Sí Cáit mo stór i nGarrán a' Bhile.

Curfá

3.
Is binne a ceól ná lon is ná smól,
'S ná phileméil ar chraoibh na saile;
Mar loing faoi sheól ar thoinn gan cheo;
'Sea chím mo stór i nGarrán a' Bhile.

Curfá arís

14

Kate of Garnavilla

1

Were you ever in Garnavilla
Or did you see her in Garnavilla
The cheerful young woman of the golden curls?
Tis Kate, my treasure, in Garnavilla

2

She is whiter than a swan on a lake
And than snow atop the round heather
Her kiss is sweeter than dew on a rose
Tis Kate, my treasure, in Garnavilla

chorus

3

Her music sounds sweeter than blackbird or thrush
And nightingale on a willow-tree branch
Like a ship under sail on sea without fog
Sure, I'm seeing my treasure in Garnavilla

Repeat Chorus

The Legacy of Mary O'Donnell
Cahir to Newfoundland
By Karol DeFalco

Mary O'Donnell was the matriarch of a large, internationally influential family that originated in Cahir. Mary was born O'Donnell and married an O'Donnell. She and Thomas O'Donnell were married at Cahir on 9 February 1812 and had thirteen children, all of whom were baptised in Cahir between 1813 and 1838. A Thomas O'Donnell is listed on Barrack Street, Carrigeen, Cahir, in "Griffith's Valuation" of 1852.

After her husband's death, Mary emigrated to Newfoundland, Canada. She went to Newfoundland to be housekeeper for her first child who had arrived at Newfoundland in 1844. Amazingly, of Mary's thirteen children, eight went to Newfoundland; and of the eight, six went into religious life – four as priests and two as nuns. What a legacy!

The oldest child of Mary O'Donnell was Jeremiah who was baptised at Cahir on 11 July 1813. He was ordained in 1840 and arrived in St. John's, Newfoundland, in 1844 to be a curate at the Cathedral of St. John the Baptist. It was Jeremiah for whom Mary was the housekeeper.

From 1858-1860, Jeremiah was a teacher at the newly formed boys' school, St. Bonaventure's College. From there, he was assigned back to the Cathedral of St. John the Baptist. In 1861, while trying to disperse a mob engaged in a demonstration, he sustained a gunshot wound to the leg.

Jeremiah stayed at St. John's until 1868 when he was assigned as Parish Priest to Harbor Main, Newfoundland. He remained there until his 1882 retirement at which time he relocated and resided with his brother, Fr. Patrick, at Conception Harbor, Newfoundland. Jeremiah died there on 27 February 1891. His funeral left from the Railway Depot, and the "*Evening Telegram*" of March 2, 1891 (Monday) carries this account:

O'DONNELL, Very Rev. Jeremiah
The Whole People Mourn Him.
A great multitude of people went down to the railway depot this afternoon to pay their last tribute of respect to the late **Very Rev. Jeremiah O'Donnell**, by accompanying his remains to their last resting place - Belvedere. The train did not arrive until a quarter to four.

In addition to Jeremiah, Mary's three other sons who became priests in Newfoundland were:

*Richard O'Donnell, who was baptised by Fr. Patrick McGrath at Cahir on 31 March 1822. The sponsors were James Lonergan and Mary Cody. Richard was still in Cahir in 1847 when he sponsored a niece at her baptism. By 1861, Fr. Richard was in Newfoundland and was with his brother, Fr. Jeremiah, on the night of 13 May 1861, when Jeremiah was wounded, trying to disperse a demonstration in St. John's. Fr. Richard became parish priest at Assumption Parish, St. Mary's Bay, Newfoundland, and the church's baptism register shows him performing the sacrament from 1871-1883. He died at Newfoundland on 16 May 1889. One of the communities under his administration was Mussel Pond which changed its name to O'Donnell's, apparently in appreciation of the priest from Cahir.

*Patrick O'Donnell studied at Mount Melleray, Co. Waterford, and then at St. Patrick's College in Carlow from 1858-1860. He emigrated to St. John's, Newfoundland, in 1861. For two years, he studied there at St. Bonaventure's and was ordained in 1863 at the Cathedral of St. John's. Having been assigned to Harbor Main, Patrick was a curate for his brother, Jeremiah, and later became parish priest there, serving from 1863 to 1877. On 16 January 1906, Fr. Patrick O'Donnell died at Avondale, Newfoundland,leaving a house and stable in that community as well as a thirty-one acre farm called 'Mount Patrick' at Dock Ridge. Fr. Patrick is buried under the floor of the church at Harbor Main.

*David O'Donnell, who was baptised on 7 June 1838 at Cahir, was the youngest of the thirteen O'Donnell children. Sponsors were John Cody and Catherine Morrissey. He was ordained at St. Patrick's College in Carlow in 1864. Like his family members, David emigrated to Newfoundland where he served as parish priest of Witless Bay. A young Fr. David died unexpectedly at Witless Bay, Newfoundland, on 25 April 1871, aged 32. He is buried at Belvedere Cemetery, St. John's, Newfoundland

O'Donnell Nuns

As for the two O'Donnell nuns, who were daughters of Mary O'Donnell and sisters of the above four priests, the older was Alice O'Donnell. She was baptised at Cahir by Fr. Stephen M. Lonergan on 2 October 1831. Sponsors were John McGrath and Margaret Hanrahan. In 1854, Alice entered the Presentation

Order at St. John's, Newfoundland, and was professed at Cathedral Square in 1856 as Sr. Mary Bernard. In 1860, Sr. Mary Bernard was sent to Witless Bay, Newfoundland, to found a Presentation Order convent and became Mother Superior there, serving in that position until 1916. After a long life, she died on 6 April 1924 and was buried at Witless Bay. From the Presentation Archives, here are Sister Mary Bernard's own words, describing the Presentation Order at Witless Bay on Sunday June 3, 1860:

> Sunday 3rd June 1860 was a day that can never be forgotten by the people of Witless Bay and its neighbouring settlements, who witnessed its glorious manifestation of faith and devotion. It was for a long time the intention of his Lordship Dr. Mullock and the venerable Dean Cleary to introduce here a community of the Presentation Order to take charge of the education of the poor female children and to thus scatter in this locality some portion of that blessed seed which has been so beautifully distributed over most parts of the island.... The road for miles leading to the place was completely lined with people from the earliest hours and triumphant arches were erected at various places with flags in countless numbers, giving the most holiday-like and joyous appearance of the whole line of country and to the settlements. As soon as the carriages with the Clergy and Nuns came in sight, the people demonstrated their joy in a degree which I have never seen surpassed. It seemed as if every man in Bay Bulls and Witless Bay had brought out a sealing gun. The firing was so well and spiritedly kept up along the lines, and shouts of welcome and gladness, rung from the whole people with such heart and soul as showed their intense gratitude for the great boon then conferred upon them and their just estimation of its value. I have never seen His Lordship [Bishop Mullock] on any such occasion received by his people with greater enthusiasm. Surely such a people prove themselves worthy of the solicitude and affection he bestows upon them and which cannot be better proved than in the establishment of such Institutions of that of Witless Bay has now the happiness to possess.

The Witless Bay convent is now a listed historical building, and according to Newfoundland Built Heritage, "Holy Trinity Convent and Chapel is historically valuable because of its long history in the community of Witless Bay. In 1860, when the convent was established, an attached building was used as a school for girls and was run under the authority of Mother M. Bernard O'Donnell and staffed by the Presentation Sisters. Initially school accommodations were provided for one hundred children and within the first year, ninety two were enrolled. This school helped form and maintain the Roman Catholic education system in the community, under the guidance of the sisters. The school building has since been demolished, but the convent and chapel associated with it remain." (Photo courtesy of Nat Bourke and Marie O'Connor)

The younger of the two Cahir O'Donnell sisters, who went into religious life in Newfoundland, was Bridget. She went into the Presentation Order in 1858 and was professed in 1861 as Sr. Mary Joseph. She became Mother Superior at Renews, Newfoundland. The 1877 annual of the Renews convent reported that, "...the Convent School was opened. Sixty five children were in attendance.", and according to the Municipal Heritage Site, "By the following summer there were more than one hundred pupils registered. Some of the sisters who taught in Renews are buried in the Presentation Cemetery, including Sisters O'Donnell, Mulally, Gealy and Kineally who were among the first sisters at convent."

Renews Cemetery

Both nuns and parish priests are buried at the Presentation cemetery at Renews:-

This small burial plot is located on a knoll behind Holy Apostles Roman Catholic Church in Renews and is generally referred to as the Presentation Cemetery. It is the final resting place of two priests and twelve nuns who served this parish from the mid 1800s onward. The Presentation Sisters initially established a convent at Admiral's Cove (now Port Kirwan), Fermeuse in 1853. The first Presentation Sisters, mainly from Ireland, arrived there under the patronage of the local parish priest, Father James Murphy. About 1867, Father John Walshe moved the parish centre from Admiral's Cove, Fermeuse to Renews. However, it appears it was not until 1876 that the Presentation Sisters were relocated to the new convent that had been for them built a short distance from the parish church in Renews.

(Newfoundland's Grand Banks website)

Sr. O'Donnell's gravestone reads:-

O'DONNELL

MOTHER JOSEPH

DIED JAN. 19, 1896

AGE 61 YEARS

R.I.P

Two Additional O'Donnell Children

In addition to the above six O'Donnell children who entered religious life in Newfoundland, two more of Mary O'Donnell's thirteen children emigrated to Newfoundland. Her son, Thomas, had been baptised at Cahir on 18 July 1829. Sponsors were James Donnell and Mary Morrissey. Thomas was in Newfoundland by 24 February 1857, when he married Mary Theresa Little, the sister of Newfoundland's first Prime Minister, Philip F. Little, who served in that office from 1855 to 1858. Thomas and his wife had four children, born between 1857 and 1864. In 1864, Mary Theresa died; and about five months later, Thomas was dead, leaving the four children as orphans, aged 0-7. The parents were buried in Belvedere Cemetery, and the children were placed in the care of their mother's family. Three of the children died at the ages of 14, 20, and 23 and were buried with their parents. The fourth child is believed to be Alice O'Donnell who was the heir to the 1906 estate of her uncle, Fr. Patrick O'Donnell, of Harbor Main.

The last in this list of Mary O'Donnell's eight children who emigrated from Cahir to Newfoundland was Margaret. She married Michael Leamy in Cahir on 6 October 1842. Witnesses were John O'Donnell and Helen O'Donnell. The couple had seven children baptised at Cahir between 1845 and 1858. Although in 1852 this family appears to be living at Ballynamona, Cahir, for the first ten years of the marriage, the couple resided at Barrack Road where their first three children, including a daughter named Mary, were born. Mary was baptised at Cahir on 21 June 1847. Sponsors were Richard O'Donnell and M. Fogarty. By 1865, Mary was in St. John's, Newfoundland, where she entered the Presentation Convent at Cathedral Square on the 8th of February. According to the 21 February 1868 edition of "*Waterford News and General Advertiser*", reporting from Newfoundland, "Miss Leamy, daughter of Michael Leamy of Cahir", was professed on February 11th, bringing a granddaughter of matriarch Mary O'Donnell into religious life. The reception took place at the Presentation Convent, St. John's, Newfoundland. She had been invested in a black veil and took the name Sister Mary John Baptist. The newspaper article suggests that Miss Leamy is the niece of Rev. Fr. O'Donnell "of this mission". According to the archives at Presentation Convent, St. John's, Sister M. John Leamy died on 6 April 1916 and was buried at Witless Bay next to her aunt, Sr. M. Bernard O'Donnell. Sister Leamy was the third of the descendants of Cahir's Mary O'Donnell to be in Witless Bay, Newfoundland.

The cemetery at the Roman Catholic church in Witless Bay, showing the gravestones of two descendants of Cahir's Mary O'Donnell: Sister M. John Leamy (granddaughter) and Mother M. Bernard O'Donnell (daughter). Other headstones show the surnames Kelly, Hanrahan, O'Driscoll, Walsh, Noonan, and Power, indicating an Irish predominance. (Photo courtesy of Nat Bourke and Marie O'Connor)

What was Newfoundland like at the time of the O'Donnells' arrivals? Three of the above O'Donnell descendants – David O'Donnell, Alice/Sr. Mary Bernard O'Donnell, and Mary/Sr. Mary John Leamy - resided at Witless Bay, Newfoundland; and Wikipedia gives a taste of life of Irish Catholics in Witless Bay: Irish fishing servants had begun to arrive in Witless Bay in the 1700s, yet in 1755 Roman Catholicism was still outlawed and the priests disguised themselves as fishermen. By 1836, the population of Witless Bay was 542 of whom 540 were Roman Catholic, but it wasn't until 1845 that the first Roman Catholic church was built. In 1860, Presentation Sisters, including Alice (Sr. Mary Bernard) O'Donnell, arrived at Witless Bay and opened the convent and girls' school.

Mary O'Donnell – Matriarch

The matriarch of this impressive Cahir family, Mary O'Donnell, died on 14 December 1875 at the residence of her son, Fr. Jeremiah. Her death record lists her as 84 years of age. She was buried at Belvedere Cemetery and rests there with at least sixteen members of her family, including children, grandchildren, and great grandchildren. Her obituary follows:

Royal Gazette December 21, 1875 (Tuesday)
DIED. ... On Tuesday last, at Harbor Main, aged 82 years, Mary, the widow of the late Thomas O'Donnell, Esq., late of Cahir, County Tipperary, Ireland. The lamented and venerable lady was the mother of the respected and esteemed Clergymen - the Very Rev. J. O'Donnell, the Rev. R. O'Donnell, and Rev. P. O'Donnell, and of the deceased Rev. D. O'Donnell, and of the Superiores, at present, of two Houses of the Presentation Order of Nuns in this country. - R.I.P.

Interestingly, the obituary gives only the names of her sons who are priests. The names of the nuns and Mary's other children are omitted.

In 1999, Bert Riggs, an archivist with the Centre for Newfoundland Studies at Memorial University, reflected on Mary O'Donnell in a column called "A Backward Glance" in the December 14th edition of the "St. John's Telegram". In his column, Riggs referred to Mary as "in all likelihood a hardworking woman, dedicated to her family and to her church, very similar to thousands of other Irish women who emigrated to Newfoundland. In one way, though, Mary O'Donnell was quite remarkable....The O'Donnells made quite a mark on the religious life of Newfoundland. Several nieces and nephews also joined religious orders in Newfoundland, Ireland, and the United States. It is highly likely that no other family has had so many of its siblings enter religious orders, and it is equally unlikely that their feat will be matched in the years to come." AMEN!

~~~~~~~~~~~~~~~~~

Note:-
Coincidentally, according to the Irish Times of 1 August, 2017, Sr. Emma Rooney, originally from the Presentation Sisters' Newfoundland Province, has recently taken up residence in Cork's inner city at Nano Nagle Place where immigrants are given free English lessons. The circle of life: Cahir to Newfoundland and back to Ireland

Sources:
1. Transcriptions of baptism records from St. Mary's, Cahir
2. Transcriptions of marriage records from St. Mary's Cahir
3. "A Backward Glance", *St. John's Telegram* (Newfoundland), Dec 14, 1999
4. *Griffith's Valuation* of Cahir, 1852

5. *Evening Telegram* (Newfoundland), March 2, 1891
6. Transcriptions of baptism records from Assumption Parish, Newfoundland
7. Transcriptions of headstone inscriptions at Belvedere Cemetery, Newfoundland
8. Personal correspondence with Wanita Bates, Presentation Convent archives, Newfoundland
9. Facebook page for "Newfoundland Built Heritage"
10. 1877 annual of the Renews convent, Newfoundland
11. Renews, Municipal Heritage Site
12. *Waterford News and General Advertiser*, 21 February 1868
13. Presentation Cemetery, Municipal Heritage Site
14. "An Irishwoman's Diary", Colette Sheridan, *Irish Times* August 1, 2017
15. Wikipedia, Witless Bay
16. *Royal Gazette*, Newfoundland, 21 December 1875
17. *Harbor Grace Standard & Conception Bay Advertiser*, 30 August 1879
18. *The Origin and Political Activities of the Orange Order in Newfoundland 1863-1890*, Eleanor Kyte Senior
19. Newfoundland's Grand Banks Website

Cahir Women and the Great Famine (1)
Starvation - Soup Kitchens – Charity - Picnics
By Ed O'Riordan

How could I look to you mother,
how could I look to you
for bread to give to your starving child
when you were starving too?

(Amelia Blandford Edwards 1831-1892)

Destitution and wretchedness didn't arrive suddenly to the women of Cahir district with the coming of the potato blight at the beginning of the Great Irish Famine in 1845, nor did those afflictions disappear magically on a date in 1850 when historians say the Great Hunger was over. Hunger and desperation had been women's constant assailants for many decades, and a random search through pre-famine archives reveals scenes that one might usually expect to read about during the cataclysmic years of the 1840s. A reoccurring topic in Famine and pre-Famine publications is one of women with their children taking an active part in accessing food - whether this entailed labouring, seeking alms, scavenging in fields, or plundering the flour-carts.[1] Many of the Great Famine images from the *Illustrated London News* depict women working in fields, often searching for potatoes, or starving women with dying children begging for food or queuing at soup kitchens or the workhouse door. Famine poetry frequently highlights the effects of lingering hunger from a woman's and mother's viewpoint. Cahir was

Woman with dying child.
Illustrated London News, 13 Feb. 1847

---

1 Official reports and newspaper accounts didn't always reveal the breakdown by gender. It is necessary to accept that the famine reports of crowds, hordes, groups, etc., are female as well as male.

one of several parishes in Clogheen Union, Co. Tipperary, and an 1849 report - mentioned in these pages - shows that the number of women 'inmates' in the Union Workhouse at Clogheen was higher than that of men, and the number of 'Paupers' from Cahir parish in the workhouse was higher than any other parish.

Lady Glengall's Evidence 1823

In order to understand the condition of the female population of the Cahir district in the decades prior to the Great Famine, it is worth looking at the important evidence of the then Hon Lady Glengall in the July 1823 *Report on the Employment of the Poor in Ireland.* Lady Glengall informed the commissioners that she had been instrumental in establishing the Fever Hospital and a factory for the employment of females in her neighbourhood who had no other means of employment. In her opinion, both the males and females were anxious for employment, but the women were less liable to work for unsuitable wages. She said :-

> The industry of the female peasantry is impeded by various causes. Their poverty places implements of labour out of their reach, and the general poverty by which they are surrounded renders it impossible to procure employment. They are anxious to procure spinning wheels, hackles and looms, and everything of that kind but they are out of their reach. They are in a state of great destitution; they are perfectly naked as to clothing, and without any comfort of convenience, or any possible way of gaining their livelihood; and unfortunately they see people naked, and with nothing in the world but a blanket to sleep on, without a bed to lie on; and they are so used to seeing it, that they are not sensible that that is not the usual and proper way for them to exist.[2]

Lady Glengall went on to say that she now had an establishment at Cahir for the employment of females and it had been of great benefit. In six months the employed females were cleaner, habits were improved, and they were anxious to be helped. There was no further mention of those who were still unemployed. *Pigots Directory*, describing Cahir, stated in 1824 that ....

---

2   *Report on the Employment of the Poor in Ireland.* 1823. Evidence of the Hon. Lady Glengall.

this ...handsome, thriving little town... can boast of numerous charitable institutions, the most extensive and beneficial of which is a linen factory, under the protection of the Cahir local association. The evils arising to females from the want of employment, induced this committee, in November 1820, to turn their attention to the foundation of a spinning school. Earl Glengall having gratuitously supplied one hundred and fifty wheels, a few trifling subscriptions were made for the purchase of flax.[3]

Starving Creatures 1827

In 1827, almost two decades before the 'Great Famine', *Saunders News-Letter* described a 'recent event' two miles from Cahir during which Mr Going's flour carts were stopped and twelve bags of flour stolen. These were not highwaymen, or desperados, nor was it a gang of profiteering men intent on plunder. The newsletter informs us that the attackers – who did not hurt the carriers – were 'starving creatures', and actively taking part in the robbery were 'wretched looking' 'women and children.' The flour was immediately divided among the starving people.[4] Approximately twenty years later, in 1846, the same article would have sufficed to describe a similar event at Woodroofe, Cahir, when flour carts from the mills were attacked by a 'mob of men, women and children' who made off with eleven bags of flour. The usual military escort had been withdrawn the day before.

---

3   *Pigot & Co's Provincial Directory of Ireland, 1824*
4   *Saunders News-Letter*, 12 June 1827

Woman and her children accompanying the men watching the meal cart from Cahir which is laden with sacks of meal. *Pictorial Times* October, 1847

Evidence of Rev. Fr Tobin P.P. Cahir 1836

In 1836, a 'Poor Enquiry' had been held in Ireland to investigate the national and interminable question of poverty in Ireland. Rev. Fr. Michael Tobin, Parish Priest of Cahir and Mortlestown, responded to the commissioners' questionnaire and stated that "Women and children find no employment but in harvest, the weeding season, in spring, and particularly at the digging of potatoes." He said further that:-

> Bad potatoes and salt is the diet of the majority; a few, when employed, endeavour to provide a little sour milk; their clothing in general is coarse and shabby; numbers are obliged to remain indoors on Sunday for the want of covering.[5]

---

5   (Poor Enquiry 1836, Parliamentary Papers Volume 31) Supplement of Appendix (D) First Report of Commissioners for inquiring into the Condition of the Poorer Classes in Ireland, 1836.

Distress on Glengall Estate

In April 1846, the *Dublin Evening Post* carried a report on one of the many attacks on the Cahir flour carts and on the bakeries in Clonmel. If it had not been for the personal intervention of Mr Bernal Osborne of Newtown Anner who promised the rioting crowds food and employment, and made good on his promise, the riots and attacks might well have been more serious. For most of Cahir District the landlord was The Earl of Glengall, and it was to him that women and their families looked for support when the potato crops failed. In Cahir, as elsewhere, the response of the landlord to the Famine dictated just how those families survived.

According to the above mentioned *Evening Post*, the Lieutenant of County Tipperary - Lord Donoughmore - was absent at the time of the April 1846 riots, and in his absence, the Earl of Glengall was Vice Lieutenant of Tipperary; but both these noble Lords, according to the *Post*, were supporters of the notion that all reports of famine and hunger and potato shortage were fabricated.[6] The following week, The *Freeman's Journal* sent an investigative reporter to South Tipperary, and he described what he had found there. In Cahir, he met Rev. Stephen Lonergan - coadjutor to the parish priest, Rev Fr. Tobyn. Fr. Lonergan gave a "very deplorable account of the wretchedness that prevails in and about the town." The reporter confirmed the description and wrote, "...this, coupled with my own observation, leaves no doubt of the fact." Destitution outside of the town was also dreadful, many had no food while others had barely enough for a couple of weeks. Responding to the cry that nothing was being done by the landlords, the reporter wrote:-

> The Landlords are doing nothing – so it is said, but this is a mistake. The following notice, which is posted on every corner of the town of Cahir, and on the Post Office window, from whence I copied it, proves that something is being done by the landlords:-
>
> **Notice. The Tenantry on the Earl of Glengall's estate, resident in the manor of Cahir, are requested to pay into my office on the 12th of May, all rent, and arrears of rent, due up to the 25th March last, otherwise the most summary steps will be taken to recover same. John Chaytor.[7]**

---

6   *Dublin Evening Post*, 16 April 1846
7   *Freeman's Journal*, 24 April 1846

"Commentary on this is superfluous," wrote the *Pilot* newspaper in a similar article, regarding that notice, on the same date, adding:-

> In truth, the landlords at this juncture, with a few honourable exceptions, are fully carrying out, by their apathy and neglect, the character Irish Landlordism has been earning by extermination.[8]

The *Journal* reporter went on to say that he had heard that the Countess of Glengall was charitable, kind and humane and had given twenty five pounds to the Relief Fund which had been started by the shop keepers and others of the town and the better off farmers, while the Earl gave fifty pounds out of his forty thousand per year rent-roll. Yet, the reporter wrote "...in all Tipperary I have not met with so much distress as there is at this moment existing on his estate."[9]

Lord Glengall's Praiseworthy Example

It is to be expected that different newspapers of the time with their different allegiances would pen descriptions shaded by their own particular bias, and it is possible to find benevolence as well as lack of charity in descriptions of Lord Glengall in the different newspapers. The improvement works carried out on Cahir town itself were widely acknowledged by the press and one report acknowledged the Earl's patronage of the Temperance movement in Cahir. Indeed, in 1840, Lord Glengall's praiseworthy example was noted after he had provided an excellent dinner to the teetotallers of Cahir on which occasion the special guest was Fr Mathew.[10] In the *Limerick Chronicle* in March 1846, it was noted that Lord Glengall generously gave land free of charge for the building of the New Line road between Cahir and Clogheen where the road passed through his estate, in order to give employment to the labourers.[11] In December of that same year, when thousands of people had gathered throughout South Tipperary to protest at the lack of food and employment, many of the protests resulted in shops being ransacked for bread. In Cahir, they 'assembled in masses', to protest at the non payment of those who had obtained relief work under the Board of Works. The Earl of Glengall intervened and pacified the angry crowd and then wrote to the Board, demanding the immediate payment of the workers.[12]

Despite this benevolence of the Earl and Countess Glengall, the *Freeman*

---

8   *The Pilot*, 24 April 1846
9   *Freeman's Journal*, 24 April 1846
10   *Freeman's Journal*, 16 Nov 1840.
11   *Limerick Chronicle*, 11 March 1846.
12   *Cork Examiner*, 11 Dec. 1846.

special reporter had declared in April 1846, that the misery and distress at the total loss of the potato crop at Barne, Lough Lougher; and New Inn was worse than he had anticipated. He visited the small fields at Barne to speak with the people who were crying at the complete loss of their crop. When he asked what they would now do, they replied *"God is good, we have hope still".* Unfortunately for most, that hope was misplaced; after all, it was believed by many in positions of authority that the loss of the potato crop had been caused by Divine Providence.

Destitution in Ireland – Failure of the potato crop.
Pictorial Times 22 August 1846.
(Courtesy of Ireland's Great Hunger Museum, Quinnipiac University, Hamden, CT)

Eight months after the *Freeman's Journal* report, a correspondent of the *Cork Examiner,* visited Clonmel and Cahir. He described the awful circumstances near Clonmel of the half naked, starving, wretched women and children "troops of wretched children whose situation was equal to that of their unfortunate mothers, round whom they thronged in wild despair, uttering the most piteous lamentations for protection and food." The women and children had, without any male accomplices, stopped and plundered the flour carts coming into Clonmel. The writer then recounted a conversation he had with a 'gentleman from Cahir' who informed him that the mortality in and about Cahir was 'really alarming'. It was suggested by the gentleman that coroner's inquests weren't held on the deceased people because they did not die suddenly, most of the deaths being a result of lingering starvation and exhaustion.[13]

1847 saw the Waterford to Limerick Railway company making progress on the new rail-line, and at the half-yearly meeting in September, the Earl of Glengall was singled out for praise by the chairman of the company. The Earl of Glengall, he said, had assisted and facilitated the company in their endeavours in the Cahir area. In his reply, the Earl stated that in Cahir, 800 men were now employed on the railway works on wages never before heard of. If the railway did not continue to employ the thousands presently employed, he said, the upkeep of those men and families would fall upon the landlords by an increase in Poor Law rates.[14] It was welcome news indeed for the women of Cahir whose fathers, husbands, sons and brothers needed the employment offered by the railway company. And how fortunate for race-goers in 1848 when four hundred of the rank, fashion and beauty of Limerick city and neighbourhood availed of the new train-line to the Tipperary racecourse which was already 'densely crowded with rank and fashion' – of County Tipperary, presumably - when they arrived.[15]

Soup Kitchens

Prior to the establishment of the official Soup Kitchens in 1847, charitable food distribution centres had already been set up in the Cahir area, mostly by the members of the Society of Friends in 1846. For the starving women and their families in the Cahir area, it was, obviously, destitution that drove them to the soup kitchens. For the more affluent women of Cahir, it was a deep sense of decency, charity and benevolence that brought them there; the destitute women and the affluent women being brought together, possibly for the first time in their lives, by the cataclysmic circumstances which existed at the time. On three days of the week, the Countess of Glengall attended, with others, while bread and soup were being distributed in Cahir to 205 families, comprising 1028 individuals; and on every Friday, 120 families, comprising 600 individuals

---

13   *Cork Examiner,* 4 Jan, 1847
14   *Cork Southern Reporter,* 4 Sept. 1847
15   *Tipperary Free Press,* 1 April 1848

were supplied with a quantity of coal gratuitously "at her Ladyship's expense"; and 110 families comprising 520 individuals were supplied with coal at half price. "Such acts," wrote the Cahir Correspondent of the *Vindicator* in January 1847, "deserve to be recorded in the unperishable gratitude of the people."[16]

A September 1848 edition of the *Limerick Reporter* made reference to the thriving members of the Society of Friends at Cahir and wrote, "evidence of their ever active benevolence and untiring industry encounter you in every direction."[17] The generosity of the Quakers throughout Ireland was instrumental in maintaining life for many thousands of people. At Tincurry, Cahir, before the auxiliary workhouse was established there, the Friends had established a porridge kitchen. So too in Clogheen, where Mrs Grubb and the Ladies Committee had set up a soup kitchen prior to the establishment of the 'official' soup kitchens.[18]

No Place for Poor Cahir Women

Although the poor women and the affluent women would have met at the Soup Kitchens and other places where charity was distributed, it can be stated with a degree of certainty that the poor and destitute women of Cahir and district were not mingling with the attendees at Cahir Steeple Chase Races at the Cahir New Melton Course in September 1845 which were under the stewardship of Lord Waterford, The Earl of Glengall, Hon. C. O'Callaghan, and many other gentlemen from the area. Neither would the impoverished women of Cahir have been invited to the grand picnic, in July 1846, at the Earl of Glengall's 'romantic lodge' which was given by the Officers of the 8th Royal Irish Hussars "to all the gentry of the surrounding neighbourhood, where the happy scene was further enlivened by the charming music of the band of the 8th."[19]

The Cahir Races in April 1846, at the 'splendid course' on the Earl of Glengall's Kilcommon demesne were, presumably, also off limits to the impoverished women.[20] And what, one wonders, would the starving mothers have made of the Cahir Grand Steeple Chase in October 1846 which was followed that evening by a "ball and supper on a very magnificent scale.[21] The *Limerick Chronicle* had carried a one sentence 'society announcement' a few weeks earlier:- *"The*

---

16   *The Tipperary Vindicator*, 9 January 1847
17   *Limerick Reporter*, 22 September 1848
18   *Famine in the Valley*, 1995
19   *Westmeath Independent*, 25 July 1846.
20   *Cork Examiner*, 6 March 1846.
21   *Limerick Reporter*, 27 October, 1846.

Earl and Countess of Glengall have returned to Cahir Castle from the Lakes of Killarney, and are to attend the Cahir races this month."[22]

Emigrants From Cahir and Tubrid

In October 1848, a report from Clonmel described a journey of a different sort that the Cahir district, country people planned for their future. Many of those who had managed to raise a few pounds had decided to flee the country. Even those who had managed to hold on to their few acres or find work on the relief works, finally had enough of living on Indian meal and the uncertainty of the future in Ireland.

> CLONMEL THURSDAY. At an early hour this morning the town was all astir in consequence of the arrival of several bodies of country people, men, women, and children, in [horse-drawn] cars, and accompanying them, some groups with fifes and drums playing before them etc. It was difficult at first to conjecture what object they had in entering the town [Clonmel]; but doubt was soon dispelled when it was known that these were people from the west of the County about Cahir, Tubrid, etc., on their way to Waterford to take shipping for America. Indeed the tide of emigration was never known to be so strong as it is just now from this neighbourhood. Already, I am credibly informed, one hundred families, if not more, have left the neighbourhood of Tubrid to seek their fortunes across the Atlantic.[23]

Two months later, the *Clonmel Chronicle* carried this short announcement:

> **Another Sign of the Times:-** We are informed that over one thousand acres of land in the neighbourhood of Cahir have fallen into the hands of the Earl of Glengall, (head landlord) during the last few weeks, either by process of law or voluntary eviction.[24]

In many instances, the middle men who leased hundreds of acres from the Earl of Glengall, and sublet it for profit, found themselves unable to pay their debts to the Glengall Estate and gave up their contracts. The tenants on those lands were the most vulnerable as they had no agreements with Lord Glengall.

---

22   *Limerick Chronicle*, 12 September 1846.
23   *Cork Examiner*, 2 October, 1848.
24   *Clonmel Chronicle* in *Dublin Weekly Register*, 30 Dec. 1848

Illustrated London News, 10 May 1851. Image of Priest blessing the emigrants includes many women and several children, experiencing the almost unbearable pain of emigration. Old people were left behind to mourn the loss of their families.
(Courtesy of Ireland's Great Hunger Museum, Quinnipiac University, Hamden CT.)

Professor William Smyth has noted the following from an early valuation map for the townland of Glengarra, which is on the Galtees, in the parish of Clogheen and Burncourt: "The Earl of Glengall has received possession of the whole of the present occupiers of this townland and their houses are to be thrown down."[25] There are similar entries for the townlands of Ballyhurrow and Boolakennedy. The census figures for those townlands are as follows:

Townland	Population 1841	Population 1851	Houses 1841	Houses 1851
Ballyhurrow	227	83	44	13
Boolakennedy	128	34	27	7
Glengarra	214	82	40	16

In January 1849, *The Dublin Evening Post* enlarged on the matter and claimed that the number of acres from which people had been evicted on the Glengall Estate - or which had been abandoned or surrendered by emigrating tenants -

25   Professor William J. Smyth, *PhD Thesis,* UCD. 1966

was three thousand acres. Once again Lady Glengall was praised for her charity, and readers were assured that she was the means of keeping many families from the overcrowded workhouse in Clogheen. In its description of Cahir, the *Post* declared that the spread of 'destitution and wretchedness in this hitherto comparatively favoured district is almost incredible'..

> ... I am told that on Tuesday, twenty houses were tumbled to the earth; on Wednesday, twenty; on Thursday, fourteen, on Friday, twenty; and I witnessed the departure of the car this morning for the same purpose, loaded with its freight...in some of these houses there are no tenants; they have gone away either to the workhouse or to America; in others there were families, some of whose members were sick and diseased, and had to be removed whilst the bailiffs were earning their wages..."[26]

THE DUBLIN EVENING POST,

EVICTIONS OF TENANTRY.

CAHIR, SATURDAY.—Lord Glengall is just now in London; and the absence of the Countess, who is universally esteemed for her benevolent virtues and attention to the poor, is severely felt at this most inclement and disastrous season. I understand that Lady Glengall orders the distribution daily of a quantity of bread to many poor persons, who should otherwise betake themselves to the overcrowded workhouses of Clogheen, where the number of admissions has augmented exceedingly within the last few weeks. Indeed, the spread of destitution and wretchedness in this hitherto comparatively favoured district, is almost incredible. You are aware, I suppose, that Lord Glengall's estates are under the protection and management of the courts, and that Mr. Richard Pennefather, the present High Sheriff of this county, is the agent of the estates under the courts.— Mr. Pennefather is also brother-in-law of Lord Glengall; he holds an office here on Tuesdays and Fridays in each week, which is attended by such of the tenantry as have the means of meeting their demands. Up to the present moment, I am credibly informed, about three thousand acres have been cleared by the process of voluntary or forcible ejectment within the last few weeks on those estates alone! I am told that on Tuesday twenty houses were tumbled to the earth; on Wednesday, twenty; on Thursday, fourteen; on Friday (yesterday), twenty; and I witnessed the departure of the car this morning for the same purpose, loaded with its freight; and I understand that on Monday also the same work is to be performed in and about the same locality. In some of these houses there are no tenants: they have gone away either to the workhouses or to America; in others there were families, some of whose members were sick and diseased, and had to be removed whilst the bailiffs were earning their wages. I have been assured that from

Dublin Evening Post, 4 January 1849

26   *Dublin Evening Post*, 4 Jan. 1849

The Barracks

Earlier in the Great Famine, the occupiers of Cahir Barracks discovered that in spite of the staunch fortifications and stout walls that surrounded them, death could not be kept at bay. In November 1847, Captain W.B. Frizell, the Barrackmaster at Coventry, agreed (with permission) to an exchange with Captain Samuel Chambers, Barrackmaster at Cahir and New Inn, whose wife had died at Cahir, on 25 June 1846.[27] Captain Frizell travelled to Liverpool and crossed over to Ireland with his wife, Mary, on the 'Royal William' and made his way to Cahir.[28]

William Frizell had been in the military for fifteen years, and served in India on two occasions where his health had suffered from the climate. His father had been chaplain to the Duke of Kent, who was son of George III, and Queen Victoria's father. Mr Frizell senior had dedicated some of his works on the Liturgy of the Church of England to the Duke.[29]

Distribution of Bread and Soup by Cahir Troops

While women in their tattered rags would surely not have been in the audience at the garrison theatricals in June 1849, they and their families were the beneficiaries of the charity emanating from Cahir Barracks. An article in the *Limerick Reporter,* in June of that year, lavished praise on the troops of the Cahir Garrison, not just for their theatrical expertise but also for their humane treatment of the poor.[30]

Cahir might have been seen as an 'easy billet' during those years, with occasional duties protecting the convoys of flour heading from Cahir and Clogheen to Limerick or to the Clonmel barges for conveyance to the waiting ships at Waterford. In 1848, the troops would have been on alert and ready to quell any local insurrection similar to the Young Irelanders' action at Ballingarry. However, in 1849, there evolved a different characteristic of the Cahir military that deserves to be recorded. The most recent performance by the men from the barracks, according to the *Limerick Reporter* in the 1849 report, was of 'Hamlet', the leading role being played by Private Jones while Private Comer played a supporting role. "So universal was the approval" of the piece that a repeat performance of the theatrical presentation had been arranged. The article went on:

---

27   *Cork Examiner,* 29 June 1846
28   *Dublin Evening Packet,* 11 Nov. 1847
29   *Eniskillen Chronicle,* 7 July 1842
30   *Limerick Reporter,* 22 June 1849

The great benevolence of Colonel Hanky and the troops under his command is highly spoken of and is exhibited in the distribution of bread and soup to hundreds of destitute beings, whose wants are supplied at Cahir barracks almost daily. The gallant Colonel distributes wagons of bread, besides good serviceable raiment to the poor; and the troops are so generous and humane as to subscribe two pence each, weekly, for the benevolent fund. [31]

It's certainly a dichotomy for students of military and 'Great Famine' history to resolve. Soldiers who escorted the food out of the country were, some time later, feeding the poor and donating part of their wages on a weekly basis to hundreds of Cahir district destitute beings.

Captain Frizell and his wife Mary arrived at Cahir Barracks in November of Black '47 and one might assume that they played a part in the fund-raising entertainment and assisted in the distribution of food and clothing to the poor. Then, on 23 August 1849, the death was reported of Mary, fifty eight year old wife of W.B. Frizell, Esq., Cahir Barrackmaster.[32] In the absence of official registration of Births, Deaths, and Marriages prior to 1864, we have to rely on the occasional notices in Irish newspapers; cause of death is not always given.

Less than a year later, on 20 May 1850, Barrackmaster William Biston Frizell remarried, this time in St Mary's Church of Ireland, Clonmel, to Alice Duggan, daughter of Patrick Duggan, a farmer. However, William Frizell's happiness was short lived and on 15 February 1851, *The Northern Standard* carried the following notice, *"Died, February 10, at Cahir Barracks, Alice, the beloved wife of Wm. B. Frizell, Barrackmaster of Cahir, after giving birth to a daughter, which died a short time before its mother."* Alice Frizell, nee Duggan, aged 23, is buried with her baby daughter in St. Nicholas Cemetery, Clonmel.[33]

In 1851 Capt Frizell was stationed as barrackmaster at Carlow and Athy, having ended his connection with Cahir. Having replaced Barrackmaster Chambers whose wife had died in Cahir in 1846, William Frizell had suffered the premature loss of two wives and a baby daughter in his short time there, another example of the plight of women in Cahir (and elsewhere) during those years. [34]

---

31   *Limerick Reporter*, 22 June 1849 (According to *http://landedestates.nuigalway.ie/LandedEstates/* Col. Hankey became the second husband of the Earl of Glengall's sister Lady Emily Butler in 1852.)
32   *Clare Journal*, 23 August 1849.
33   http://www.clonmelgraveyards.com/
34   *Cork Constitution*, 14 June 1851.

Continued Entertainment for the Beauty and Fashion of Cahir

In December 1851, while hunger and poverty were still being endured by a great number in Cahir district, and the workhouses were still filled with people from all parts of the Clogheen Poor Law Union, ...the *Belfast Mercury* newspaper copied the following from a local paper:

> A grand entertainment was given on Friday last, by Lieutenant Colonel Hodge and the officers of the 4th Royal Irish Dragoon Guards, to the gentry of Cahir. The evening commenced with a theatrical representation, when the play of the *'Illustrious Stranger'* was admirably performed by some of the non-commissioned officers and men of the regiment, after which a ball and supper were given in the officers' mess-house, where all the beauty and fashion of the neighbourhood were assembled. Dancing was kept up until a late hour. The music was that of the regimental band, who rival Weippart [a famous composer of the day] in their style of giving polkas and waltzes.[35]

Starvation – Soup Kitchens – Charities – Picnics

By the time the Great Famine was over, Cahir district was a very different place than it had been previously. The population of Cahir electoral division had been reduced by 14%, from 7,185 in '41 to 6,192 in '51. The population of Mortlestown electoral division had been reduced by an incredible 42%, from 1,830 to 1,057. The combined loss from just two electoral divisions was 1,766 representing a 20% loss overall. (These are the numbers for electoral divisions and not the population decrease for the Parish of Cahir and Mortlestown which would have been greater.) Evicted families found little sustenance in the countryside, and those that survived losing their homes and being afflicted with diseases, often migrated to the nearest large town, masking the actual population loss in those towns. Hundreds of women and girls found their way to the workhouse, but for countless others, death was inevitable.

---

35   *Belfast Mercury*, 30 December 1851

Three generations of women struggling to maintain life during the Great Irish Famine.
Source: *Irish Times* Book Review (10 October 2015) by Christine Kinealy of *Compassionate Stranger, Asenath Nicholson...*

Cahir Women and the Great Famine (2)
Doctors and Workhouse - Letter from the Workhouse
By Ed O'Riordan

Dispensary and Fever Hospital Doctors in Cahir District

It would be remiss of any account of women and the Famine if it neglected to mention the sacrifice made by the medical profession in their care of women and their families in Cahir District before, during and after the Famine.[1]

According to Mr. George Fennel, at an 1825 hearing in a case between Surgeon Thomas Beale of Caher Fever Hospital and Rector of Cahir, Rev. Augustus Cavendish, Mr Fennel first made the acquaintance of Dr Beale in 1815 and was of the opinion that no man could pay more attention than Dr Beale did 'to the duties of his office'. Dr Beale had been appointed as physician and apothecary to the Cahir dispensary and fever hospital in 1815. Prior to Dr Beale's appointment, a Mr Douglas had been surgeon and Mr Walshe was the apothecary.[2] Rev. Cavendish had arrived in Cahir a few years later, and it appears he allowed himself to be influenced by malicious rumour about the running of the fever hospital. An earlier hearing of the Grand Jury had described his claims as vexatious and referred them to the Management Committee who dismissed the claims. Dr Beale weathered the storm of indignation created by Rev. Cavendish (including Rev. Cavendish's letter to the *Clonmel Advertiser*) and continued as the esteemed Doctor/Surgeon at the fever hospital for almost thirty years. In 1827, Dr Beale married Mary, the daughter of Nicholas Chaytor, Esq.[3] Their son, Thomas Chaytor Beale, died from Yellow Fever in 1860 while posted as acting assistant surgeon with the army in Gambia.[4]

In 1830, Dr Beale and Rev. Cavendish sat together on a committee formed to combat the distress that existed in the town of Cahir and neighbourhood.[5] Then, in December 1843, Doctor T. Beale, after many years as 'surgeon to the Cahir Dispensary', died.[6] Some weeks later, at a general meeting of the governors with the Earl of Glengall in the chair, Doctor Michael Daniel - or Daniell - [of Cahir] was unanimously elected as Medical Superintendent of Cahir

---

1 There were other doctors throughout the district not connected to the Dispensaries or Fever Hospitals who are not mentioned here.
2 *Dublin Morning Register*, 08 July 1825
3 *Cork Constitution*, 17 April 1827
4 *Saunders's News-Letter*, 22 September 1860
5 *Clonmel Herald*, 3 July 1830
6 *Dublin Monitor*, 22 Dec. 1843

Fever Hospital and Dispensary.[7] He had been enrolled as a member of the Royal College of Surgeons in London in June 1841.[8]

Dispensary System

Prior to the establishment of the Poor Law Unions in 1838, and for some time afterwards, the dispensary system was supported by those who could afford to make annual contributions and who would not avail of the free advice and medicines given out by the dispensary. The Grand Juries (fore-runners of the County Councils with a role also in the administration of justice) granted an amount equal to the local subscriptions. The doctor's life alternated between work at the dispensary, work at the fever hospital, and later, in towns where workhouses had been established, working at those institutions. They augmented their salaries by their private work. The doctors also travelled into the rural parts of their districts when necessary, as part of their public duty. During the Famine, they must have witnessed horrific scenes, being for the most part powerless to help other than to offer meagre comfort and to direct those women and families who could make the journeys to enter the fever hospitals and the workhouse. During the Famine, women and their families were at risk from relapsing fever, typhus fever, bloody flux, dysentery, and cholera. These diseases were no respecters of class, creed, rank, gender or profession and doctors in particular were exposed to the dangers every day.

Dr. Daniel's wife, Frances Hatchell of Dublin, had predeceased him in 1841 just one year after their marriage.[9] Her untimely passing may well have been the result of child birth complications, though this is unclear. In September 1845, at Tubrid Church, he remarried, this time to a local woman, Mary Jemima Rice, daughter of Henry Rice of Scart, Tubrid.[10] They went on to have one son, Henry, and one daughter, Margaret. Dr. Daniel is named as a subscriber to the Cahir Relief Fund in 1846. He was a son of Captain Hugh Daniel who was agent to the Glengall estate for many years and Adjutant to the Tipperary Militia. Hugh Daniel was the secretary of, and also a contributor to, the relief fund.[11] It appears that Dr Daniel's mother was the daughter of Stephen Going of Clonmel.[12]

---

7   *Tipperary Free Press*, 3 Jan. 1844 (Name is given variously as Daniel and Daniell.)
8   *London Medical Gazette*, Vol 28. P.560
9   Death notice in *Dublin Morning Register*, 13 November 1841, states she was "wife of Surgeon Michael Daniel of Cahir". Marriage cert in Dublin Church of Ireland Marriage Register.
10 *Dublin Evening Post*, 2 Oct. 1845
11 Subscribers list to Cahir Relief Fund in *The Tipperary Free Press*, 1 July 1846. Notice of Hugh Daniell's death in *The Waterford Chronicle*, 30 April 1867, describes him as 'Captain and Adjutant of the Tipperary Artillery'. Dr Michael Daniel's marriage registration in October 1845 to Mary Jemima Rice states that his father Hugh Daniell is 'Adjutant of the Tipperary Artillery'.
12 Notice of Hugh Daniel's marriage to Miss Going. *Saunders News Letter* 25 Nov 1817.

Death of Dr Daniel

In 1847, Dr Michael Daniel, Cahir, made the ultimate sacrifice in the care of his patients. His name is added to the list of the many heroic doctors in Ireland who died during the Great Famine. The notice of Dr Daniel's death in the *Tipperary Vindicator* stated on 19 February 1847 that the good doctor had died of fever contracted in the discharge of his professional duties. He was Medical Superintendent of 'Caher Fever Hospital and Dispensary' and Surgeon to the Tipperary Regiment of Militia.[13] The *Coleraine Chronicle* on 6 March noted:

> The physician of the Cahir dispensary died last week of fever caught attending his patients. A more valuable officer than Dr. Daniel never existed. The number of poor dying of dysentery and bad food is truly dreadful throughout the whole country, although every human aid is extended.

Cahir womenfolk and their families had availed of the professional services of Dr Daniell from 1843 to 1847. Just one month later, Dr Daniel's mother, died in Cahir. As was not uncommon at the time, her identity seemed dependant on her husband's, and, just as she had been described in the notice of her marriage in *Saunders New-Letter* in 1817 without a first name but simply as 'daughter of Stephen Going' she was now recorded in *The Pilot* newspaper as 'Mrs. Daniel, wife of Captain Daniel, Tipperary Regiment.'[14]

After ten years of widowhood, Mary Jemima Daniel (nee Rice) remarried, this time to Isaac Strahan, the governor of Clonmel Gaol.[15] Unfortunately, she was to be widowed again when Isaac died in 1861.

Dr Daniel named on Tubrid Headstone

It is not clear where Dr Daniell is buried; however, his name is on a gravestone in Tubrid cemetery which remembers his son Henry, his daughter Margaret, and his wife Mary Jemima. His grandmother, Mary Daniel (died 1826), is buried in Old St Mary's graveyard Clonmel as is his grandfather, Michael Daniel (died 1832), who had been adjutant to the Tipperary Militia before his (Michael's) son, Captain Hugh Daniel, was promoted to that position.[16]

---

13 *Tipperary Vindicator*, 27 Feb. 1847
14 *Saunders Newsletter*, 25 Nov. 1817; *The Pilot*, 26 March 1847
15 *Dublin Evening Mail*, 18 Sept. 1857. Mary is described in the marriage notice as being widow of Dr. Daniell and daughter of Henry Rice Esq.
16 clonmelgraveyards.com

The wording on the Tubrid Gravestone is as follows:
IN LOVING MEMORY
HENRY DANIEL WHO DEPARTED THIS LIFE JAN 18TH 1867
AND OF HIS MOTHER
MARY J. STRAHAN WHO DIED DEC. 1886.
ALSO **HENRY RICE** OF SCART WHO DIED FEB 21ST 1871
AND OF HIS WIFE **SUSAN RICE** WHO DIED FEB. 20TH 1873
ALSO OF **ISAAC STRAHAN** HUSBAND OF THE ABOVE MARY
WHO DIED DEC. 22ND 1861
ALSO **MARGARET** DEARLY BELOVED WIFE OF **J.J. O'C O'BRIEN**
AND DAUGHTER OF THE LATE
DR. M. DANIEL OF CAHIR
WHO DIED JUNE 3RD 1906[17]

It may be presumed that the casual use of the word 'who' on the last line of the gravestone has kept the era of Dr Daniel's death hidden from many people for many decades; it could easily be assumed from the headstone that Dr Michael, rather than Margaret, was the one 'who died' in 1906.

17   http://historicgraves.com/graveyard/tubbrid/ts-tbrd

Dr. Valentine Flood

By coincidence (or by design), the stone at Tubrid, on which Dr. Daniel's name is inscribed, is side by side with the gravestone/memorial slab erected to the Tubrid Fever Hospital doctor, Valentine Flood, who also looked after women and their families and who, on 18 October 1847, also died of fever.[18] That memorial stone at Tubrid Graveyard reads:

THIS STONE HAS BEEN PLACED HERE BY THE CLERGY

OF BOTH DENOMINATIONS AND THE PRINCIPAL MEMBERS

OF THE RELIEF COMMITTEE OF TUBRID

WITH A FEW OTHER FRIENDS

AS A MEMORIAL OF THEIR GRATITUDE

FOR THE VALUABLE PROFESSIONAL SERVICES AND OF

THEIR RESPECT FOR THE MEMORY OF

VALENTINE FLOOD ESQR M.D., M.R.I.A.

AND PHYSICIAN TO THE TUBRID HOSPITAL

WHO DIED OF FEVER

CAUGHT IN THE FAITHFUL DISCHARGE OF HIS

DANGEROUS DUTIES IN THAT ESTABLISHMENT

AND WHOSE MORTAL REMAINS ARE BURIED

UNDERNEATH.

OB. *18 Oct. 1847*

In December 1847, The *Dublin Medical Press* carried notice of a fund-raising effort towards the support of Dr Flood's widow and five children, who had been left totally destitute and "bereft of the means of support."[19] The *Medical Press* went on:

> Dr Flood, in addition to his academic and medical degrees, was a fellow of the college of Surgeons in Ireland. He was lecturer on Anatomy and Physiology for many years in the Richmond school of medicine in this city [Dublin]. He afterwards lectured at a private school in London, in which metropolis his talents as an Anatomist and Physiologist were highly appreciated, but his health becoming delicate, he was advised to try his native air, and

---

18   The Valentine Flood memorial slab and the gravestone on which Dr Daniel's name is inscribed were brought to light by a team working under the direction of U.C.C Geographer and Tús Operations Coordinator, Mark Rylands.

19   *Dublin Medical Press*, 1 December 1847.

at the recommendation of the Board of Health was subsequently appointed Physician to the Fever Hospital at Tubrid. Besides various contributions to the Medical Periodicals, his memory will be perpetuated by the following works:

1.*Treatise on the Brain.* 2. *Treatise on the Nervous System.* 3. *Treatise on Hernia.* 4. *Treatise on the Anatomy of the Arteries.*

In the accounts above, and in countless other cases of doctors contracting fever while tending the sick, the wives and children were the ones left to carry on, some relying on family for support, but others, like the widow of Dr Flood, having to rely on friends and public subscriptions. However awful the circumstances of their early widowhood, perhaps, in the context of the Great Famine, their circumstances were not as grim as the lives of hundreds of thousands of their fellow female citizens.

Dr Bagnell Appointed

There may well be other doctors in the area who died during the Famine. The death of a 16 year old Cahir medical student was reported in January 1847 in the *Freeman's Journal*. The notice stated that Robert Smithwick of Monaraha Cottage, Cahir, died at his late father's home.[20]

Following the death of Dr Daniel, an election was held at a meeting of the 'Subscribers to the Fever Hospital' in Cahir. It is worth noting that the Cahir subscribers still held the power of appointment even after the establishment of the Poor Law Union. Dr. Robert Bagnell was appointed as physician to Cahir Fever Hospital in March 1847.[21] It was now Dr Bagnell who took on the onerous task of looking after the sick and poor of Cahir and district. His salary was £80 per year, but a notice in the press reveals that in 1854, at a meeting of Clogheen Board of Guardians, the salary was increased to £100.[22] That short notice demonstrates that the Poor Law Guardians were responsible for payment of the doctor's salary.

In March 1855, a 'complimentary' resolution was unanimously adopted at a meeting of the Cahir Dispensary Committee at their Committee Rooms, Cahir. Dr Bagnell had given notice of his intention to resign having taken a position as Surgeon to North Tipperary Militia.

---

20 *Freeman's Journal*, 8 Jan. 1847
21 *The Pilot*, 22 March, 1847.
22 *Westmeath Independent*, 20 May 1854

"That Dr. Bagnell having resigned the duties of Medical Officer of this Dispensary District, the Committee cannot too strongly express their unqualified approbation of the zeal, assiduity, and efficiency with which he performed the medical duties of the district during a period of eight years, and his uniform kindness and attention to the recipients of medical relief." By order of the Committee..

Robert Franklin, Hon Secretary.[23]

Dr Bagnell was replaced by Doctor John Stokes M.D. who had already been, since 1848, the doctor at Tincurry auxiliary workhouse.[24] Dr Stokes who was a founding member of the Tipperary branch of the Medical Protective Association was married to Mary, the daughter of Margaret and William Burke of Cahir.[25] His name appears in press reports throughout the years at inquests, autopsies, etc. In 1877, he was actively involved in the   successful efforts to have a new convent erected for the Sisters of Mercy in Cahir.

Ophtalmia in Tincurry

At the Clogheen Union (including Cahir) auxiliary workhouse at Tincurry in June 1853, the doctor's report recorded that forty-two persons that year were attacked with Ophthalmia, a disease of the eyes. Dr. Stokes was able to report that twenty-seven of the afflicted children were discharged, totally cured. Others were not so fortunate and lost the sight of one or both eyes. In his time at the children's workhouse, Dr Stokes would have had to deal with the 1848 outbreak of a very 'malignant form of scarlatina', and he requested that no more children were to be sent there for the time being. During a measles outbreak in February 1849, thirteen boys, thirteen girls and six babies died. Some died at Tincurry and others died at Clogheen where they had been sent to hospital. By the 6th of March, Tincurry was home to 529 children. That week, between Clogheen and Tincurry, 11 boys, 9 girls and 6 babies died from measles.

When the auxiliary house at Tincurry was being closed in 1853, Dr. Stokes reported that ten year old Catherine Burke was suffering from measles and dysentery and would be a danger to the health of the Clogheen house. She had to remain at Tincurry for some weeks with one other child, John Griffin, who was suffering from scrofula on the knee-joint. It had been ordered that a nurse

23 *Dublin Daily Express*, 12 April 1855
24 *Saunders Newsletter*,23 April 1855, and O'Riordan, *Famine in the Valley*.
25 Death of Margaret Burke in *Waterford Standard*, 31 May 1876, and *Dublin Medical Press*, 7 Oct. 1857.

was to remain behind to care for him, as all others left. The last member of staff at Tincurry was that nurse, and the last patient to leave for the Clogheen workhouse was ten year old girl Catherine Burke. Little John Griffin never recovered. He was the last occupant of Tincurry Children's Workhouse and was the last of the Tincurry children to be buried in the nearby cemetery. [26]

Cholera

The work load of the workhouse doctors can only be guessed at, but these figures of hospital cases from the Clogheen Board of Guardians in April 1849 indicate the enormity of the workload in their daily lives. In *Clogheen Workhouse Hospital, Diarrhoea, 56; Fever Cases 50; Cholera cases, 9; other complaints, 81; In Tincurry Workhouse Hospital, 61. In Clogheen Town Fever Hospital, 5. Total 262.* The figure of nine cholera cases belies the situation in Cahir in 1849 when Cahir was mentioned as one of the places in Ireland where cholera -which had spread across Europe- had taken its toll. It was to the credit of the Cahir authorities variously called the Town Commissioners and the Cahir Board of Health, that they were to the fore in dealing with the dreadful situation. The *Dublin Evening Mail* carried a report that on 28 April in Cahir, of the 106 cases that had been identified, forty-one of those had been cured and discharged, fifty-nine had died, and six were still being treated.[27] At a meeting of the 'Sanatory Association' in Dublin earlier that month, the chairman mentioned Nenagh and Cahir as being two of the towns where cholera was prevalent. He also noted that 'Cahir' had written to him for guidance regarding the disease and he had advised that they follow the "Glasgow mode of district visitation".[28] In March a deputation from Cahir Town Commissioners attended at a Board of Guardians meeting to request that a hospital be prepared to deal with any outbreak of cholera in the area. They also requested an order that paupers on outdoor relief should be obliged to " clean and remove the nuisance of the town, so necessary for the prevention of contagion." In reply the Guardians stated that they had no able-bodied male paupers on outdoor relief in the Clogheen Union.[29]

26 *Board of Guardian Minute Books for Clogheen Poor Law Union* –at Tipperary County Library – and a pamphlet on Tincurry Workhouse compiled to coincide with the erecting of a memorial to the Children of Tincurry by Councillor Seanie Lonergan, Cahir.
27 *Dublin Evening Mail*, 30 April 1849
28 *The Advocate or Irish Industrial Journal*, 4 April 1849
29 O'Riordan, E., *Famine in the Valley*, 1995

Dr J.V. Cormick

By coincidence, on the date of publication of the *Dublin Evening Mail* figures given above (30 April 1849), the Cahir Commissioners issued a notice of their gratitude to Doctor J.V. Cormick.

> The Board of Guardians being called upon by the disappearance of Cholera, to discontinue the services of Doctor J.V. Cormick, we, the Commissioners and members of Caher Board of Health, feel great pleasure in recording our perfect satisfaction of his valuable services as Medical Officer, and of his indefatigable diligence and zeal in the carrying out of Sanatory Measures for the preservation of the Health of the Town and vicinity, during the awful visitation of Cholera.

The signatories were all prominent gentlemen of Cahir including, William Sargint, Richard Grubb, Thomas Going, Samuel Jellico, etc.[30] In September, the sad death notice of Elizabeth, Beloved Wife of Samuel Jellico, Esq., of Cahir, appeared in the *Tipperary Vindicator* and gave cause of death (in Dublin) as Cholera.[31]

The news of the Cholera in Ireland was also carried in the UK newspapers. A correspondent of the *Morning Chronicle* wrote that the cases on one day in Cahir numbered fifty-four and the deaths thirty three.

> It should be remarked [said the *Chronicle*] that Cahir is one of the cleanest and best regulated towns in the county of Tipperary, yet the progress of the epidemic, has been more rapid there, and the mortality greater, in proportion to the population, than perhaps any other part of Ireland...[32]

---

30 *Tipperary Free Press*, 28 April 1849
31 *Tipperary Vindicator*, 15 Sept. 1849
32 *Morning Chronicle*, 4 April 1849 (the word cholera was very often capitalised)

SKETCH IN A HOUSE AT FAHEY'S QUAY, ENNIS.—THE WIDOW CONNOR AND HER DYING CHILD.

This Co. Clare image of a mother praying over her dying child was certainly repeated many times in Cahir district and other parts of Clogheen Union. The conditions in the house are shocking to our modern eyes, and yet, the workhouses were designed so that people had to reach this level of destitution before attempting to find refuge in those institutions. Image from *Illustrated London News*, 5 January 1850. (Courtesy of Ireland's Great Hunger Museum, Quinnipiac University, Hamden, CT.)

The Workhouse

Cahir and the surrounding areas were part of the Clogheen Poor Law Union which was set up in 1841, and it was to the Union workhouse in Clogheen (near St. Theresa's Hospital) that impoverished Cahir women and their families went as a last resort. An 1849 report from the Board of Guardians offers some interesting figures regarding the numbers in the workhouse: In Clogheen Workhouse - 458; Auxiliary accommodation in Clogheen - 40. In Tincurry Children's Auxiliary workhouse - 494. Conditions in the workhouses were deliberately bleak to ensure that people entered there only as a last resort. The following is from *Famine in the Valley*, 1995.

"Reference was made to conditions in the workhouses on many occasions and the Guardians were divided in their opinions as to the acceptability of the conditions that prevailed. Some felt that Clogheen was a model workhouse, while others, including the inspector, felt that it left a lot to be desired. It is unusual to get an inmate's view of life in the workhouse during the famine years, apart from the occasional complaint about bad stirabout being recorded.

Letter to the Workhouse

However, on the 22 April 1848, a pauper named Michael Doody was called before the Board to substantiate charges that he had made against an assistant nurse (a pauper) and others. *The Tipperary Free Press* reporter was present at that meeting, and he described what took place.

'Doody was called into the board room and told to state his complaints. His ease of manner, self possession, and style of address told that he had seen better days and society different from workhouse associates.

Doody - My lord and gentlemen, although I am now in this workhouse I have been well bred. I have received a fair education, and studied something of the medical profession, but adversity compelled me to seek a livelihood in a different way, and I became a boot and shoe maker. I worked in a respectable establishment, and I could support my family decently until trade fell away, when I, with many others, was discharged, and I was forced to seek this asylum. The practices in this house were so revolting to my feelings that I mentioned them to my confessor, and he advised me to state them to the board. I am prepared to be sworn. I do not know whether I can corroborate all I will say by other witnesses, but my lord, if my word should be doubted, you can examine the parties accused and see what they will admit.'

He took from a pocket a paper and read as follows:

'Clogheen, April 22, 1848

Sir, The workhouse of the Clogheen Union is intended by the Legislature as an asylum for the destitute poor of the neighbourhood; the exterior of it is grand and inviting, but the interior is a scene of tyranny, cruelty, and inhumanity, which is destructive to human life. The portion of the food and drink given to each person daily is not sufficient for one meal, which I would swear on oath, and that small portion is fraudulently distributed. Some are gluttonously fed, and many are perished by lingering hunger. This practice is so managed by the paupers themselves that the master cannot investigate the conduct of a rude, stupid house of paupers, who are terrified by hunger and death. The poor children committed to your care are notoriously perished, for the pauper nurses sell and eat the very small portion of nourishment which you offer them, for whiskey and other purposes. From the 1st of March until the 1st of April, I have seen from 6 to 12 children dead daily. On the 23rd March or thereabouts, I have seen 16 dead together, 14 of whom were helpless children. I have seen fathers and mothers who could not find their children dead or alive. I attempted twice to report this inhumanity to you, but you refused to listen to me. Merciful God! Would you permit so much human life to be destroyed through indolence or wilful neglect?

An Inmate.'

The report in the *Tipperary Free Press* (3 May 1848) continued with Mr. Fennell cross-examining Mr. Doody on behalf of Dr. Gallogly [Clogheen Workhouse and Fever Hospital doctor]:

'What are your particular charges and against whom?'

Doody-
'My children were in hospital and I occasionally went to see them; having observed the gross neglect of the nurses, I sat up with them all night, and had an opportunity to see what passed. I have seen the bread and milk allowed the patients, sold by the nurses to other paupers. I have also seen whiskey drank in this house by the nurses.'

A pauper nurse named H……. was then interviewed. She maintained that the money for her whiskey came from her daughter who worked for Parson Palmer (Tubrid). Other witnesses verified Mr. Doody's account of events, but the board decided that the food which was sold by the pauper H…… was food that the sick children could not eat, and that no injury was sustained by the children from her doing so. Mr. Doody insisted that on a previous night he had heard a row in which all concerned "must have been drunk". This report from Michael Doody, taken with other occasional entries in the minutes of meetings, about overflowing stinking cesspits and food being returned to suppliers as unfit for use, paints a most horrifying picture of what life was like in a 'model workhouse'.[33] "

It is interesting to note that the number of paupers from Cahir in the workhouse system in November, 1849, exceeded that of any other Electoral Division in the Clogheen Union. The full list is as follows: Cahir 220 (22% of total); Derrygrath, 5; Ardfinnan 13; Tullamelan, 10; Newcastle, 21; Ballybacon, 21; Tullahorton, 33; Tubrid, 76; Whitechurch, 58; Clogheen, 218; Ballyporeen, 184; Kilbehenny, 67; Union total – 1005

The numbers were further classified by the guardians as follows: Able-bodied women, 148; Able-bodied men, 75; Infirm women, 55; Infirm men, 32; Girls from nine to fifteen, 220; Boys from nine to fifteen, 220; Children from five to nine 188; Children from two to five, 37; children under two, 28. Total 1005. [34] (Reports at different dates showed higher numbers overall but did not include the breakdown given here)

33   Edmund O'Riordan, *Famine in the Valley*
34   *Cork Southern Reporter*, 8 December 1849

1932 Photo of the ruin of the entrance building of Clogheen Workhouse. The *Irish Times* of 9 November 1922 reported that Clogheen workhouse had been burned down by armed men on Tuesday of that week. Free State troops had been billeted there and had vacated the house on the previous Sunday night. Through those gates and through the doorway in the background, the destitute women of Cahir and all those classified by officialdom as 'paupers' entered and exited since 1842. Based on the figures above, approximately 100 women and female children from Cahir were in the house in November 1849. In 1851, Clogheen and Tincurry housed 1,789 paupers. (*Cork Southern Reporter*, 19 April 1851) Assuming the percentage remained constant, 175 of that number would have been women and female children from Cahir. From here, the Cahir Female Orphans began their long journey to Australia in 1848. (Photo Source: Cronin/ Weber collection. By kind permission of Pete Weber, California.)

~~~~~~~~~~~

Women Reacting to Cruel Treatment in Workhouse

There is a growing debate in Irish Famine studies relating to the suggestion that women suffered more than men during the Great Famine. Perhaps, some might argue, women suffered more emotionally than men at times of famine; they were often deserted by their husbands or were left as widows, suffered more from evictions in the sense that they were the ones now unable to put the food on the table, mind children, give birth to those children, etc.

It might be believed also that women are less inclined to rebel and to fight injustice, by virtue of their gender, being described as the 'weaker sex', the 'fair sex', and seen as being more gentle than their menfolk. However, there is ample evidence from modern historical research that women, while possibly suffering more in the famine, were also able to fight their corner when occasion demanded. A report from the *Cork Reporter* in 1848, described how hundreds of women in Cork workhouse objected to the comments of a workhouse inspector who had ordered some 'female paupers' to remove some of the tables and to clean them. The objections began as a lot of murmuring, progressed to loud shouting; and finally, in what was described as an insurrection, the eight hundred women began to hurl stones and break glass in a demonstration of the anger they felt. One can only imagine the sufferings of those women prior to being incarcerated in the workhouse, possibly having lost loved ones, some having been deserted by husbands, evicted from their homes, having existed for a time by the food distribution at soup-kitchens, and now separated from their remaining family. A pompous gentleman exercising authority and criticising them as they ate their meagre helpings of food was just too much.[35]

Tipperary Women Rebelling

Tipperary women were not found wanting either when occasion demanded. In Nenagh, according to the *Tipperary Vindicator* that same week in 1848, the women rebelled, in this instance against the substitution of rye bread in place of white bread. The women objected by vociferously objecting to the introduction of 'black bread' and refused to eat it. Those in charge decided to punish the women by stopping their milk allowance; but that action caused more instead of less discontent, and a 'company of the 79th Highlanders' had to be brought in to restore order.[36]

Clogheen Workhouse 1851

Conditions and training for women in the Clogheen Union Workhouse would seem to have improved from 1851 onwards. In August 1851, Joseph Kettlewell, Clerk of the Clogheen Union, wrote the following to the Kilkenny Guardians:

> In accordance with the request contained in your letter of the 15th instant, I beg to inform you that the female industrial department of the workhouse is thus conducted:- In three day-rooms the processes of carding wool and cotton, and the spinning of thread of all kinds, are carried on by the general body of women – that from those women, the girls between the ages of about 15 to 20

---

35 *Cork Reporter in Newry Examiner and Louth Advertiser, 18 November 1848*
36 *Tipperary Vindicator in Newry Examiner and Louth Advertiser, 18 November 1848*

years who have made most progress, and are most distinguished by excellence of character, are selected by the matron, and instructed in all the details requisite of a thorough knowledge of all branches of industry carried on in these rooms; after which they are taught warping, etc., and are transferred to the principal female day-room, in which linen, chambray, Russian duck etc., are woven; and, being placed in the first instance to attend a loom they are in due course taught to weave and beam etc. Three of the pauper girls thus trained are at present Officers of other Unions, and the accounts received of the benefits conferred on the Unions in which they are placed, are most gratifying. ... no charge whatever made at present for clothing our own paupers, but that we are in a position to supply every article of clothing and bedding to another Union, and I am this day answering an advertisement, offering to undertake six months contract for supplying with clothing and bedding, a Union in which there are three thousand paupers. ... [37]

Population Changes 1841 to 1851

Because the registration of deaths did not become compulsory in Ireland until some years after the Famine, it is not possible to accurately ascertain how many people died in, or emigrated from, Cahir and district during that period of our history. However, it is worthwhile examining the demographic changes (from all causes) evident from the figures supplied by the census commissioners for the years 1841 and 1851. Below is a table showing not only the population figures for the electoral divisions in the Clogheen Union, but also the number of houses at each census date.....

37   *Kilkenny Journal and Leinster Commercial and Literary Advertiser.* 30 August 1851

Electoral Division.	Population 1841	Population 1851	Houses 1841	Houses 1851
Ardfinnan	2,669	1,942	384	277
Ballybacon	1,602	1,118	247	177
Ballyporeen	4,362	2,944	720	555
Burncourt	1,929	1,280	322	214
Cahir	7,185	6,192	1,136	957
Clogheen	5,464	5,155	896	667
Coolagarranroe	2,545	1,723	442	330
Derrygrath	2,300	1,661	343	239
Kilcoran	3,393	1,472	570	253
Mortlestown	1,830	1,057	296	169
Newcastle	2,639	2,226	402	356
Tubrid	3,103	2,819	485	384
Tullaghmelan	3,028	2,059	487	341

Figures from the Census of 1851, the year in which some suggest the famine was over, show that in that year, the numbers in the Union Workhouse at Clogheen had increased to 1322 people, 827 (62.5%) of that number being female. In Tincurry auxiliary workhouse 306 (56%) of the 545 residents in 1851 were female.[38]

Baptism Register St. Mary's Catholic Church - Cahir

The Baptismal Registers at St. Mary's Parish Catholic Church in Cahir reveal the following Baptisms for each year 1843 – 1852.

Year	'43	'44	'45	'46	'47	'48	'49	'50	'51	'52
Total	321	339	293	299	237	233	230	192	199	160

Some baptisms may not have been recorded by the priests at the time but the figures are certainly indicative of a dramatic fall-off in the numbers. Death, evictions, emigration, residence in the workhouses, and perhaps, a growing reluctance by younger people to marry, all contributed to the lower numbers.

---

38 Edmund O'Riordan , *Famine in the Valley* 1995

Numbers at Tincurry

At Tincurry, just west of Cahir, the children's workhouse – referred to earlier in connection with Dr. Stokes - was established by the Clogheen Union Guardians in 1848 to alleviate the pressure on Clogheen main workhouse. Initially, men and women were sent to Tincurry as well, but, later on, a decision was made to populate the Tincurry workhouse as originally intended, with boys of the union and subsequently with boys and girls of the Union. Tincurry was also designated an Agricultural training school and many a knowledgeable farm worker in Cahir area in the post famine period would have received their training at Tincurry. A November 1848 edition of the *Tipperary Vindicator* carried a report which gives some indication of the different treatment of boys and girls at Tincurry regarding the work carried out and diet provided. Of the 436 children then in the house - down from five hundred in April - there were 225 boys and 211 girls. Thirty one of those children were in the hospital and seventy-nine of the total were under nine years of age. It was originally planned that children who became ill would be transferred back to Clogheen, but the distance proved too great for sick children to travel, so a doctor and nurse were employed by the auxiliary house. Doctors were usually 'visiting doctors' and probably on call, while the nurse would have lived at the Tincurry workhouse. The male officers of Tincurry were listed as follows: a wardmaster, schoolmaster or agriculturist, a chaplain, a porter and a doctor. Female officers were: a matron, schoolmistress, assistant schoolmistress and a nurse.[39] Other than the officers, fifteen adults lived at the auxiliary workhouse and saw to the efficient running of the establishment; nine of those were female. The gender based division of labour was as we might expect, a division which continued into the twentieth century. The six men were two tailors, a shoemaker, a mason/whitewasher, an assistant whitewasher, and a night watchman. The jobs assigned to the women were as follows: three hospital assistants, one laundry superintendent, one in the store, one scouring floors, one in the kitchen, and two employed 'washing children etc.' It could be argued that the female staff played a more important role than the men in the daily lives of the children.

The children worked each day, the boys alternating between cultivating the twelve acres and attending at school. The boys were allowed play ball after supper. Those boys who worked hard at school and in the fields were

---

39 *Tipperary Vindicator*, 11 November 1848 (Article: 'Clogheen Union, Reproductive Employment')

rewarded with an extra 4 ounces of bread each evening. The girls' time was divided between school and work. Those engaged in scouring floors, washing and cooking were given an extra 2 ounces of bread each day. The remaining girls, who were engaged in mending clothes and knitting, received no extra allowance.[40] *The Farmers Gazette* suggested that 'early training' in scouring floors, mending clothes of the auxiliary workhouse, sewing and knitting, helping in the kitchens and occasional weeding in the fields would bestow an 'almost incalculable' advantage on the girls in preparing them for life after Tincurry.[41] Earlier research on the subject of girls receiving such training reveals the following:

> For the girls, domestic service was all that was available, though there is reference in the Clogheen Union workhouse minute books to wool being bought and the girls being put to work. It would appear that the Commissioners felt that the girls' future lay in being servants. Anne Lanigan in ' The Workhouse Child' notes that both the Poor Law and the Education Commissioners condemned the "concept of teaching workhouse children sewing crafts of such specialised intricacy. Their destiny lay in common domestic service. Therefore 'rough household duties should occupy the first rank' in their industrial training."[42]

> Boys too were sent out of the house to work, and it was common for people to apply for young workers, though this practice was to become more prevalent in the years after the famine, as the need for workers grew. For the lucky ones this meant a place to live, as they were all too often orphans, and gave them a few pennies a month. For many others however, it was little more than slavery.[43]

Tincurry Children in Training

James Keane was the agriculturalist employed at Tincurry. His 1848 report shows that the twelve acres were cultivated on best agricultural practices, the boys digging, trenching, sowing, weeding, draining, and harvesting. The boys also

---

40 Ibid.
41 *Farmers' Gazette*, quoted in Cork Examiner, 27 September 1848
42 O'Riordan, E., *Famine in the Valley,* and Anne Lanigan, 'The Workhouse Child' in *'Thurles: The Cathedral Town',* (William Corbett and William Nolan, Eds)1989
43 O'Riordan, E., *Famine in the Valley* , 1995

received instruction in agricultural theories including geology, soils, manuring, crop rotation etc. At harvest time, approximately forty of the stronger boys were given reaping hooks and set to work on the several acres under oats. Picture the scene, forty boys reaping the crops on the farm at Tincurry at the foot of the Galty Mountains. Following them across the fields were the girls who were employed binding sheaves and building stooks. Then came the small children, who were engaged in gleaning – gathering the fallen ears of grain which lay on the ground.[44] The Tincurry girls returned to Clogheen before the boys, and by 1853 all had returned to life in Clogheen Union Workhouse.

Plaque erected at Tincurry by Cllr. Seanie Lonergan and Ed O'Riordan in memory of the children of 'Tincurry Auxiliary Workhouse' and all who cared for them. 1848 -1853.

---

44 *Tipperary Vindicator*, 11 November 1848. (Article: 'Details of Agricultural Operations on the Land Attached to Tincurry Workhouse')

Cahir Female Orphan Emigrants 1849
By Ed O'Riordan

Several of the Cahir girls who had been engaged in binding sheaves and building stooks at Tincurry Auxiliary Workhouse in 1848, were neither in Tincurry nor Clogheen when Tincurry finally shut in 1853 . They, along with four thousand other Irish female orphans, had left Ireland to seek what they hoped would be a better life in Australia. In 1848, a scheme called the 'Earl Grey Scheme' had been implemented by the Poor Law Commissioners in Dublin which directed the Guardians of the many workhouses throughout Ireland to identify orphan girls who would be willing to emigrate to Australia. At a meeting of Clogheen Board of Guardians in March 1848, the matter was raised when Mr G. Fennel argued that in spite of the definition given by the Commissioners, he was of the opinion that girls whose fathers were dead could be considered orphans "in which case numbers could be transhipped" to relieve the heavy burden on the rate-payers. The other Guardians present argued against Mr Fennel and voted against his proposal. However, throughout Ireland a great number of girls whose mothers were still living were encouraged to emigrate. Clogheen and Cahir were obliged to follow suit. Mr Fennel had won his argument.

From Cahir to Wooloomooloo

This list and information regarding the thirteen young orphan women from Cahir who were in Clogheen Union Workhouse and Tincurry Auxiliary Workhouse in 1848/49 and who were sent out to Australia is from www.irishfaminememorial. org[1]:

Catherine Kennedy, age 18, from Cahir, Catholic, daughter of James and Margaret (Margaret living in Cahir), no relatives in colony, sailed on 'William and Mary' to Sydney 1849. Farm servant, can read. Employed by H. Tebbutt at £8 per year. In 1851, her indenture was cancelled for assault by mistress.

Catherine Doody, aged 15, a Catholic, daughter of Michael and Bridget Doody – both deceased, went out on the 'William and Mary' to Sydney in 1849. Catherine was a nursemaid, able to read and write. No relatives in Colony'. She was employed by a family named Dunn at 'orphan wages'. For neglect of duty,

---

1   All from: http://www.irishfaminememorial.org/orphans/database/
     ?page=9&surName=&firstName=&nativePlace=&parents=&age=0&religion=&ship=11

her wages were withheld for a time until she was well behaved, but she was paid in 1850. [It is worth considering the possibility, even though there is no definite evidence to support the theory, that this young Doody girl was a daughter of the Michael Doody who, in 1848, reported to the Board of Guardians on conditions in the Clogheen workhouse. See *Cahir Women and The Famine (2)* in this book. A Catherine Doody was baptised in Cahir in November 1833. Parents Michael Doody and Bridget Walsh]

Bridget Halloran, aged 17. Native place – Cahir. A Catholic, daughter of Edward and Catherine – both deceased, went out on 'William and Mary' to Sydney in 1849. No relatives in colony. Unable to read or write. Employed by John Hicknoe as a nursemaid at eight pounds per year.

Bridget Luddy, aged 18, a Catholic, Cahir, daughter of Edmund and Bridget - mother living in Clogheen [possibly in workhouse]. Went out on 'William and Mary' 1849. Bridget was a nursemaid, with no relatives in the colony. She was employed by H. Wilson at £8 per year. Married Matthew Bryan at Goulbourn in 1851 and had 12 children.

Catherine Healy, aged 18, Cahir, Catholic, daughter of Nicholas and Catherine. A nursemaid, had an uncle in colony. Employed by G.J. Armitage in Sydney at £8 per year. Married a Cornish 'free settler' John Joseph Vercoe in 1853 and had seven children. Catherine died aged 70 in 1905. Her name appears on the Sydney Famine memorial. ("The memorial to the Great Irish Famine and the young women who came from the workhouses of Ireland to Australia between 1848 and 1850 on a special emigration scheme is the vision of the Irish community in Sydney".[2])

Margaret Lynch, aged 17, Cahir, Catholic, daughter of William and Ellen - Ellen living in Clogheen [presumably Clogheen workhouse]. A nursemaid, can read, no relatives in colony. Sailed on 'William and Mary' with her sister Bridget to Sydney 1849. Employed by John Dawson at £8 per year.

Bridget Lynch, aged 19, from Cahir, a house servant, sister of Margaret, Catholic, daughter of William and Ellen – Ellen living in Clogheen [possibly workhouse]. Sailed on 'William and Mary' to Sydney 1849. Worked with her sister Margaret for Mr Dawson. Married Thomas Gilroy 1851.

---

2   *http://www.irishfaminememorial.org/en/about-monument/*

Judith (Julia) McGrath, aged 15, from Cahir, Catholic, daughter of Thomas and Mary, (Mother living in Cahir). Sailed on 'William and Mary' to Sydney 1849. House Servant, cannot read or write, no relatives in colony.

Mary Mulcahy, aged 16, from Cahir, Catholic, daughter of Michael and Mary. Sailed on 'William and Mary' to Sydney 1849. Farm Servant, can read, no relatives in colony. Her indenture with Mr J Nowlan was cancelled for being disobedient and insolent.

Bridget Scanlan, aged 16, from Cahir, Catholic, daughter of James and Margaret (both deceased). Went out on 'William and Mary' to Sydney in 1849. Nursemaid, cannot read or write, no relatives in colony. Employed by Alex Moore at £8 per year. Married Edward Randell in 1855, 3 children by 1859. Sister to Johanna on same ship.

Johanna Scanlan, Aged 18, From Cahir, daughter of James and Margaret (both deceased), sailed on 'William and Mary' to Sydney 1849. House Servant, can read, no relatives in colony. Employed by Michael Harnett at £8 per year. Married Thomas Smith in 1851, 3 children. Thomas died 1856. Johanna married again, this time to Daniel Mahoney in 1860, 3 children. Johanna died in 1887 and is buried in an unmarked grave. Sister to Bridget who travelled on same ship.

Judith (Julia) White, Age 16, from Cahir, Catholic, daughter of William and Margaret (both deceased). Sailed on 'William and Mary' to Sydney 1849. Farm Servant, read and write, no relatives in colony, employed by S.S. Gould, Wooloomooloo at £8 per year. In May 1851, indenture cancelled in dispute over wages.

Catherine Kearney, age 18, from Cahir, Catholic, daughter of John and Ellen (both deceased), Nursemaid, cannot read or write. Employed by S. Moses, £8 per year. No relatives in colony.[3]

Many of the letters that appeared in the Australian press in the years of the Female Orphan Emigration scheme reveal the intolerance and the unwarranted stereotyping that pervaded the cities where the Irish girls were placed. There are also letters in praise of the Irish Female Orphan Emigrants. The girls spent some time at Hyde Park Barracks depot; and then, employers were invited to

---

3   *http://www.irishfaminememorial.org*

apply for orphan girls who might be suitable employees.[4] A small number of those letters will suffice to demonstrate the opposing viewpoints.

Sydney Morning Herald, 19 October 1848

FEMALE ORPHANS BY THE EARL GREY. *(From Tuesday's Government Gazette.) PERSONS desiring to obtain servants or apprentices from amongst the female orphans who have arrived in the Earl Grey, are requested to send in written applications for the same, on or before the 23rd day of October instant, addressed to the Agent for Immigration at the Office in Hyde Park Barracks, by whom they will be submitted to the Committee appointed to superintend the disposal of the orphans, and to act as their guardians. If sent by post the application should be forwarded under cover, addressed to the "Clerk of the Executive Council." In each application there should be set forth the applicant's Christian name and surname, his or her calling, his or her address in full, the nature of the service which each female applied for by him or her would be required to perform, or whether he or she would rather that such female should be bound to him or her under an indenture of apprenticeship or under an ordinary agreement of service. It will be understood that in accordance with the general rule which has been for some time observed by the Government in the disposal of Female Immigrants, the orphans placed under the charge of the Committee will not be allowed to accept situations in inns or other houses of public entertainment. The orphans will be landed, and lodged in the Institution at Hyde Park, where, on some future day, of which due intimation will be given, they may be inspected by such applicants under this notice as shall have been approved of by the Committee. Signed: Francis L. S. Merewether, Agent for Immigration, and Chairman of the Orphan Immigration Committee.* [5]

---

4   For details on Hyde Park Depot, see:
     https://sydneylivingmuseums.com.au/exhibitions/female-immigration-depot-1848-1886
5   *Sydney Morning Herald,* 19 October 1848

Sydney Morning Herald. 28 February 1850

IRISH ORPHAN GIRLS. To the Editors of the Sydney Morning Herald. February 28, 1850. GENTLEMEN, Two letters have recently appeared in your paper on the above subject, on which one or two remarks may not be out of place. To take the last first, I find "a Bushman" is very angry that parties of them are not sent to Wide Bay and the Burnett districts. He urges, strongly and truly, the enormous moral wickedness likely to arise from an exclusively male population, and would like parties of these girls to be sent there, that the stock keepers and shepherds may take to themselves wives. It is rather strange, however, that friend Bushman did not recollect that the mere presence of men and women is not all that is required to consummate a marriage. He surely cannot imagine that the Government will send hundreds of orphan girls to places where there is no possibility of marrying them, and every imaginable inducement to them to live in a state of concubinage! The idea is too monstrous to be entertained by any but a savage. Let the graziers in the districts spoken of be unanimous in providing for a clergyman to reside among them, and then it will be time enough to call in the authorities to send them orphans. Another of your correspondents complained of what he was pleased to call "Hiberno phobia." I think he would have more accurately described this as Romano-phobia. Such of our citizens as walk upon Hyde Park are constantly exposed to this feeling being stirred up. Everybody remarks on the regiment of these girls which is constantly marched into the Romish Chapel; and there is at least one half of our population who are irritated that out of the 1300 orphan girls who have been imported at public expense, more than 1100 have been Roman Catholics. If we transplant Tipperary to New South Wales, we know full well that we shall have its habits with its people, and as the police have quite enough to do already, we don't want this. In conclusion, I will tell your correspondent who speaks of " Hiberno-phobia," a little fact that may put him on his guard. It is this - that the lower orders of the Roman Catholics are now heard to boast in Sydney, that though the Protestants have succeeded in stopping the importation of over whelming numbers of grown up Romanists, yet that the priests have beaten them by getting out these girls, who they anticipate will, with their offspring, give us, not many years hence, a Popish ascendancy in New South Wales. [6]

---

6   *Sydney Morning Herald*, 1st March, 1850

The Melbourne Argus, 15 Mar 1850

IRISH ORPHAN IMMIGRATION. *Advices have reached the local government, of another ship load of female orphans, from Ireland, being on their way to this province; it becomes, therefore, an imperative duty on the colonists to offer a public remonstrance against this outrageous prostitution of the immigration fund. … we feel assured that we are but expressing the universal voice of the public in declaring the present system of Irish female orphan immigration a serious injury to the community, and a wanton abuse of the funds intended by the colonists to procure the immigration of virtuous and reputable parties. Without reverting to, or recapitulating the reasons previously assigned in our columns why Irish female orphan immigration should not further be proceeded with, we feel it to be our duty to state that further experience has but shown that the evils we before referred to are increasing, and that now, from the general disinclination of the colonists to have anything to do with them as servants, they hang on hand at the depot till a very considerable proportion of their number join the ranks of the prostitutes infesting the more public streets of the city. Nor are we alone in our experience of this infliction for, as we learn from the public journals, precisely the same result has followed the Irish Orphan Immigration both to Sydney and Adelaide. It is necessary, therefore, that immediate steps should be taken for the transmission of a strong protest to Earl Grey against the use of the colonial immigration fund for any charitable purpose whatsoever and the sooner they are proceeded with the better.[7]*

=====================

In July 1850, *The Sydney Freeman's Journal* responded to the dreadful character assassination of the girls and wrote *"The most shameful and groundless charge of immorality made against the orphans by the 'Argus' and re-echoed by the City Council of Melbourne, has been taken up and most triumphantly refuted by the Irish residents in Port Philip. From the written evidence of the Chief Constable, the Sergeants, and members of the Police Force produced at the meeting of St. Patrick's Society, it has been proved that not more than three or six at most, out of the thirteen hundred orphan girls landed at Melbourne turned out disreputably. The Mayor and Immigration Agent certified the same, and spoke in high terms of the moral character of these girls.[8]*

7   *The Melbourne Argus,* 15 Mar 1850
8   *Freemans Journal Sydney,* 11 July 1850. (reprinted 23 Jan 1904)

Cahir Women in the News 1827-1935
By Karol DeFalco and Edmund O'Riordan

Catherine Smith/Smyth

According to the *Tipperary Free Press* of 13 June 1827, the house of Thomas Hannigan, a publican opposite the Caher Barracks, had been robbed of wearing apparel, silver spoons, a silver watch, and about £2. The clothing was found in the possession of a woman named Smith. She and two young men named Dorney and Leamy were taken into custody. A week later, the same newspaper reported that Catherine Smyth, David Leamy, and John Dorney had been committed to gaol, charged with robbery of the Hannigan house.

Mrs. Hughes

The death of Mrs. Hughes was reported in *The Limerick Chronicle* on Wednesday, December 5th 1832. The article stated that Mrs. Hughes was the wife of Henry James Hughes, Esq. of Killemly who was the Captain of the Cahir Yeomanry. Mrs Hughes died at her home in Cahir. About ten o'clock on the previous Monday night, she had been upstairs, reading a prayer book.

> "Her headdress caught fire from a candle which was placed on the table; the fire instantly communicated to other parts of her dress; she then endeavoured to extinguish the fire by wrapping herself in the curtains of her own bed. Shortly after, Mr. and Mrs. William Walpole, who live next door, having heard a noise in Mrs. H.'s apartments, hastened to know the result, together with Mrs. Hughes' servants, and they found the lady lying on the floor near the room door, enveloped in flames, in a weak state and almost exhausted. The curtains had, by this time, also caught fire. Surgical aid was immediately called in; but all to no purpose, Mr. Hughes was on a visit to Ballydine - the seat of his brother-in-law, Capt. Power. A messenger was dispatched with the melancholy intelligence, who arrived at Ballydine at five o'clock in the morning, and Mr. Hughes had the poor consolation of arriving in time to see his wife alive; she retained her senses to the last moment, and peaceably resigned her soul into the hands of her Redeemer

at twenty minutes past one o'clock on Tuesday. She earnestly recommended with her last breath, her children, of whom she was passionately fond, to the special care and protection of her dear husband. Mrs. Hughes was in her 37th year; she was married in the year 1818, and has left three sons. Her mortal remains were interred at eight o'clock Thursday morning, in the interior of the old church, Caher. Though it was understood that the funeral would be a private one, it was numerously attended by the gentry and clergy of the town, and many other respectable persons from distant parts of the County. The lady was descended of an ancient and highly respected family, and was the daughter of J. Butler, Esq. of Coolguile Castle, and grand-daughter of Theobald Butler, Esq. of Wilford, who was, upwards of seventy years ago High Sheriff of the County Tipperary – Theobald was the near relative and intimate friend of the present Marquis of Ormond's father. Mrs. Hughes was also the cousin of the late Edward Power, Esq. of Gurteen, and sister-in-law of the present Capt. James Power of Ballydine, Deputy Lieutenant of the County Waterford. Mrs. Hughes in her figure was extremely genteel and handsome, and was possessed of a kind and amiable disposition, which endeared her to all who had the pleasure of her acquaintance. It is needless to add, that she is universally and deservedly regretted by all classes of persons. Melancholy to relate, Mrs. Hughes is the *third* person who suffered a similar fate, and who died within the last month in Caher, in consequence of their clothes having caught fire!

Miss Anne O'Meara

On Friday, August 14, 1840, the *Limerick Reporter* reported on the "Loyal National Repeal Association"[1] meeting at the Corn-Exchange in Dublin at which "Mr. O'Connell entered the meeting, and was received with loud cheers". The secretary had been honoured with the following letter and list of repealers, submitted by Miss Anne O'Meara. The letter had been written in Cahir on 2 August 1840. In it, Miss O'Meara stated that she had enclosed 30 shillings from subscriptions collected from twenty-nine Cahir women, "with my own",

---

1   The Loyal National Repeal Association was formed to campaign for the repeal of the 1800 'Act of Union' which created the United Kingdom of Great Britain and Ireland and effectively dismantled the Irish Parliament.

for the Repeal Association. Miss O'Meara said that she would submit another remittance and wrote, "You will have the goodness to have us enrolled in the ranks of the Repealers". The other twenty-eight signatories were Miss Holohan, Mrs. Burke, Miss Cody, Miss E. O'Connor, Miss Roach, Miss Butler, Miss O'Shea, Miss Dillon, Miss Morony, Miss M. Burke, Miss J. Ryan, Mrs. O'Meara, Miss Ellen Lonergan, Miss Tobin, Miss Lonergan, Miss Mary O'Connor, Miss Catherine Maher, Miss Ryan, Miss Julia Butler, Mrs. Ryan, Miss Eliza Hassett, Miss Margaret O'Shea, Miss Cantwell, Mrs. Robinson, Mrs. Tobin, Miss O'Donnell, and Mrs. Boland. Daniel O'Connell said he was:-

> "very proud of having the honour to move that the ladies, whose names they had heard, be enrolled as associates and he was sure it would be carried by acclamation (hear,hear and cheers for the Cahir Women.) He would also move that the secretary be requested to write to Miss O'Meara, thanking her for the communication that had been received, and expressing the deep respect of the association for the patriotic exertions which those young ladies had made (hear, hear.) And further, that Miss O'Meara, be requested to communicate to them the sentiments contained in the secretary's letter, as well as the fact of their names being enrolled with respect and gratitude (cheers.)"

"Nymph of the Pave"

In January 1844, Sarah K. "a nymph of the pave", was charged with robbing Officer William Augustin Hyder, of the 10th Hussars at Caher Barracks, of a Bank Post Bill for £25. Mr Hyder deposed that his room in the Cahir barracks was forced open at night and the bank note and other items were stolen. The bank note was returned to Officer Hyder a few days later from the mess waiter who found it in a billiard room attached to the barracks. On the witness stand, Officer Hyder underwent a humorous cross examination by the facetious attorney, Mr Smith, who asked Hyder about his relationship with the celebrated Hyder Ali Khan and other matters more closely related to the robbery.

A young woman in the service of the Bridewell keeper, where Sarah was confined, testified that Sarah made a confession to her while in custody. The jury returned after a short while with a verdict of guilty. Poor Sarah K. was transported for seven years. *Tipperary Vindicator*, 16 March 1844.

(It seems extraordinary that the young woman, Sarah, was able to get through the gates of a military barracks, past the armed sentries, across the parade grounds, enter the barracks building, and force open the door to the officer's room!) In an unconnected incident in 1845, William Augustin Hyder of 10th Hussars was charged "with conduct unbecoming an officer and a gentleman", that in 1842 he had deceived his commanding officer at Ballincollig, Co. Cork. Even though Hyder was acquitted, the court stated that they "could not refrain from animadverting in the strongest terms of disapprobation on the violent, coarse, and uncalled for language, which he, the prisoner, has had recourse to in his defence, in allusion to the character of [one of the witnesses]."

Cork Examiner, 17 November 1845.

Cahir Military Barracks which, according to Officer William Augustin Hyder, was broken into by 'Nymph of the Pave', Sarah K in 1844

"Immoral Behavior"

The Waterford Mail of 23 May 1860 reported a court proceeding "which has caused not a little stir in the town and neighbourhood of Cahir". A "colony of improper women" used "horrid obscenities" leading to the "greatest public annoyance that any town could possibly be subjected to". This group of at least eleven women, residing at a plantation adjoining the cavalry barracks, were arrested by a party of the military men under the direction of Colonel Knox, "very much resembling martial law!" The women were then turned over to the constabulary. Prior to the round-up, people walking along the road had been subjected to "the filthiest language or being offended in a still worse degree." After previous arrests, "the wretched outcast females from distant localities appear at Cahir again and again to replace those who might be undergoing imprisonment." The women arrested this time were charged with being women of bad character. They confessed to their "immoral behaviour" and admitted they had no place of residence and no ability to pay bail. They were imprisoned for six months. Although the writer of the article is glad of the "riddance", he deplored the tactics used by the military, stating, "[Even if]... the women were the very worst moral characters that could be herded together ...the arrest was...an unjustifiable assumption of power [of the military] which the law could not tolerate." He closed the article by saying,

> "Though we, in common with those who were immediately annoyed, regret the existence for so long a time such a lamentable nuisance, and must heartily congratulate the neighbourhood upon the riddance it has experienced, still we cannot but think the law sanctions not any such course as collecting a number of people together, and hurling them over indiscriminately to the constabulary, merely because they belong to that wretched class of the community whose frailties and evil conduct are so much to be deplored."

Catherine O'Donnell

According to the *Waterford News and General Advertiser* of February 21, 1868, Miss O'Donnell, daughter of James O'Donnell of Cahir, took the name Sister Mary Joseph Aloysius at her profession and reception held at Presentation Convent, Cathedral Square, St. John's, Newfoundland, on 11 February. Further research indicates that Miss O'Donnell was one of eight children born to James O'Donnell and his wife, Mary Dalton, of Clonmore. Sister Mary Joseph Aloysius had been baptised 'Catherine' on 9 October 1844 at Cahir. She entered the convent on 23 July 1865. Her death occurred on 23 January 1909, and she was buried at Cathedral Square, St. Johns, Newfoundland.

Mrs Mary Dillon, Mrs Bridget English, Mrs Fitzgerald

In an attempt to secure salaried teachers at a National School established by the land agent, he, Mr Butler, threatened to evict families whose children attended the convent school. Mrs Mary Dillon and Mrs Bridget English were two women who had children enrolled at the convent school. According to the *Waterford News and Star* of 7 September 1871, Mary Dillon, mother of six children, was ordered to Cahir Lodge. She claimed in court that if she did not send her children to the agent's school, she would be refused the Christmas charities and "would have to look out for a house for myself and my family". In addition to a husband and six children, Mary had two lodgers, "two poor widows as nice and quiet as women could be."

Mrs Bridget English had three children and a husband in America. She had received no coal from the Charteris Estate at Christmas. Mrs Fitzgerald, mother of five children, suffered the same fate. The report concluded with "some dozen of mothers waited outside who were refused the Christmas charity coals".

Misfortunates

The stories of Cahir women are often harrowing. The following cases, involving young girls, were reported in *The Waterford Standard* and at The Petty Sessions of 1879. The editors of this book have decided not to print the girls' names.

* *The Waterford Standard* in 1876 reported that E.F. was arrested as the mother of a dead child found in a ditch by Constable Connor. The constable deposed – at an inquest in Cahir - that the woman "came to his home on Wednesday and told him that she had on the previous night given birth to the child in the stable of a farmer in the neighbourhood, where she was at work, and that the child was still-born and she buried it. She accompanied witness to the place where he found the child wrapped in an old apron. Dr Stokes, of Cahir, deposed that he made an examination of the body, and he believed that the child was still-born and never breathed. He also stated that there was gross neglect shown to the girl, and that a savage could not have been worse treated. The coroner directed the jury to find a verdict in accordance with the doctor's evidence, that the child was still-born, and he remarked that it was for the police and other legal officials to take any steps they may think necessary on any other matter connected therewith. A verdict as directed was found."

The Cahir Petty Sessions archives of 1879 include the following:-

*E.K., aged eight, was found with "no visible means of subsistence and no surviving relative". She was sent to St. Louis Industrial School in Thurles until "she attains the age of sixteen".

*E. & M. W., aged eight and nine, having "no proper guardianship" and described as destitute, were sent to Rosanna Industrial School in Tipperary.

Mrs. Gaussen

An advertisement in the *Dublin Daily Express* on 17 January 1880: Cook and General Servant – Will be disengaged on the 1st of February, a smart, active, cleanly woman, who is a good, comfortable plain cook; wants a place where another servant is kept; understands pastry, soups, and made-up dishes; is leaving at her own desire, in consequence of a change in the house; a small regular family and a quiet place more an object than high wages; will be found most attentive to her business, and trustworthy, and very careful of everything under her care; no objection to a small washing; the country preferred. Address T M, in care of Mrs Gaussen (with whom she is still living), Castle Cottage, Cahir, County Tipperary.

Lady Louisa Knox

Lady Louisa Knox of Cahir Abbey advertised in the *Dublin Daily Express* (15 September 1880), noting that she resided in the country and was offering £40 a year for a pantry boy.

Mrs. Mulcahy

Dublin Daily Express, 13 October 1883

Housemaid in a gentleman's family – A respectable young Girl requires a situation as above; understands the making up of fine things; is a good plain needlewoman, if required; will be disengaged at the end of the month; no objection to town or country, and can be highly recommended; two years in present place. Please address M K in care of Mrs Mulcahy, Bridge Street, Cahir, Co Tipperary.

Dead Body

Dublin Daily Express, 20th June 1891

The dead body of a woman who had apparently been maltreated was found yesterday at Cahir in which place a troop of Hussars was billeted the previous night.

Young Women's Christian Association

To raise funds for the YWCA, a bazaar was held in 1894 in the "large room, Cahir Castle". *The Waterford Standard* of 25 July 1894 reported that the room was lined with stalls: refreshments, farm produce and flowers, fancy work, hat competition, and art. A substantial gain was made from the sale of fruit and eggs. A beautiful photo of the Cahir Church, taken by a Major with the 10th Royal Hussars, was "a ready sale". A lady brought an electric battery "which gave rise to no little amusement". The article concludes with "the bazaar... very successful, and that a good sum of money was realised..."

Mrs Murphy wins Court Battle

There was great rejoicing over the success of an elderly, illiterate woman of the Galtees - who lived in a one roomed, thatched cottage with one window - in her heroic fight against the attempt to hustle her out of her ancient freehold at the base of the Galtees. According to *The Nationalist* (January 1898), Mrs Murphy received many congratulations over the shower of gold sovereigns she received. Other tenants on the estate had to abandon their claims to graze sheep and cattle because their ancestors – some 80 years ago – "too confidently trusted in the then Lord of the Manor, when ...they yielded up their free right of common, without having preserved the proper evidence of depasturage (grazing) ...Mrs Murphy happily for herself, had a firmer footing..."

Abandoned Baby

On May 19, 1900, *The Nationalist* reported that a Miss O'Brien from Clonmel had come before the Board of Guardians with a delicate looking infant in her arms. Miss O'Brien said that the baby had been deserted and asked the guardians to take the infant into the workhouse. In reply to questions, she stated that she did not know to whom the baby belonged. A young woman had left the baby with Miss O'Brien on Wednesday week and promised, once employed, a month's wages for its keep. The young woman went to America, sending 2s 6d from Queenstown before departing. The name of the young woman, and her address of Cahir, was given to the Board of Guardians who then refused to accept the child. It is thought that because the baby's mother was from Cahir, which fell under the Clogheen Board of Guardians, the baby would have to be supported by that Board rather than the Clonmel Board of Guardians.

Miss Cecil Violet Denny

The marriage of Miss Cecil Violet Denny was announced in the *Waterford Standard* on 16 August 1902. She was the daughter of C E Denny, Esq. and Mrs. Denny of Ballybrado. The groom was Captain Gordon MacCampbell, RFA, and the wedding was held on Saturday, August 9th "at the beautiful parish church of Cahir", followed by a reception at "Ballybrado , where all the guests present were most hospitably entertained". Much praise was given "to Mrs. Edward Smith who, with the kind assistance of the Misses Devenish and other friends of the bride, designed and arranged the lovely decorations of the church, which were composed of white flowers, foliaged plants, flags, and garlands entwined with the artillery colours."

"The bride, who looked quite charming, was given away by her father. She wore a very becoming dress of white crystalline silk having a train from the waist, which was covered with a flounce of accordion plated mousseline de soie, inserted with motifs of lace. The bride had a wreath and spray of myrtle, and her mother's embroidered tulle, which was fastened by a four-leaved diamond and emerald shamrock brooch, the gift of the bridegroom: also a beautiful necklace and pendant of peridots and white enamel which was given by her father. The bridesmaids were – Miss E M Denny, Miss O Denny, and Miss E R Denny, sisters of the bride; Miss B W Denny and Miss Mackenzie, cousins of the bride. The bridesmaids' dresses were composed of cream silk voile, with bolero and motifs of cream lace. The hats were of white crinoline straw, draped with lace and trimmed with yellow roses. They carried shower bouquets of yellow roses and ferns, and wore brooches having the artillery monogram in enamel and gold, the gifts of the bridegroom. The bride's going away dress was of … navy blue serge, with collar and blouse of string-coloured lace, and a burnt straw, trimmed with a wreath of corn flowers and Eau de Nil satin ribbon.

The newspaper article concludes with a list of more than one hundred wedding gifts and the names of the gift givers. Noteworthy is the carriage clock given by the farm labourers. As a wedding gift, silver was definitely in. Among the silver items, the couple received six silver scent bottles and three silver salt cellars. Other gifts, which today seem like unusual wedding gifts, included:

Mr and Mrs Murdoch – silver buttonhook and shoehorn
Mrs Mackesy – lace handkerchief
Miss L B Rice – tennis racket
Mrs Daniell and Miss Grubb – silver thermometer
Dr and Mrs Walsh – leather address book
Mr Mooney – silver egg cup
Mr and Mrs Summers – silver ink bottle
Mr and Mrs Farquharson – fan

Mrs Hutchinson – silver buttons
Mr and Miss M Hutchinson – hunting crop
Butler at Ballybrado – fountain pen
Miss C Browning – gold whistle
Mrs E M Power – Bible, prayer book, and hymn book
A Fitzpatrick – silver stamp box
Mr and Mrs Richardson – silver pincushion
Mr Ellarry Beddoms – silver rose bowl and cigarette box
Miss Hassard – silver bell
Mrs Palgrave Simpson – brass candlestick and match stand

'Ladies of Cahir' Protest

An article entitled "The Persecution of Nuns in France" appeared in the *Cork Examiner* of 21 August 1902. It reported, "The ladies of Cahir signed a protest against the persecution now being enacted by the government of so called Catholic France by turning adrift to the outer world the good and holy nuns of that country from their convents and happy homes." The article went on to say, "We the women of Cahir Co Tipperary Ireland unite heart and soul in sympathy in prayer and in protest with the brave women of France struggling to protect their altars and their homes. Our hearts burn with shame to hear of such scenes enacted in a country once so great and once so Catholic. We utterly condemn the wanton persecution of those holy nuns whose lives are spent in ministering to the very poorest of the poor and utterly execrate and brand as villains and cowards the men who, in defiance of all liberty and justice, are oppressing God's church and God's poor and warring against women and children."

School Children Injured

According to the *Cork Examiner* of 7 May 1904, there was an accident on Tuesday in which children and servants of Cahir Convent were injured when their wagonette overturned at a sharp corner on the road between Clogheen and Cahir. All the occupants were thrown out. The party had been returning from Shanbally demesne where they had seen the King and Queen. Mary McGill, aged about 21, "deaf and dumb", and a servant at The Mercy Convent Cahir died at 3am on Thursday at the Clogheen Union hospital. Prior to the accident, Miss McGill, who was born in Scotland, served as a domestic at the convent at Mountanglesby, Clogheen.

Also injured in the accident was Patrick Whelan, a gardener about 60 years of age and "deaf but not dumb". He was kindly admitted to the Cahir Military Hospital which was just 300 yards from the scene of the accident. The day after the accident, trepanning (hole drilled in skull to release the pressure of blood build-up following trauma to the head) was successfully performed by Drs Walsh (Clogheen), Cusack (Cahir), and Whitty (the Barracks). Mr Whelan was showing some improvement.

The Blooming Girls

In March 1911, *The Advocate* reported the impressions a visitor from Australia experienced having come upon "...a galaxy of youth and beauty who were dancing and making merry in the Cahir area. The girls and boys were stepping, jigging, and reeling on a portable wooden platform, the fiddler occupying a most exalted position on a donkey cart. The style of dancing was different from that practised in Australia and the mazy waltz was conspicuous by its absence. It was a great source of amusement and pleasure to see the strapping Tipperary boys and the blooming girls jigging. As the third couple led up and bowed to a blushing Tipperary girleen and a strapping six footer whom someone called Mike, I almost fancied I could hear them humming the phrases of the 'Ould Irish Jig'."

A Cahir Divorce

The editors of this book have decided to not print the names of the Cahir participants mentioned in this news article. *The Northern Whig* of 13 January 1914 reported that at London Divorce Court, Joseph Wright, who had been a gunner in the Royal Horse Artillery at Cahir but was "now of Woolwich", sued for divorce from his wife C. Wright. Joseph Wright testified that the couple were married at St. Mary's Church at Cahir in November 1909 and that shortly after, his wife gave birth. Wright said the baby was not his, and he left his wife. He alleged his wife's misconduct with J. O'D., and evidence was introduced, stating that the two people involved in the misconduct were "seen about together". The divorce was granted.

Cahir Women's Anti-Conscription Pledge

During the First World War, Britain hoped to draft Irish men into the military to fight on the Western Front. On June 9, 1918, events were held all over Ireland for the purpose of getting women to sign petitions, opposing the plans for conscription and refusing to take the jobs of men who had lost their employment because of their refusal to be drafted. The *Freeman's Journal* reported that 1,204 women signed in Cahir! "In the evening, they walked in procession from the Convent grounds to the Church where Benediction was given, and the Rosary was recited."

Irishwoman's Sad Death
Miss Josephine Tierney, aged 40-45, fell from an Irish mail train as it travelled swiftly through Flintshire, having left Holyhead on Saturday at 12:28 and headed for Euston. *The Derry Journal* of 22 July 1929 went on to say that the woman's body showed severe head wounds. She possessed a return ticket from Cahir and was headed on to Leeds and St. Joseph's Convent. Her plan was to visit an uncle. Another account stated that Josephine was the niece of Sir Thomas Ryan.

Mrs Charles Denny
Waterford Standard, 3 November 1934
The general regret caused by the passing of Mrs. Denny, Ballybrado, Cahir, was made strikingly evident on Saturday last when the funeral was attended by a most impressive cortege, representative of all classes and creeds in the district.

The late Mrs. Denny, who was the widow of Charles Edward Denny, J.P., Ballybrado, was held in the highest and most affectionate regard by those who knew her. She was of a most charitable and benevolent disposition, setting aside a large portion of her income for giving to the poor of the district. Her loss will be deeply felt, for she knew personally many of those whom she so generously helped through life, and the benefit of her knowledge and advice was freely given to those who asked for it.

Gaelic games for Cahir Girls but no "foreign dances"
"Nationalist" 29 July 1935
On Thursday evening the Cahir colleens defeated Cashel at a friendly camogie game at Townparks. The Cashel team had never before been beaten and had won the Breen Medals in open competition, so that they came to Cahir fully confident of success. The game was fast and interesting and although the Cashel colleens showed some brilliant flashes yet, the Cahir defence proved too good and the runaway victory that was expected by the visitors was turned

into defeat by good play and determination on the home side. Miss O'Mara, for Cahir, scored five goals and Miss Barrett one goal, while Cashel could only reply twice. A tower of strength on the Cahir side was Miss Quirke, who kept goal, and her exhibition in saving and pucking the ball was a treat.

Gaelic pastimes have been on the wane in Cahir for a long time and it was only a few months ago that camogie was started. The home team's victory was one of outstanding merit and they are to be congratulated on gaining a victory over such well known exponents of the game as Cashel.

Mr. T. Ryan, Secretary, Co. Camogie Board, was the referee and after the game congratulated Cahir on the success they had achieved. It was a grand thing to see the girls playing their native game and he hoped they would continue to live up to the ideals and traditions of their country. They should live up to them off the field, as well as on. There was not much use in playing Gaelic games if they danced foreign dances. It was a deserving victory for Cahir to win over such a famed team as Cashel and he hoped they would keep up the spirit of the game always. Four teams, he said, were not affiliated – Cahir, Bansha, Ardfinnan and Dromline – but at a meeting of the Co. Board in Thurles on Wednesday he had got permission to affiliate them. He would put up a set of medals for competition between the four teams. The Cahir team was represented by the Misses Quirke, McGrath, Butler, Barrett, Tierney, Daly, O'Donoghue.

"Don't Start the Revolution Without Me!"
Cahir Women and the Land League
By Josephine O'Neill

Women of the Land coming together to assist their neighbours during the Irish National Land League years. (Courtesy of the National Library of Ireland)

The next time you turn left at the corner of Castle Street into the Square, try to imagine a detachment of cavalry with drawn sabres, as they struggled to uphold the rule of English law against a rebellious army of Land Leaguers. Surprisingly enough, the forces of law and order lost that skirmish.

If you are ever in Scarrough or Rehill Woods, remember a group of poor struggling women who were continuously prosecuted in court for collecting firewood. If you are out and about on the plain of Clonmore, try to guess why an army of 1,000 farmers assembled to protect Mrs. Fenton's crops. Then there was the funeral that nobody turned up to, apart from the corpse. All of these events happened in Cahir in the turbulent closing decades of the 1800s.

Towards the end of the 19th century, huge changes affected the lives of Cahir women on several fronts. These changes were economic and social, with Home Rule and agitation for land rights to the forefront.

On a local level, the person who had the greatest effect on the lives of all who lived in Cahir and surrounding districts was an Englishwoman, Lady Margaret Charteris. Like many of her class at the time, Lady Margaret's comfortable life was made possible by extracting as much rent as possible from her tenants. However, that way of life was about to change forever.

A New Radicalism

In October 1879, the Land League was founded in Mayo by Michael Davitt. Charles Stuart Parnell became its first president. Land Leaguers vowed to achieve the three "F"s: fair rent, free sale and fixity of tenure for Irish tenant farmers while the long-term aim was to achieve peasant proprietorship. Land Leaguers were determined to outlaw rack-renting (the practice of extracting exorbitant rents) and to defend tenants against eviction. A new word, "boycott", entered the English language, as League members advocated shunning "land grabbers" or those who took over the holdings of evicted farmers. In 1880, the Ladies' Land League was formed when Anna Parnell, sister of Charles, returned to Ireland from America to lead it.

The response in Cahir to the formation of the Land League appears to have been immediate and enthusiastic. In 1879, five thousand tenant farmers met on the Square demanding a remission of a half year's rent! Meanwhile, *The Nation* reported that £32 was sent by the "priests and people of Cahir" to the Evicted Tenants Fund. A meeting was planned, but realising how many supporters would attend, the organisers postponed the event until the end of the month to arrange transport. All trains coming to Cahir were full on the 25th of September, and the crowd "amassed in its full strength over the wide expanse of the Square." They recalled the suffering brought upon Cahir in past times "by the villainy of land agents" and demanded the abolition of unjust laws which perpetuated landlordism.

Brawny Peasantry

According to *The Freeman's Journal*, September 28th, 1881, the "estimate of twelve thousand persons made by one of the speakers was far from excessive." Powerful bands of the "brawny peasantry of Tipperary" flocked to Cahir with "flags flying and bands of music." Streets were spanned with green banners bearing patriotic mottos.

Cahir Land League "wanted to secure to the occupier the peaceable possession of his home and the fruits of his industry." "Irish men and Irish women" were addressed, and Fr. Mooney, parish priest of the town, saw the occasion as "the laying of the immediate foundation of the emancipation of the farmers of Ireland." He urged them to "build a solid, perfect, impregnable branch of the Land League in this parish." Following the speeches, Joseph Fenton of Clonmore proposed that those gathered on the Square take the following pledge by holding up their hands: "We hereby solemnly pledge ourselves not to bid, take hold or occupy a house or land from which a tenant has been evicted for non-payment of an unjust rent; never to work on such land and never to purchase cattle or crops sold under these conditions." The movement grew steadily in Cahir, and in October 1880, six hundred Cahir Land League members marched in Clonmel. By November, with more than 700 members, progress was described as "remarkable in the last degree throughout the various districts of Cahir Land League."

Irish National Land League Membership Card
Ireland for the Irish – Down With Landlordism.
Keep a Firm Grip of your Homestead – The Land for the People

➻ Objects ✚ of ✚ the ✚ League. ❋ ❮

The Irish National Land League was formed for the following objects :—

FIRST—To put an end to Rack-renting, Eviction, and Landlord Oppression.

SECOND—To effect such a radical change in the Land System of Ireland as will put it in the power of every Irish Farmer to become the owner, on fair terms, of the land he tills.

The means proposed to effect these objects are :—

(1) Organization amongst the people and Tenant Farmers for the purpose of self-defence, and inculcating the absolute necessity of their refusing to take any Farm from which another may be evicted, or from purchasing any Cattle or Goods which may be seized on for non-payment of impossible rent.

(2) The cultivation of public opinion by persistent exposure, in the Press and by Public Meetings, of the monstrous injustice of the present system, and of its ruinous results.

(3) A resolute demand for the reduction of the excessive rents which have brought the Irish People to a state of starvation.

(4) Temperate but firm resistance to oppression and injustice.

The Objects of the Irish National Land League were printed in the back of each membership Card.
(Both images Courtesy of Eileen Flynn)

Sources of Radicalism

In 1880, Fr. Mooney appeared before the Royal Commission regarding the Land Act of 1870. He stated that he had been parish priest in Cahir for 17 years and claimed that rents on Lady Margaret's estate were double those in Griffith's Valuation (an 1850 valuation of land for the purpose of assessing Poor Law rates, but used frequently as evidence that rents were excessive). Fr. Mooney conceded that the landlady made allowances for loss of cattle and built houses and drained land but noted that she also increased her rent to cover her outlay. He described her as "a perfect absentee landlord", but it's

Rev. Fr Maurice Mooney P.P. Cahir 1865 – 1891
Land League Activist who claimed that the
members of Cahir Ladies Land League were a
most essential portion of the community

not clear whether this was said tongue in cheek, given that he referred to the fact that she owned and maintained a "palatial residence" in Cahir. Although she is described as kind and benevolent to the poor and had supplied a water system to the town, he maintained that "some residences of farmers are sad to look at." By September 1880, Fr. Mooney was referring to "the merciless extraction of impossible rents." He, himself, was helping evicted farmers and asking that they be given "a few weeks to thresh their corn."

Agricultural depression, cattle disease and foreign competition had brought Irish and Cahir farmers to their knees. Lady Margaret held sway over 16,616 acres in South Tipperary, which helped her to maintain her splendid house in Cahir as well as a house in Grosvenor Square, London, and a country seat in Berkshire. Rents from farmers and householders were collected by her agents. Appearing in court for a reduction of rent in 1881, one of her tenants begins his defence by saying "I only know my landlady by name." Lady Margaret only made two visits to Cahir during her lifetime. It is claimed that she had a fear of sea travel.

In 1881, Lady Margaret appears on the Land League list of boycotted rack-renting landlords. Her life in London was filled with social engagements, "all the fashionable events of the time", royal receptions and garden parties, diplomatic gatherings, operas and society weddings. She was very generous in her choice of wedding gifts to people of her rank. Gifts included gold candlesticks, diamond pendants and bracelets, gold brooches and sapphire and diamond hat pins. In 1891, she provided a stall of miscellaneous objects for the Irish Distressed Ladies' Fund. One wonders if she considered the distressed women of Cahir.

Lady Margaret Charteris – Cahir Estate
(Courtesy Joe Walsh)

Don't Start the Revolution Without Me

This period in Cahir history is clearly the story of a town becoming politicised to gain justice for tenants and labourers. Cahir women, as the wives and mothers of Land League members, were part of all the activities and demonstrations. The names Miss Kennedy and Miss O'Gorman appear in Cahir Ladies' Land League branch in June 1881. Other members of the Cahir Ladies' Land League Committee included Mrs. Nora O'Donnell, Miss Kate Hennessy and Miss Johanna Fitzgerald, and the "young ladies" of Ballylooby and Duhill sent cheques to Anna Parnell for the Prisoners' Fund.

Determining that "a nation cannot be evicted", Fanny Parnell, sister of Charles and Anna, promised that money would be "sent freely to such tenants as may be turned out of their holdings." In one year alone, the National Ladies' Land League helped 4,000 evicted families. A local example of this is seen in a letter from Cahir to Virginia Lynch (secretary) and Anna Parnell thanking them for their help and "timely assistance in this hour of need and threatened eviction from farms." When Kate O'Donoghue from Ballyporeen wrote to Anna Parnell promising "to be faithful to the principles of the Ladies' Land League as far as is in our power", she was echoing the sentiments of Cashel and Cahir Ladies' Land League.

At a meeting of Cahir Ladies' Land League in 1881, those present resolved to condemn in "the sharpest manner the cruel and cowardly action of the government in arresting Fr. Sheehy" (a Land League priest). They continue, "We tender to him and all our countrymen who have been victims of coercion, our warmest sympathy."

Roy Foster, historian and author, "Modern Ireland 1600 – 1972" claims that "one of the most important and least recognised achievements of the Land League was that it provided a political baptism for a generation of Irish women."

Progress

The Land League campaign was beginning to achieve impressive results. Cahir tenants went to the estate offices in 1881, "not in ones or twos" but in a united group to tender fair rents set by Griffith's Valuation. Only one landlord from Clonmel accepted. All other tenants were "sternly refused" and the Cahir tenants left the offices "in all cases determined not to pay one farthing more." There were very few cases of backsliding and these individuals were "isolated or sent to Coventry." Reports from Cahir also claim that "parties who were timid or indifferent came forward and demanded to be included" in the Land League.

Margaret O'Connor got her rent reduced and J. O'Brien, who owned eight acres, two roods and thirty-five perches, got her rent reduced from £15 to £12 per year.

However in 1882, progress must have been made because the following reductions were recorded without using Christian names:

Tobin rent reduced from £19 to £15.
Connors from £49 to £39.
Keating from £53 to £39.
Anglim from £35 to £29.

In 1882 at a meeting in the churchyard, local land leaguer Patrick O'Donnell urged the farmers, artisans and labouring classes of Cahir to support Parnell.

Solidarity for Mrs. Fenton of Clonmore

The first arrests of Land League members in Tipperary took place in Cahir on May 13th 1881. Patrick O'Donnell and Joseph Fenton were arrested in Clonmore at 3 a.m. by a large force of constabulary. They were put on the 7.30 train to

Naas jail to serve a three-month sentence for unlawful assembly. Supporters arrived at Cahir railway station to see them off. Mr. O'Donnell, bidding farewell to his friends, shouted "Stand by your guns", a remark which was received with cheers and calls of, "We'll step into your places", "Cheers for the Land League" and "Down with landlordism."

Catherine Fenton, wife of Joseph, described by Fr. Mooney as "amicable and noble", was left with seven children to look after. The Land League stepped in to provide assistance, and the farm work was done in Clonmore while the two men were in prison. The *Clonmel Chronicle* reported that Mrs. Fenton was not short of helpers. Up to 1,000 supporters with 200 horses gathered to "set turnips, trench potatoes and do whatever work was necessary at this season of the year." It must have been astounding to see "the procession of horses and carts laden with ploughs, harrows, seed sowing machines, pitch forks, spades, shovels and other farming implements" arriving to help Catherine Fenton.

The State of Ireland. Tilling the farm of an imprisoned Land Leaguer 1881
Local people came to the aid of Catherine Fenton of Clonmore, Cahir when her husband,
Joseph, was imprisoned for Land League activities.
Image: Courtesy of the National Library of Ireland

When the work was done, they marched back to Cahir led by the Ballylooby Pipe and Drum Band, returning to "their respective localities in an orderly manner." While her husband was in prison, Catherine faced eviction by her landlord, Lady Margaret Charteris. Catherine joined James O'Meara, Thomas O'Meara, Michael Looby, James Moroney and Edmond O'Donnell on a journey to Clonmel to tender one year's rent at 50 percent reduction, to the sub-sheriff who was about to sell their farms. Sale of the farms was postponed as they appealed to Lady Margaret on the basis that other landlords had reduced rents.

Patrick O'Donnell's time in prison does not seem to have dampened his spirit. Shortly after his release, he was back in court to defend tenants when Lady Margaret attempted to sell ten farms. A force of 60 police under arms was present at the court. The sheriff informed the court that from the day the farms were advertised, "No offer had been made to him." The passive resistance of Cahir Land League was working. Patrick O'Donnell was defiant: "If you attempt to sell or dispose of my interest in said farm, I shall hold you and each and every one of you responsible for any loss or damage I may thereby sustain." In the case of the Fenton farm, the sheriff claimed that all the conditions of rent and costs due had not been fulfilled. Lady Margaret's agents "reconsidered the facts of the case and the stand taken by the tenants." O'Donnell reported that he was "delighted to be afforded an opportunity of delivering a blow in the proper direction." He claimed that the "landlord's party were discomforted." He wrote to the Ladies' Land League in Dublin about the events of that day. There is also evidence that Michael Tobin from Cahir applied to the Ladies' Land League for help with court appearances.

Tally-Ho Cahir Tenant Farmers

According to Edmund O'Riordan, "Realising the power they had if they acted as one body, Shanbally Estate and Cahir tenant farmers conducted League Hunts across their landlords' estates, disrupting the way of life that the elite thought was theirs by some divine right." The weekly *Irish Times* reported that, in December 1881, "between five and six hundred men and boys accompanied by about fifty dogs, hunted the country between Cahir and Clogheen." As many as 60 hares and rabbits were killed and these were, it was stated, "to be sent to the suspects at present in jail" (for Land League activities). A local landlord, Mr. Fennell, was even obliged to give up hunting because he had been stopped by his own tenants from riding over their lands.

Women's Role in the Struggle Recognised

Some clergy supported the Land League movement, while others did not. Criticising the Ladies' Land League, Archbishop McCabe of Dublin asked his priests "not to tolerate in your societies the woman who so far disavows her birth right of modesty as to parade herself before the public gaze in a character so unworthy of a Child of Mary." Archbishop Croke of Cashel came to their defence, as did Fr. Mooney of Cahir. He was way ahead of his time in underlining the importance of women in the struggle for the three "F"s. The *Clonmel Chronicle* reported his words of April 1881: "The day has come when a speaker from a political platform can address the audience and say 'ladies and gentleman', because the ladies are now looked upon as entitled to take a prominent part in the present movement. The Ladies' Land League is a most essential portion of our community!"

Several women appeared in court for their involvement with the Ladies' Land League: Bridget Regan, Mary Carmody, Bridget Kenneally and another woman were called to Clonmel court. Two of them were fined £2 or one month's imprisonment and two more were fined £1 or a fortnight's imprisonment. The National Land League covered their expenses.

Court Reports of a District in Turmoil

The *Tipperary Free Press* and *Clonmel Chronicle* reported on events linked to the land struggle. In 1880, a farmer who took over a farm where there had been an eviction was reportedly able to "get nothing done." He claimed that his wife had taken butter to Cahir twice and was unable to dispose of it. Cahir Land League also put pressure on a Cahir land-grabber who dispossessed a widow and five children. He was forced to surrender the farm. In 1885, following an eviction from a farm owned by Lady Margaret Charteris, a "huge procession" went to the farm led by Poulmucka Fife and Drum Band and Cahir Brass Band. A black flag was raised 20 feet high in the vicinity of the property. *Atlas of the Irish Revolution* records that between March 1881 and July 1882, there were ten Land League arrests in the Cahir area.

Mixed Reports on Labourers' Plight

The *Daily Express* of September 1881 noted that many labourers employed by Lady Margaret Charteris were "well contented and happy in their positions", having been granted "comforts too rarely enjoyed by their class." Those labourers' wives were encouraged to promote thrift in themselves and their families and on pay days to lodge weekly deposits. In proportion to these lodgements, a large premium was added to enable them to buy clothes, etc. They wore "comfortable dresses and had cheerful appearances", according to the reporter.

However, a number of labourers attended a Land League meeting in 1881 for the purpose of acquiring information on the best way to obtain half-acre plots. There is also strong evidence of many Cahir labourers refusing to work on farms where evictions had taken place, even though the wages offered were far above the norm, "refusing most tempting offers of higher wages."

Court Appearances

Apart from the land agitation activity, times were grim for the ordinary women of the district, where survival often meant brushes with the law. In 1879, several women were found guilty of removing timber from Scarrough Wood, Rehill and Kilcommon: Bridget O'Brien, Mary Guiry, Bridget Brien, Ellen Brien, Ellen McGrath and Margaret O'Shea. Trespassing on Lady Margaret Charteris' mountain were Bridget Brien, Bridget Donnell, Mary Kinehan, Mary Cleary, Ellen Hickey, Johanna Hartigan, Ellen White, Mary Finn and Ellen Gorman. All were fined six shillings or seven days' imprisonment.

A Generous Landlord is Praised

Not all landlords were deaf to pleas for rent reduction. Andrew Hennessey of Knockgraffon wrote to the *Clonmel Chronicle* in 1881 to say that his landlord, Joseph Cook of Raglan Circus, Somerset, was prepared to accept a rent of 25 percent under the Griffith's Valuation because "it was only just that he, the landlord should share in part of the losses of his tenants through the agricultural depression." His generosity of spirit was acknowledged by Mr. Hennessey who said "It would be wrong of us not to let the public know of such generosity."

Andrew Hennessey acknowledged that even before the formation of the Land League, Joseph Cook allowed full compensation for losses and gave his tenants "leases forever." This is in stark contrast to the tenants on the Charteris estate who initially were offered a 10 to 15 percent reduction "only in special cases." Offers of rent at Griffith's Valuation rates were declined.

Sabres Drawn

In May 1881, *the Clonmel Chronicle* reported that 2,000 persons, including large numbers of tenant farmers, marched into Cahir fronted by a brass band playing "The Bold Fenian Men." They were protesting the sale of a farm in Ballylooby. Tensions were at boiling point, so the full might of the law was called up, and infantry, police and cavalry from the 26th Hussars with their sabres drawn made their way up Castle Street. From there, they wheeled left into the Square where they were met by a hail of broken crockery, mud, rotten eggs, stones and clods of earth. The sale was subsequently abandoned, and the interest in the holding was bought later by the Irish Land League.

The threat of boycotting was a serious one and it was applied to many sections of society as well as to 'evicted farm' occupancy. Even Police were shunned. In May 1881, three sub-constables arrived at Cahir railway station on their way to Rehill and Ballyporeen. "All the efforts of the police in Cahir failed to get them a conveyance to their stations."

On 10th August 1882, Cahir Brass Band played national airs on the Square, "in token of rejoicing for the release from prison of Mr. John Dillon (Land League MP)." Also in 1882, a meeting in Cahir churchyard called for peasant proprietorship. In 1883, Michael Davitt who had founded the Land League, visited Cahir.

Evictions

We do not have a comprehensive list of evictions in Cahir. Tipperary was the county with the highest level of evictions during the famine, and the spectre of eviction survived in the living memory of Cahir farmers. Tenants lived with the insecurity of dispossession. During the 1880s, Cahir landlords no longer faced individual tenant farmers but a united tenant group, acting in solidarity brought about by the Land League. In spite of, or because of this, evictions continued. In 1881, Thomas Holohan, who paid a rent of £54, even though his property valuation was £29, was evicted with his wife and seven children. The Ronayne family was evicted from Garinavalla. In 1881, writs were served on five tenants, including Thomas Lonergan. In 1884, Michael Lonergan, Pierce Lonergan and Michael Burke, Whitelands, Cahir, faced eviction.

In 1885, Patrick Guiry was evicted from Ballinamona, Cahir. Boycotting did not work in this instance because the tenant who took over the farm had a forge and Lady Margaret Charteris' agent gave him all the business from Cahir

Military Barracks. He also received work from the Murdock family, owners of the house which is now Kilcoran Lodge Hotel. Patrick Guiry served one month hard labour in prison for calling the man who took his farm a "land grabber."In 1886, Mr. John O'Connor MP spoke in Cahir. He referred to the Burke eviction by Lady Margaret Charteris at Farranagark and the O'Brien eviction from Loughoher, where families were "thrown from the homes that had sheltered them for so long." He stated that "nothing more cruel disgraced the black annals of landlordism than the eviction of Patrick Cronin, his wife and eleven young children put on the roadside by Lady Margaret Charteris." Patrick Cronin received a notice to pay, but he did not have the rent and borrowed the money. As he did not pay on the appointed day, the family was evicted. John O'Connor urged the tenants to show Margaret Charteris that if she asked for unjust rents that "she shall be obstructed in the attempt, and also obstructed in the attempt to throw any more poor people on the roadside." He urged them to stand "side by side and present a solid front to the enemy", promising that they were "marching on to victory."

There are plenty of local examples of the eviction of women. In January 1881, Maria Burke of Carrigeen, a widow, appealed her eviction from her holding of two acres. Her defence was that the eviction notice was signed by Major Hutchinson as agent for Lady Margaret Charteris and not by Lady Charteris herself, rendering it defective. The judge held that the notice to quit was sufficient and that the debt was contracted by her in her personal capacity since her husband's death.

Judith O'Brien's son gives a harrowing account of the family's eviction from their home and farm. "The house was cleared out and whatever children were there were led out into the yard and then the bailiffs went in and pulled down the roof and when my mother saw what was being done and the timbers cracking about her ears, she fell into a weakness. The agent then drew the men from the house when he saw my mother faint and he let my father stay there. We lived in the barn and made a kind of hut under the chimney for a few weeks." The family lived in the hut for five years. Rent for the 12 acres was paid by Judith's brother, David Tobin.

Edmond Walsh, son of Margaret Walsh of Ballmacadam, wrote an account of the arrival on their holding of the agent Major Hutchinson in April 1881 with 26 men of the constabulary and a troop of the 28th Hussars. He states that "as the eldest son and the representative of my mother, I offered to pay the rent that was due provided a suitable reduction would be given and the law costs withdrawn." Edmond Walsh denied charges of intimidation and claimed that when writs were served on five other tenants of Lady Margaret Charteris, the servers were not intimidated. Margaret Walsh also took Lady Margaret to court for selling bad seed to the tenancy resulting in the loss of the crop.

The *Freeman's Journal* managed to find the funny side to this grim stand-off. It reported that the only animals found on the Walsh farm by the bailiffs were three bonhams and a large Billy goat. The goat was tastefully and elegantly decorated with green sprays of ivy and holly, tied with green ribbons. On his large horns was a pasteboard with the greeting "Welcome Major." Nobody was willing to approach the animal for fear of a good, sound butting. The long arm of the law in all its pomp and circumstance wended its way via a back street to the barracks, according to the *Journal*.

"Do your worst! We are prepared to go to jail!"

By January 1888, feelings had run so high, according to *The Nation* newspaper, that many men and women were charged with unlawful assembly. On January 10th in Cahir, the following individuals were charged: Pierce Lee, William Smith, Patrick Foley, Michael Casey, Thomas Casey, Thomas Sullivan, John Hogan and Matthew Lonergan. Presiding Judge Bolton intimated that he would withdraw similar charges against four local "young ladies" Ellen Collins, Mary Morrissey, Ellen Morrissey and Diana Davin. This drew a spirited reply from one of the Morrisseys: "Do your worst, we are prepared to go to jail and suffer for Ireland!" As the parties left the court they were cheered.

Reports from Dublin stated that a named land-grabber in Cahir had to have police guarding him day and night. It was also reported that one tenant paid the rent asked by the land agent and when his mother died, "not a single person attended her funeral" in Cahir. In 1886, the weekly *Freeman's Journal* covered the eviction of Patrick Burke, his wife and 11 children from their holding at Grangemore. The agent refused the offer of money and the family was not admitted as caretakers. When a writ was sent from Dublin, nobody would deliver it "owing to intimidation prevailing in the district." Additionally, Mr. Peter Rudge, sent to Cahir to collect rents, was refused the use of every office and hotel in Cahir.

Cahir women were charged with unlawful assembly and assault on military and police in connection with evictions. Bridget Regan, Mary Carmody and

Bridget O'Brien joined Patrick Kennedy, Seamus Roche, Edmund O'Brien and Martin Hartigan in court.

1890s - The Fight Goes On

The struggle for land continued through the 1890s. In 1890, a large meeting took place in Cahir in support of the Tenant's Defence Association (established after the Land League).

In January 1891, the only land courts were held in Cahir and Clonmel. The *Munster Express* reported that 25 tenants from the estate of Lady Margaret Charteris cut "a sorry figure" from the Galtees and Skeheenarinky. "Most of them appeared hard worked, badly fed and wretchedly clad."

Life for women continued to be difficult. For example, Margaret O'Gorman went to court in 1890 in an attempt to hold onto her premises. Mary Kennedy, Mary Hassett, Alice Duggan and Mary Wall are some of the names of the many women who were brought to court in the 1890s for "taking wood from Lady Margaret's mountains."

In 1897, Patrick O'Donnell was still speaking about the "pernicious system of absentee landlordism." He had been jailed in 1881 for his Land League activities. The *Irish Daily Independent* reported that in July 1900, "one of the largest demonstrations held since the Land League days" took place in Cahir. Mr. John Dillon urged the tenants to "get rid of landlords" in order to have a peaceful and prosperous Ireland.

Conclusion

So what became of the main players in Cahir Land League? Fr. Mooney who died in 1891, does not come out well in church history *Waterford and Lismore* by Fr. Patrick Power. Power claims that, "his activities or lack of them more than once brought upon him the reprimand of his bishop and, often, the disapproval of his people." The women and men of Cahir Land League might not have agreed with that sentiment.

As for the organisers from the townland of Clonmore, all of whom were tenants of Lady Margaret, we have the following information. Patrick O'Donnell was unmarried and living with his unmarried sister, Maria, in the 1901 Census. Apparently Michael Tobin, secretary of the Cahir Land League, is listed as living with the O'Neill family of Clonmore in the 1901 and 1911 Census. Michael Burke, Clonmore, who was recorded as a very efficient treasurer, lost everything.

Local knowledge indicates that he and his wife and children owed so much to a particular shop in Cahir that they handed the key of their house into the shop in exchange for tickets to America. Joseph Fenton who led the thousands in the Square in taking the Land League oath was dead by 1885. He had been unwell and in spite of the efforts of his brother, a doctor, had not regained his health before he went to prison in 1881. His time in prison may have had an impact on his health and contributed to his death four years later.

Lady Margaret Charteris did not return to Cahir for 31 years. In 1908, a reporter from the *Clonmel Chronicle* seemed disappointed with the welcome afforded to her, claiming that "if the townspeople had got better notice, a better display than that which took place would have been the result." An account is given of her "smilingly bowing her acknowledgements" and "waving her hand to all her admirers." She attended the annual school fete and the *Chronicle* claims that her presence there "gave great pleasure." Upon her death, her estate had an estimated worth of £332,000 (over €32 million today). One wonders if the people of Cahir would have preferred the lady to provide "great pleasure" or a greater share in the vast estate built on their labour. Her son, Richard lived in the 'palatial' Cahir Park House until his death in 1961.

By the end of the 19th century, the mass movement founded by Michael Davitt was well on the way to achieving its stated aims in Tipperary and elsewhere. A combination of factors resulted in the introduction of the Land Acts, which eventually led to peasant proprietorship. The old order unravelled. We who live in more comfortable times have all but forgotten the struggle of ordinary people against the might of the British establishment. Nevertheless, the lesson of solidarity in the face of injustice should still resonate across the generations. It is also clear that the women of Cahir and district played a pivotal part in achieving the freedoms we enjoy today.

Sources

Editor: Seamus Martin, Ballydrehid
National Library of Ireland, Land League Papers.
National Library of Ireland, Ladies' Land League Papers.
Clonmel Chronicle.
Weekly Freeman's Journal.
Edmund O'Riordan, author of "Landed Classes During the Great Irish Famine"

in *Atlas of the Great Irish Famine*, 2017
Joe Walsh, Cahir
Find My Past (website)
Irish Newspaper Archives.
Land and Violence in 19th Century Tipperary, Denis Marnane.
Atlas of the Irish Revolution
Tipperary Free Press
Mike Costello, Clonmore.

McCraith vs. Quinn (Quin)
Cahir's Criminal Conversation Case
By Ciara Coughlan

In August 1872, a scandal gripped Cahir, the details of which were laid bare in the theatre of court. The judge and jury of the Wicklow assizes were charged with considering a 'criminal conversation' case, with both the complainant and the defendant being men from Cahir. Such was the anticipation surrounding the case, the *Nenagh Guardian* reported that "the utmost interest seemed to be excited in the proceedings, and much anxiety evinced to obtain seats in court. The admission was, however, regulated by ticket and no overcrowding took place during the day."[1] Criminal conversation was a civil action which allowed a husband to sue his wife's lover for damages. These originated from blackmail agreements in the late seventeenth century and were somewhat popular among the wealthier classes until its abolition in 1857. Abolition did not extend to Ireland however, where it remained in place until the twentieth century.[2] Criminal conversation actions remained relatively rare however, and it was observed in 1859 that Ireland 'was celebrated not only for the chastity and purity of its women, but also for the honour of its men. It was seldom indeed that [a crim con] action was brought under the notice of the public.'[3] Thus, while the McCraith vs. Quinn case was somewhat unusual, it reveals much about women's position in Irish society at that time.

National Attention

Throughout the extensive accounts of the case, which were reported in several newspapers of the time including the *Nenagh Guardian, Belfast Newsletter,* and *Wicklow Newsletter* and *County Advertiser*, the presence and voice of the accused woman is strikingly absent. At no point is she permitted to give any explanation for her actions. This is despite the fact that the case would have resulted in her being at the centre of a nationally reported scandal that would have made her an exile from her family and community. Her fate, and how much she was monetarily worth to her husband, was decided by a male judge and an all-male jury.

---

1 'Important Action for Crim Con', *Nenagh Guardian*, 3 August 1872
2 Howlin, Niamh, 'Adultery in the Courts: Damages for Criminal Conversation in Ireland ', (December 20, 2015), in K Costello and N Howlin (eds), Law and the Family in Ireland 1800-1950
3 Howlin, 'Adultery in the Courts: Damages for Criminal Conversation in Ireland', p. 2

Husband's Evidence

It is the husband, Major Thomas McCraith, whose evidence was used to frame the case, evidence which paints himself as a dedicated husband whose devoted but unfortunate wife was tricked away from the home by an artful, handsome seducer. He said:

> I am a Major in the North Tipperary Militia and a magistrate of the county; the defendant is my first cousin; his residence is at Loughloher Castle; my uncle died in 1869; I married Miss Phillips in 1866; she as the daughter of Mr. W.L. Phillips of Mount Phillips, in the county of Tipperary; her father is dead; her mother is still living.... I had known Miss Phillips about two years before I married her; the marriage was one of affection on my part and I had no reason to doubt that it was so on her part... at the time the defendant [Captain Quinn] was an officer in the Artillery;' I had always regarded him as a brother.[4]

It appears that McCraith and Quinn had been close, with Quinn even acting as the best man at the McCraiths' wedding. In 1872, Laura and Major Thomas McCraith had a child, Laura Mary, whose own remarkable story is told in another chapter of this book. Quinn remained a regular visitor to the McCraith's home and eventually, one of McCraith's sisters, who was also living in the family home, reported that she had witnessed a kiss between Laura and Quinn. McCraith also reported finding trinkets that he believed Quinn had gifted to his wife. He forbade his wife from seeing Quinn but shortly afterwards caught them meeting in secret.

> One day after our return home she set out to drive alone to Cahir; I rode to Cahir shortly after and saw her driving through the street in Cahir; she went down a road not in the direction of home; she had not told me of her intention to drive in that direction but that she was going to pay a visit to a lady in Cahir; I did not follow her on the road until I had seen her followed by Captain Quinn; he passed in the same direction; they continued along the high road of Garnavilla and stopped at a certain point; I saw him turning his back around, and I suppose he saw me; he rode towards me... I asked him why he was following my wife through the country, and

4   'Important Action for Crim Con', *Nenagh Guardian*, 3 August 1872

disgracing me and my family; I struck him; he said nothing in reply to what I had said; I struck him repeatedly with a heavy ash plant until the stick broke; he defended himself; I was on my horse at the time; I caught him by the neck and round the throat tried to pull him off his horse; he was nearly off when my wife got out of the phaeton and came up to save him.[5]

Following this incident, Laura was sent to live with her mother, and the court heard that she had written her husband a letter. The court was not permitted to hear the contents of the letter however, and so we do not know what Laura may have said in her own defence. Laura returned eventually to her husband and McCraith fell ill with small pox shortly after. Quinn seemed to have been in India at the time. But upon Quinn's return to Ireland, the couple eloped to Boulogne, France and stayed at a hotel where "it was proved they lived as man and wife."[6] This appears to have been the last straw for McCraith. Shortly after, he brought Quinn to court.

Innocent Victim or Fallen Woman

The contrasting descriptions of Quinn and Laura McCraith and their comparative guilt during the course of the trial reveal much about how women were viewed in 19th century Ireland. Quinn was described as "a fashionable looking and fascinating young man and belongs to a family having the reputation of being good-looking...he is a Grand juror and a magistrate of the county Tipperary; he moves in the best society; and has a very handsome demesne,"[7] despite having "artistically and deliberately planned"[8] the seduction of his friend's wife. Meanwhile, the jury were firstly shown a portrait of Laura which "represented her a beautiful creature, a fine young woman with her little child by her side. She was taken with a beaming countenance, graced by nature's choicest gift, a mother's affection."[9] But then she is also continually depicted as without agency - a "fine woman" turned to a "wretched" and "low woman" by her almost accidental abandonment of her husband and child."[10] A witness to the prosecution met Laura, who he described as the "fallen and degraded woman,"[11]

---

5   Ibid.
6   'The Tipperary Crim Con Case', *Nenagh Guardian*, 9 November 1872
7   'Important Action for Crim Con; Thomas McCraith vs William Quinn', *Wicklow Newsletter*, 3 August 1872
8   'Important Action for Crim Con', *Nenagh Guardian*, 3 August 1872
9   'Important Action for Crim Conversation', *Nenagh Guardian*, 3 August 1872
10   ibid.
11   'Important Action for Crim Conversation', Thomas McCraith vs William Quinn', *Wicklow Newsletter*, 3 August 1872

following the elopement in France and he noted that "there appeared to be no hope for her – she is exiled from her friends and relations, and day by day she must fall lower and lower in the scale of society, without any refuge from her shame."[12] Going forward, "the wretched woman, who...wandered away from her child and husband... had only her seducer to look to for support."[13] Thus Laura is depicted as both an innocent victim of her seducer and also a fallen woman who deserved her isolated fate.

Not a Word or a Witness

Laura must have known that her actions would lead to her ostracisation from the community and the loss of contact with her daughter. It surely could not have been an accidental step on her behalf. However, Laura is entirely absent from the trial and so her perspective was not evident to the observing public. This was common at the time, as Sir George Bowyer, MP for Dundalk, stated in 1854 that "... although the wife was upon her trial, and its issue might involve her utter ruin and destruction, she had no part in the proceeding. She was not heard at all ... The most abominable charges might be brought against her by witnesses in the action, and enforced by all the eloquence and ingenuity of counsel; she might thus be held up to the world as a being utterly degraded; yet she was neither allowed to produce a single witness, nor to say a single word, either in vindication of her innocence or in mitigation of the imputed guilt."[14]

Major McCraith Cross Examined

It is only during cross examination by the defence that we come the closest to an insight into Laura's side of the story. The defence implied that there was a deep animosity between Laura and McCraith's sisters, who were also living in the family house. They claimed that "Mrs McCraith was annoyed and persecuted beyond endurance by Major McCraith's sisters."[15] The lawyer also asked of McCraith: "did you say any hard words to Mrs McCraith in her mother's or brother's presence?" to which McCraith replied "No, beyond saying that she was a low woman for going out in her pony phaeton without a servant; and I said that I would not have her living in my house if she went on so." The lawyer also asked "Did you catch hold of her or strike her?", which McCraith denied

---

12 Ibid.
13 'ibid.
14 Howlin, Adultery in the Courts, Damages for Criminal Conversation in Ireland, p. 8
15 'Important Action for Crim Conversation', Thomas McCraith vs William Quinn', *Wicklow Newsletter*, 3 August 1872

except for an occasion when he was so angered by her that he pushed her aside to leave a room.[16] The defence argued that "McCraith showed upon his own evidence that he was a man of ungovernable temper, tyrannical to his wife and contended that it was his coercion and jealous temper that forced his wife from his house."[17] While these may have been exaggerations, they still paint a picture of an environment with domineering sisters-in-law and a controlling husband where Laura would possibly have felt isolated and trapped. However, we will never be able to say for certain, as like the majority of women in history, she has been rendered voiceless and invisible by the historical record.

Outcome

The court ultimately awarded McCraith £5,000 - a substantial sum of money but only half what he had sought. He died five years later at Loughloher at the age of 48. In his 1877 will, he named his sister, Honoria McCraith, and friend, Louis Ffennell, as the guardians of his and Laura's daughter, Laura Mary. He forbade his "unfortunate" wife any access to her.

Six months after Thomas McCraith's death, Laura McCraith and William Quinn married.

MARRIAGE.

QUIN AND McCRAITH—On the 6th inst., at the Church of the British Embassy, Paris, by the Rev. Canon Robert A. Maunsell, M.A., William Quin, of Loughloher Castle, Cahir, Esq., to Laura McCraith, *née* Laura Phillips, of Mount Phillips, co. Tipperary.

Marriage notice of William and Laura. Cork Constitution 17 Sept. 1877

William Quin died in France in 1889. The administration of his will was granted to Laura Philips (Quin's mother-in-law) a widow who was the guardian of the executor, still a minor.[18] Who this minor was I have been unable to ascertain, although it was possibly Quin's stepdaughter born 1870, or a child which the exiled couple had together.

---

16 'Important Action for Crim Conversation', *Nenagh Guardian*, 3 August 1872
17 ibid.
18 'The Children of Rev. Rev. John Pennefather', Family History Website by Alison Stewart, http://alison-stewart.blogspot. ie/2011/12/children-of-rev-john-pennefather.html

Tragic Case

This was certainly a tragic case and the public nature of its resolution undoubtedly caused great distress to all those involved. While Laura's decision to leave her family, including her small daughter, seems on the surface unpardonable, we see glimpses of the environment that may have driven her to seek a route out. But we will never know why she left with Quinn, even though a version of the tale was told in great detail in the press. She was rendered voiceless and powerless thanks to the rigid rules of society and its expectations for her as a woman. Her fate was decided by powerful men without a chance to even plead her case.

Author – Artist – Photographer
Laura Mary McCraith
By Josephine O'Neill

When her 1870 birth was registered, Laura Mary had not yet been given her first names, so she was registered as Female McGrath, the daughter of Thomas McGrath (McCraith) and Laura Phillips. The birth date was given as 1 September at Loughloher, and Thomas' occupation was listed as 'Gentleman'. Laura Mary was the only child of Thomas and Laura – a Church of Ireland family.

The 1872, Laura Mary's mother left her husband, leaving Laura Mary with him; but when Laura Mary was just six years of age, her father died at Loughloher. In his will, Thomas entrusted the guardianship of his daughter to his sister, Hanoria McCraith, and Louis Ffennell.

Laura Mary was educated at Cheltenham, first by Miss Annie Proctor who had been the first principal of Cheltenham Ladies' College. The school had been founded on the premise that girls should be taught the same subjects as boys. Following her time with Annie Proctor, Laura continued her education at Elmfield, Bayshill, Cheltenham.

Following her education, Laura Mary began her career as an author, publishing under the name L.M. McCraith. Some of her early publications include "In Old Gardens" (1895) and "Historic Houses" (1896).

Marriage

Laura Mary was residing in Loughloher when she married John Henry Blakeney at Dalkey Parish Church, Dublin. The 26 August 1897 edition of the *Bath Chronicle and Weekly Gazette*, Somerset, announced the marriage, stating that the bride, the only child of the late Major McCraith, entered the church on the arm of her cousin, Mr. J.H. Ryan, and was given away by her aunt, Miss Honoria McCraith. The newspaper article describes the bride's veil as "attached by an arrangement of orange blossom and heather from Tipperary".

After the wedding, the couple resided in England. At the time of the 1901 Census, John H. and Laura M. Blakeney were residing at 36 Bristol Road in Edgbaston, Warwickshire. He was a surgeon who was born in London. Although the census return listed a visitor, a cook, and a housemaid, no children were at the house.

During these early years of their marriage, Laura continued to write. *Concerning Leicester House and Its Memories* was published in 1899. Other publications of this time were *A Forgotten Great Irish Woman* (1900) and *The Touch of the Wand* (1903).

Although the Blakeneys had no children at the time of the 1901 Census, a son, John Robert McCraith Blakeney was born in 1904. His birth was registered at King's Norton, Worcestershire, just two miles from Edgbaston.

Move to Cheltenham

About 1907, the Blakeneys relocated 45 miles south to Cheltenham where they remained until the war. Laura published *Does Ireland Want Tourists?* (1908) and two works in 1909: *The Irish Novel* and *At Geoffrey Keating's Grave.* In 1910, *Athassel Priory and Its Patrons* was published.

In the 1911 Census return, John Henry Blakeney and Laura Mary McCraith-Blakeney were visiting her aunt, Harriet Ker, in Kingstown (Dun Laoghaire), Dublin, while their son – by then a six years old student - remained at Cheltenham with the servants. In that Census, Laura Mary was listed as an author who spoke both English and Irish.

Return to Loughloher

During the war years, Laura Mary published *Romance of Irish Heroines* (1914) and was the Lady Superintendent of the Cheltenham nursing division, consisting of sixty-five ladies. In 1915, she was appointed Commandant of the Cheltenham St. John's Voluntary Hospital for soldiers; and in 1916, she and her husband donated a silver chalice to St. Paul's Church in Cahir. After the war, Laura Mary returned to Loughloher. Her husband, J.H. Blakeney, surgeon, is listed in Ireland's Medical Directory at Cahir for the years 1922, 1924, 1925, 1926, and 1928.

One of Laura's very good friends was none other than the Rev. Wm. P. Burke, author of *History of Clonmel,* which was written in Cahir during his curacy there, as the preface testifies. Laura and Canon Burke spent many hours together, discussing the area's heritage, comparing notes and ideas. In her *Cashel of the Kings* (1921), she thanks Burke for the loan of invaluable books of reference, his interest, corrections and help.

Extract from *The Suir from its Source to the Sea*

Laura M. McCraith (1912)

Past the reaches of Ballydrehid, the river pursues its course over three weirs to the pleasant little town of Cahir. The upper waters of the Suir above Cahir are accessible only by rowing boats, which may be lifted over these weirs. Cahir is the centre of a rich corn growing district, directed by a large and influential Quaker community. The milling industry brought prosperity and population to the valley of the Suir in the eighteenth century and especially to Cahir which was known as the Quaker town. As of old, the mills of Going & Smith Ltd. still grind corn and form centres of activity and employment which serve as unmixed blessings and sources of prosperity to Cahir, now a thriving little town of some two thousand inhabitants. The lovely green banks of the Suir are nowhere lovelier or greener than in Cahir Park. Its beauties need to be seen to be realised to the full. It is a question whether Cahir Park is more beautiful on a hot summer's day, when the cattle stand knee deep in the broad, clear river and when trees and pastures wear their richest dress of living green or in late autumn when the scarlet coats of huntsmen and the dappled white, black and tan of fox hounds appear and disappear through groves of golden oaks and coppices carpeted with yellow bracken in which laurels keep their summer livery.

Laura was interested in the arts. She was a photographer and accomplished artist; and in 1896, she published *The Genius of Irish Music*. In addition, she had an interest in theatre. A letter dated June 2, 1923, from Laura to Lennox Robinson of the Abbey theatre has been found. It congratulates him on his play, "The Round Table – That play so full of insight that once seen, it never leaves a woman's memory."

Dr. John Henry Blakeney died in Worcester, England, where – according to his obituary in the 19 March 1927 edition of *Cheltenham Chronicle* he died the previous Saturday night. He had been doing locum work for a practitioner there and contracted influenza which progressed to pneumonia and heart failure. In addition to his wife, he was survived by his son who had recently finished exams at Trinity College, Dublin.

In the 1930s, Laura resided in Dublin. The Dublin directories list her under the category of "Nobility, Gentry, Merchants, and Traders". The directories of 1931-1934 report her residence at Saint John's Road, Sandymount.

Laura R.I.P.

The *Gloucestershire Echo*, of 4 February 1937, reported that Laura Mary McCraith-Blakeney of Avona, Howth Road, Raheny, Dublin, had died on 27 September 1936. She died at Dublin North, with an estate of about £8000. Her bequests included £1 to each worker who attended her funeral, £5 to her coachman Edmond Maher, and £1 per each year of service to her servants.

Laura's writings spanned over thirty years. Apart from her better known books, she also contributed to publications, expressing her strongly held views on contemporary issues such as Irish women and their vote. Her literary legacy renders her one of the most under-rated Irish authoress of her time.

References:

Genealogical research by Karol DeFalco.

Cahir Heritage Newsletter – Joe Walsh.

Liam Roche

Extract from *The Suir from its Source to the Sea* courtesy Paul Buckley

Women's Role in the Rituals of Death
Keening -- A Dying Practice
By Mary Caulfield

The customs and rituals surrounding death and burial were a central part of traditional societies around the world and were carried out with precision and ceremony. The rituals of the Irish wake involved laying out the body, keeping watch, keening the dead, feasting and funeral games. It was the women who dealt with the more intimate side of death and dying especially when it came to laying out the corpse. It was the women who washed the body, a practice dating back to ancient Greece; it was the women of Troy who washed the body of Hector. In Ireland, it was the women who laid out the body and tied the *marbh fhaisc* (the death knot) a piece of cloth binding the jaw to keep the mouth closed. It was they who placed pennies on the closed eyelids and threaded a rosary beads through the joined fingers; *the dough white fingers / shackled with rosary beads* as Seamus Heaney described them.[1] These same practices are referred to in a book about life in the English Midlands in the late 1800s. *...the chin was tied up, the plate of salt placed on the breast of a corpse, and the new pennies used to weigh down the eyelids.*[2] On the remote Great Blasket Island, a grieving Peig Sayers, on her own, washed and laid out the body of her young son, Tomás, who drowned when he lost his footing and fell into the sea. His body was carried to the house by the fishermen who searched for him, who then left, their work done.[3]

During the final moments, signalled by the death rattle, female relatives and local women kept vigil at the bedside of the dying person keeping watch. (The Irish language word for wake is *faire,* meaning watch.) One of Paul Henry's Achill paintings, titled *A Prayer for the Departed* depicts a group of women in black shawls, kneeling at the bedside of a recently deceased woman – these were the watchers.[4]

Keening the dead is as old as mankind, practised across cultures and continents, from ancient Greece to Achill Island. Pottery from ancient Greece depicts wailing women around a corpse with the men standing in the

---

1   'Funeral Rites', Seamus Heaney.
2   *Lark Rise to Candleford,* Flora Thompson.
3   *An Old Woman's Reflections,* Peig Sayers.
4   A Prayer for the Departed, Paul Henry. Hunt Museum, Limerick.

background. In the Old Testament, the Prophet, Jeremiah, in reference to the destruction of Jerusalem, says, "Call for the wailing women ... that they may come, and send for the most skilled of them. Let them make haste and take up a wail for us; that our eyes may run down with tears"[5].

In North America, keening was practised among tribes such as the Tsawataineuk Tribe of Kingcome Village, British Columbia, Canada. The keeners were described as professional mourners, usually three, who took turns wailing, day and night. One account describes an old Native Canadian woman, whose face was scratched and bleeding, wailing loudly.[6] Interestingly, entries in The Schools Folklore Collection (1938-39), from schools in South Tipperary, give similar accounts of keening women; "an old woman was paid to come to the house and keen". The entries also refer to the fact that sometimes three women would come to the wake and do the keen.[7]

Caoine

The keen is a lament for the dead, derived from the Irish word, *caoine,* meaning to cry although a Hebrew word, *cina*, which signifies lamentation or weeping with clapping of hands, sounds similar.[8] Keening is the funeral cry; the primal scream; guttural, wild and unearthly. Numerous accounts of keening are to be found throughout Irish history. As early as the 12th century, Welshman, Giraldus Cambrensis, wrote that the Irish musically expressed their griefs. The *caoine* or lament, forms an important genre of 18th century poetry in the Irish language. For example, in *Caoine Art Uí Laoghaire,* Eibhlín Dubh Ní Chonaill laments the death of her husband. Another example is in the religious poetry of the time, *Caoine na dTrí Muire.*

In parts of the West of Ireland, the keen was performed three times: at midnight, at dawn and before the coffin was carried from the house. Somebody would ask, "Is it the time to cry him/her"? Before the advent of clocks, a mourner would check the sky to confirm that it was midnight. Gathering around the coffin, the keeners, usually women, with hair hanging loose, would begin by clapping and throwing their arms in the air before starting their wild unrestrained funeral cry. Older people recall the keen as a discordant, high pitched, wailing sound meant to be upsetting.

5   Kevin Toolis, *My Father's Wake.*
6   Margaret Craven, *I Heard the Owl call my Name,* 1967
7   *Irish Schools Folklore Collection,* (1938-39) Duchas.ie
8   *Irish Penny Journal,* (Vol. 1 No.31) 1833 Dr. O'Brien.

There were three parts to the keen: the salutation in which the person's name was repeatedly called; the dirge in which the genealogy, rank and virtues of the dead were rehearsed with questions addressed to the deceased such as, "Why did you go? Why did he leave me?" and a repetition of phrases such as *go deo, deo*. Finally, it was the *gol* (the cry). As well as lamenting the deceased, the people present mourned their own losses, bereavements and disappointments, thereby releasing pent up anxiety. This was cathartic and healing at a time when counselling and anti-depressants were unavailable.

In the Barony of Erris in North Mayo, older people remember hearing men perform the keen. One local person described a man clapping his hands and keening, in English, while another man, standing in a doorway, complained, "He's no good to cry him", before starting his own version in Irish, while he circled the house outside.[9]

In a BBC documentary, presenter Marie Louise Muir, sums up the effect that keening at an Irish wake had on her,

> It shocked and surprised me how difficult I found listening to these recordings .To my ear, as a classically trained musician, they were off note. That unsettled me. It's akin to nails being scraped down a blackboard. Every atom of my body cringes against it. You just recoil ...it's expressing how you're feeling.[10]

Bean Chaointe

Mr. and Mrs. Hall, an English couple who toured Ireland in 1840, witnessed Co. Kerry funeral ceremonies which they found to be most peculiar, remarkable and interesting. They wrote that the body was laid out on a bed and salt was placed near the corpse. Then the women of the household ranged themselves on either side of the corpse and the keen (caoine) commenced. They rose with one accord; and moving their bodies in slow motion to and fro, their arms apart, they kept up a heart rending cry. The cry was interrupted for a while to give the bean chaointe, the leading keener, an opportunity of commencing her lament. At the close of every stanza of the dirge, the cry was repeated, and then dropped, and the woman then continued with the dirge, and so on to the close.[11]

---

9   Caitlin Bn. Ui Sheighin, Ceathru Thaidhg, Co. Mhuió.
10   Marie Louise Muir, *Songs for the Dead*, B.B.C 4, 20th AUG. 2016.
11   Hall's Ireland: Mr. and Mrs. Hall's Tour of 1840. (Vol. 1)

The lament for the slain Hector, in Homer's Iliad, has echoes of the aforementioned:

They weep, and place him on the bed of state.
A melancholy choir attend around,
With plaintive sighs and music's solemn sound:
Alternately they sing, alternate flow
The obedient tears, melodious in their woe.[12]

Feasting, which involved food and drink, the drink often of the home brewed variety, was an essential part of the wake. Clay pipes (dúidíns) were passed around on a white enamel plate with plug tobacco in the centre, often shared when there was a scarcity. Frederick R. Higgins' poem entitled; *Padraic O Conaire Gaelic Storyteller,* captures the atmosphere of the wake,

They've paid the last respects in sad tobacco
And silent is this wakehouse in its haze;
They've paid the last respects; and now their whiskey
Flings laughing words on mouths of prayer and praise.[13]

Cahir

In relation to Cahir, while there were many midwives who carried out the task of laying out the dead, forty year old Ellen Heffernan, Church Street, performed other duties. She resided next door to what was until recently Condon's Public House. According to the 1911 Census, Ellen was the mother of two children and her husband, a tinsmith, worked at this trade in the Military Barracks. In their house, which is now a hairdressing salon, local people remember seeing shelves full of tin utensils.

Ellen was paid for the job of laying out the body and reciting prayers over the corpse. This recitation may have involved keening the dead. She always dressed in black and carried salt which she placed on the lips of the deceased. The use of salt was to ward off evil spirits. The belief was that the same portal that allowed the spirit to pass into the next world, could also permit evil spirits to enter this one. According to the 1911 Census, thirty-one year old Margaret Morrissey, wife of a chemist of Castle Street, as well as being a midwife, was known to have laid out the dead.

---

12   *The Iliad of Homer,* Translated by Alexander Pope.
13   F.R. Higgins, *'Padraic O Conaire Gaelic Storyteller'.*

The home of Ellen Heffernan on Church Street,
with the tin mugs hanging outside the door (Circa 1910).
(Courtesy: Lawrence Collection, National Library)

A Cahir lady, recalls hearing her late father, William O'Neill, say that he remembered hearing, as a child in the 1930s, keening women at a wake. These women were hired and the house was that of a Fenton family on the Reiska Road, near Cahir. A native of Shanballyanne in the Nire Valley, Co. Waterford, Eileen Bolger, remembers an old lady in the village who attended wakes for the purpose of keening the dead. Pulling her shawl tightly around her, this lady would rock from side to side wailing and praying.

Keening the dead, as a practice, largely died out in the 1950s, although it continued in remote parts of the West of Ireland. Irish Travellers have been known to perform a version of keening up to the present day. The keen was frowned on by the Catholic Church, regarding it as a pagan custom. In recent years, *The Father Mathew Players* from New Inn, performed an excellent interpretation of the keen in their staging of Dion Boucicault's play, *The Shaghraun*. The depiction of wailing women around the 'corpse' had a very powerful effect on those present, highlighting how the keen awakens a deep emotion within the human psyche.

Writing in *The Irish Times*, Dr. Muiris Houston, medical journalist and lecturer, endorsed the practice of waking the dead. He wrote that in the rural area where he lives, the practice of watching over the recently deceased from the time of death to burial is still followed and that he had come to appreciate how a wake is an important part of the grieving process. He goes on to say; "waking someone close to you – literally staying awake to watch over them – seems to set up a soothing of the grief to follow".[14]

Kevin Toolis, in a BBC video, describes the Irish wake as a process by which mourners drained out emotion before they moved on to the stages of acceptance of death.

> I think the best way to deal with death is not to invent a new ritual or appoint another priest caste of bereavement counsellors or medical professionals. It is to do what we've always done and that's to gather together, as fellow mortals in the face of our mortality and seek to bridge that moment of bereavement and loss together[15].

In modern times, we struggle with the emotional and physical trauma of death. Searching for ways to deal with this, we might find that the old ways of dealing with death – long discarded as archaic, tribal practices rooted in superstition – could be revived as a way of dealing with grief.

---

14   Dr. Muiris Houston, *Irish Times* -10th April 2018.
15   Kevin Toolis, BBC Video- 5th May 2018.

FUNERAL EXPENSES FEBRUARY 3rd 1941

NO RECEIPT VALID UNLESS ON OUR PRINTED FORMS.

Burial Expenses

1941

Feb 3	Coffin		12	12	.
	1 gross pipes			10	.
	4 lbs Bacco		2	13	.
	5 lbs Cheese		1	7	6
	8 × reels Jam			12	.
	p/c Candles			2	.
	2 lbs matches			1	8
	200 Cigarettes			10	6
	3 lbs Tea			10	.
	28 lb sugar			11	9
	Duplex Chimney			1	3
	½ yd wick				4½
	Telegrams			8	7
	Insertion in	}			
	2 o Local Press			11	.
	Use of Hearse		1	10	.
			22	1	2½

Expenses include 1 gross pipes (144 clay pipes)

duplex chimney (globe for oil lamp)

Half yard wick (also for oil lamp)

Mercy Nuns at the Heart of Cahir
By Josephine O'Neill

Cahir/Clogheen Sisters of Mercy 1907
(Image Source: Courtesy of National Library of Ireland)

Do you remember?

Maybe you are old enough to remember walking in convoy down The Covered Walk to music class in the convent, hearing the rain beat against the galvanised roof or watching the gardener dig the potatoes, attending concerts in the school hall, seeing the boarders out walking around Cahir accompanied by nuns on a Sunday afternoon. Some of us recall the May Procession around the convent grounds, prayers before every class, writing 'Per Mariam' at the top of your essay, hockey in the field at the back of the graveyard, science experiments in the hut and even school on Saturday mornings!

So many of the memories of our youth revolve around school. Sometimes, when I park in the grounds of the Day Care Centre, I think I learned Latin in this very spot or did my Irish Leaving Cert examination right there. Whether you had good or not so good memories of school, the fact is that the nuns influenced our lives. Cahir convent and Scoil Chríost Rí are no more, but the memories live on.

The story of the sisters who lived and worked in the Cahir convent spans 151 years. It is impossible to truly evaluate the contribution that these women made to the education and healthcare of generations of people in Cahir and the surrounding areas. In fact, the Cahir nuns' sphere of influence extended across Ireland and indeed further afield to Wales and the USA.

Meet Cahir's Rebel Nun

High walls separated the imposing Cahir Convent from the local community with the parlour and chapel marking the boundaries of public access to the interior. Of course, notwithstanding the religious ethos of the sisters, it would be wrong to assume that an atmosphere of peace and harmony always prevailed behind the convent walls. After all, these women were human and the discipline of convent life and living with so many others in close proximity must have been challenging at times. Meet Sister Joseph, who from 1887 to 1889, wrote from Cahir convent to Bishop Piers Power to complain about the "tyranny" of her Reverend Mother.

Addressing the bishop as "My dear and respected Lord", she recounts incidents which convinced her that her superior had "availed of every opportunity to crush her." When she is ordered to go to her cell, her reaction was defiant, "I said I would not, that no one is bound to obey when the superior is commanding what we never vowed." Sister Joseph even claims that her superior said, "the veil ought to be taken" from her. She ended her letters of complaint with the phrase "yours devotedly in Jesus". Sister Joseph tells him that after yet another confrontation, "I renewed my vows this morning and am in the hands of God."

A Horse-drawn Cart over the Vee

The first House of Mercy was established by Catherine McAuley in Baggot Street Dublin in 1827. A wealthy lay woman, Catherine, worked with like-minded lay women amongst the poor of Dublin and by 1841 had received papal approval for a new religious order. The modus operandi was to set up a convent in a town. Once that was established, a small group of pioneers left and established another one and so the network grew.

Grave marker of Mary Anne Phelan who founded Mercy Convent Cahir on 21 May 1863

The Cappoquin Convent of Mercy was founded in 1850, and thirteen years later, on Whit Monday, May 1863, three sisters from the order there set out in a horse-drawn cart with "frugal supplies" to set up a Cahir foundation. Tradition tells us that to save time, the driver, who had to be back in Cappoquin before nightfall, unharnessed his horse above Baylough, and avoiding the Vee and perhaps Petticoat Loose, proceeded to manoeuvre the cart himself over the shortcut through the mountain, while the sisters led the animal.

Mother Mary Teresa Ligouri Phelan, appointed as the first Mother Superior, was accompanied from the mother house by Sisters Mary Francis Kennedy and Mary Augustine O'Connor. The three sisters set up temporary accommodation in a house on the Mall. The community began to grow with many postulants being received at ceremonies held in the parish Church.

Two of the young sisters died of pneumonia, which was attributed to the damp conditions in the Mall house, and were buried outside the sacristy of the Parish Church. When the Church was enlarged in 1888, the plot was incorporated into the building and the sisters' graves now lie under the altar of the current parish Church.

Establishing a Convent

In 1874, the sisters rented a house on Castle Street and a second house on the Mall. By this time, the congregation had grown to 24 sisters, and plans were put in place to build a convent. The 18-acre site on Pearse Street (then known as Wellington Street) was obtained from Lady Margaret Charteris through the mediation of her tenants, especially Mr Sam Burke.

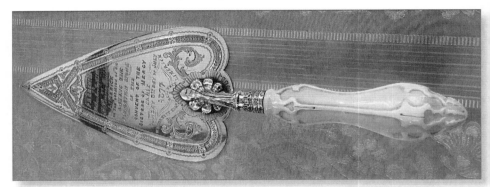

Silver and ivory trowel presented to the Sisters of Mercy in Cahir on the occasion of the laying of the Foundation Stone of Cahir Convent in 1877

From Mullinahone, Mary Anne Vaughan, known in religion as Sister Bernard, enrolled in 1866 and was professed in 1869. She personally designed and attended to the building of the Convent, which was partially completed in 1878. However, only half of the building could initially be undertaken due to lack of money. A raffle was organised to raise funds with the first prize on offer a

"beautiful pony and phaeton (a type of carriage), value £20." Other listed prizes included an easy chair, a gold ring, a sewing machine, a Douay Bible, a magic lantern, a handsome epergne (an ornamental centre piece for a table) and wax flowers under a glass vase.

As a lack of funds was still impeding the completion of the convent, the records show that the enterprising Sister Bernard began a novena. An answer came in the form of a donation from a wealthy widow, Mrs Catherine McHugh from Tipperary Town. Later, Catherine entered and donated all her property to the community. As an extension to the convent, Sr. Bernard also laid the plans for a new Chapel and "displayed her skill as a painter in the work of its interior decoration." We know that the Ballyporeen and Clogheen Convents were also planned and designed by Sister Bernard, who was a remarkably talented woman by any standard.

Cahir Convent. (Courtesy of Michelle O'Loughnane)

The first sisters in Cahir were engaged in visitation of the sick and "works of mercy". They then took over the lay-run National School, which had catered for boys and girls of the town. Education in Cahir now became segregated with the Sisters focussed on teaching Cahir girls while the Parochial School in Church Street, near the Protestant Church, became the Boys' National School.

Cahir Nuns first Primary School demolished in 1967. Courtesy of Sr. Eileen Fahey.

Cahir Expands to Other Areas

In 1863, just twenty years after the arrival of Mercy Sisters in Cahir, five Sisters, Sister Peter McCarthy, Sister Alphonsus McCormack, Sister Stanislaus O'Connell, Sister Berchmans Sheehy and Sister Joachim McCarthy left Cahir to establish the Convent at Portlaw. Sadly, two of these young sisters died of TB before they reached the age of thirty. In 1885 and 1886, branch houses were established in both Clogheen and Ballyporeen with primary schools also opening in both locations.

In 1883, the Sisters took charge of the Workhouse Hospital in Clogheen, later to become the current St Theresa's Hospital. The sisters also began to work in the Infirmary attached to the Clonmel Workhouse with training of nurses approved there in 1897. Researcher, Eamonn Lonergan provides us with a fascinating history of the evolution of this Workhouse Hospital, which would eventually become St Joseph's Hospital, now known as South Tipperary General Hospital. According to Lonergan's account, members of the Board of Guardians in the Workhouse were divided on the employment of Cahir nuns. Some argued that "the sick and dying would be better cared for by the Sisters of Mercy than by mercenary nurses" while others claimed," We are not desirous of imposing on them so humiliating a duty as their residence in this Poorhouse would entail."

Letter from Rev Fr Walsh P.P., St. Mary's Cahir to Clonmel Board of Guardians in 1883
(Courtesy of Sr. Eileen Fahey)

In December 1883, Sister M. Gertrude Foran, a native of Listowel and Sister Monica Vaughan from Mullinahone took up duty and resided in accommodation in the Workhouse. According to reports of that time, "The arrival of the Sisters of Mercy brought about an immediate improvement in the level of care available to patients in the Infirmary Wards." Meanwhile, author Bonnie Brennan reminds us that in hospitals, regular prayers, especially the Rosary, were recited daily in the wards while lay nurses were encouraged to join the Irish Catholic Nurses' Guild. Wards were placed under the patronage of a variety of saints; and religious images such as crucifixes, holy pictures and statues lined the corridors which indeed many of us remember from the not-so-distant past.

Over the Years

The Census of 1901 lists 30 nuns and no servants in Cahir Convent, which is divided into two sections with fifteen nuns per section. The convent is described as a stone building with a slate roof, 16 front windows, 36 rooms and five outbuildings. The sisters hailed from Tipperary, Limerick, Wexford, Kerry, Carlow and Waterford. Sister Catherine, the wealthy widow, whose inheritance helped to build the convent is included in the census data. The occupation for each is given as "Sister of Mercy".

In 1909, a room in the National School Cahir, was designated by the Sisters of Mercy for girls, who wished to prepare for King's Scholarship Matriculation and Service Examinations and Commercial Examinations. Mother Peter provided a commercial class in the Convent, teaching shorthand, typing, book-keeping and commerce. Twenty-six students are listed on the 1911 Census, including students from as far afield as Mayo, Leitrim, Roscommon and Cavan.

In the 1911 Census 20 religious are recorded in the Convent. Fifteen are described as involved in "works of mercy and teaching" while five are engaged in "works of Mercy", probably as lay nuns. At this stage Cahir Convent had six servants; one gardener, three farm servants and two cooks. The term nun now changes to "religious." Fast forward to 1937 and there were six nuns in Ballyporeen, 12 in Clogheen and 32 in Cahir. There were also Cahir nuns in the convent attached to Clonmel hospital.

A Secondary School is Established

Cahir Convent School c. 1898
(Courtesy of Paul Buckley, *Glimpses of the Past*)

Back row, l-r: Mary Ann Looby (Townspark), Annie Brennan (Wellington Street), Mollie O'Neill (Reiska), Mollie Kennedy (Mitchelstown Road), Alice Quigley (Suttonrath), Ellen Curran (Mountain Road), Jo McGrath(Mountain Road), Margaret Keating (Kedrah), Cathy O'Neill (Suttonrath).

Middle row, l-r: - - Sullivan (Mountain Road), - - Roche (Raheen), Ellen Buckley (Market Street), Annie Prendergast (Ballingeary), Ciss Wallace (Chapel Road), - - Roche (Barrack Steet).

Front row, l-r: Mother Louis, Anna Fitzgerald, Anne Looby (Townspark), Catherine Dooley (Barrack Street), Annie O'Donnell (Church Street), Mary Dooley (Barrack Street), Sister Cecilia.

In September 1934, Scoil Chríost Rí Secondary School was established with all subjects taught through Irish. Sister Teresa Kelly recalled the highly polished, pitch pine floors, single desks and the furniture in the four rooms as "breathtaking." Out of a handful of students present on that day, five subsequently became nuns. The staff comprised of Sister Finbarr Stokes and Sister Declan Gardiner with two teachers, Miss Cahill and Miss Liston. Sister Rosarii, one of the first students, recalls the daily prayer recited, "A Bhríd, A Mhuire na nGael, cabhraigh linn an Ghaeilge a labhairt chomh binn blasta agus do labhair tú féin í." Saint Brigid, Mary of the Gaels, teach us to speak Irish as sweetly as you did." According to author Bonnie Brennan and indeed true to many of our own memories, religious instruction was given for one half hour per day, prayers were said in the morning and before and after class with the Angelus recited at midday. On days of adoration, the navy gym-slip and jumper with red collar (which later changed to a maroon gym slip and blue blouse and later again for a wine gym slip and white blouse) were exchanged for white dresses and veils, made by a local dressmaker. Processions in honour of Our Lady were held in May, attended by all the students with the Holy Communion girls given special place of honour, while students were also encouraged to join the Children of Mary, the Pioneer Total Abstinence Association and the Legion of Mary.

The school quickly built up a reputation for excellent academic results. Day girls attended the school from Cahir, Ardfinnan, Clogheen, New Inn, Ballylooby and Ballyporeen while boarders came from Clare, Tipperary, Limerick, Cork, Kerry, Waterford, Cavan and Kildare. The 1940s saw an expansion of the school buildings with records showing that seven lay teachers contributed to Scoil Chríost Rí in the 1930s and 1940s.

Recruiting Future Nuns

In the late 1920s, the Blessed Sacrament Sisters from Pittsburgh, Pennsylvania visited various Primary Schools in Ireland to seek out young girls who would be willing to be educated in Ireland and go to the States as "apostolics." Following this initiative, an Apostolic School was established by the nuns in Cahir between 1931 and 1938 for "those desirous of entering religion in Cahir or abroad." Sister Malachy Aherne volunteered to look after prospective candidates in the Cahir boarding school. During the seven years of this school, records reveal a "steady stream" of teenage girls from many counties in Ireland, from Cork, Clare Galway and Kerry. A large number came from Kerry, in fact the records show that three sisters from the same family from Listowel came to the Apostolic School.

Having received a few years education in Cahir, these young girls sailed for the States to the Novitiate in Cornwell Heights, Pennsylvania, where they spent their formative years. After profession they attended training Colleges and qualified as teachers for "Indians and coloured people in

A mould used in Cahir convent for making Communion breads

the Southern States." The Blessed Sisters saw their mission as uplifting minority populations, long before the era of Civil Rights.

Records reveal that many years passed before these "heroic missionaries" returned home and "invariably found their parents long since dead." According to records, they "visited Cahir and the grave of the Sisters they knew in their early days and they often stayed in their Alma Mater." In terms of local representation, Sister Catherine O'Neill from Cahir worked in Los Angeles and Sister Catherine Barrett of Rafane, Cahir worked in Arizona, both as sisters of the Blessed Sacrament.

Mercy Order Family Tree

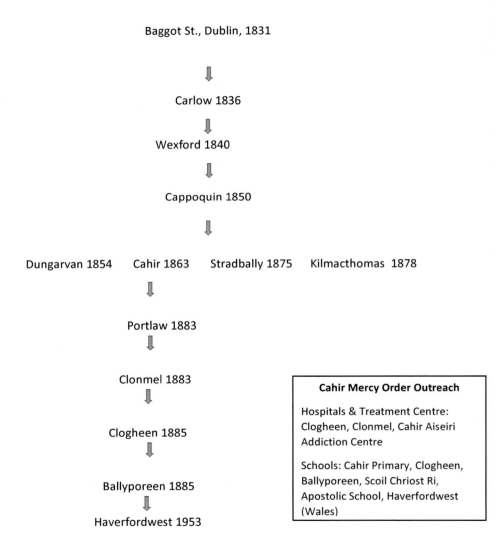

Baggot St., Dublin, 1831

⬇

Carlow 1836

⬇

Wexford 1840

⬇

Cappoquin 1850

⬇

Dungarvan 1854   Cahir 1863   Stradbally 1875   Kilmacthomas 1878

⬇

Portlaw 1883

⬇

Clonmel 1883

⬇

Clogheen 1885

⬇

Ballyporeen 1885

⬇

Haverfordwest 1953

Cahir Mercy Order Outreach

Hospitals & Treatment Centre: Clogheen, Clonmel, Cahir Aiseiri Addiction Centre

Schools: Cahir Primary, Clogheen, Ballyporeen, Scoil Chriost Ri, Apostolic School, Haverfordwest (Wales)

Life Behind Convent Walls

Annals for Cahir convent have been lost over the years and the only records available are scrapbooks and brief histories, written by individual Cahir nuns. However, we can assume that Cahir convent operated on the same principles as other Houses of Mercy.

Vocations

A vocation, meaning a call from God to religious life, brought many women to Cahir convent in search of salvation. However, a candidate also needed to come from what was deemed a "suitable" family. Postulants to the Mercy Order typically came from farming, business or professional backgrounds, where a dowry was provided by the family. In Cahir, it is worth noting that the dowries brought by choir nuns added to convent resources. Diocesan archives record the following dowries for the 1880s and 1890s: £300, £200, £33, £200 and £110. The convent was not allowed to touch the capital sum until the sister died but could use the interest. Once accepted, the sister entered the novitiate for two years. After some months in the convent, the community voted on the suitability of the postulant for religious life. Her cap and simple black veil were exchanged for a white veil and a two-year period of "withdrawal, study and reflection" began. The first year of novitiate was described as an intense spiritual year. This was followed by a year of spiritual formation and work in education or nursing, designed to help the sister decide on a future career.

When the novitiate was complete, the community again voted and a temporary profession of vows was taken. All nuns – including those in Cahir – took four vows: celibacy, poverty, obedience and service to the poor, sick and the work of education. Temporary vows lasted from three to six years. After this period, a ceremony was held in the convent chapel and the sister took her perpetual profession of vows.

The habit worn by Cahir nuns had been designed by the order's founder, Catherine McAuley. It consisted of two white garments, a helmet and breastplate, covered with a black veil, a long sleeved close pleated dress with a train, a black belt or cincture at the waist from which hung a set of rosary beads ending in an ebony and ivory cross and a wood and metal crucifix inserted into the belt in the centre front. The headdress had to be partly starched. Patterns for the habit were kept in the convent and passed from sister to sister, and Sister Genevieve made the habits for Cahir nuns for decades.

Reverend Mother

The Reverend Mother was the most powerful woman within the Convent. She was elected every three years by choir nuns. Voting was by secret ballot and she in turn nominated sisters for other positions. Next to the Reverend Mother in terms of hierarchy was the Mother Assistant and then the Bursar, who controlled the finances. The position of Novice Mistress was also very powerful because she determined which novices completed their training and identified women who would later be given positions of power.

1901…. Eight Thousand Nuns

According to Catriona Clear, author of "Nuns in 19th Century Ireland", the number of nuns in Ireland increased eightfold between 1841 and 1901, outnumbering men in religious orders. This remarkable increase came at a time when the overall population fell by over half. In 1901, there were 8,000 nuns in 368 convents around Ireland. So why did so many women choose this way of life? Historian Dr. Denis Marnane suggests the following: "If an intelligent, middle-class woman wished to do more with her life than the conventional options of marriage, home and family or indeed if she wished to remain unmarried but not lose status, then entry to a convent brought not only social status and a better chance of personal salvation. In addition, there was the possibility of a career in teaching or nursing and for some sisters, the exercise of power and influence".

Power Structures

The nuns' work in the kitchens, hospitals and schools won acclaim from hierarchy, clergy and laity alike, but Rosemary Raughter, author of "Religious Women and their History", contends that "It did not win them admission to the power structures of a patriarchal and authoritarian Church". One would argue that this was in keeping with the conventions of the time, when women generally occupied a lower position in society than men. According to Maria Luddy, Emeritus Professor, Warwick University, "the view of women as secondary and inferior to men was deeply embedded in Irish society. In the realm of religion, it was couched in theological language and internalised in prayer and practice". True to the historical context of the time, the convent conformed to class structures and a two-tier system was in operation. In the Mercy guidebook, the lives of choir and lay nuns were considered distinct. According to historian Rosemary Raughter, lay sisters were generally from humble backgrounds and carried out domestic tasks of the communities. From wealthier backgrounds, choir nuns were well educated and "carried out the public work for which the communities had been established."

Children of Mary Garden Party at Cahir Convent 1933
(Courtesy of Paul Buckley)

Lay Nuns

Lay nuns were addressed as "Sister" whereas choir nouns interestingly enjoyed the prefix of "Mrs". For example, Mother Bernard Vaughan, who was largely responsible for constructing Cahir convent, was known as "Mrs Vaughan." According to Denis Marnane, the "category of lay sister was a means of integrating domestic service within the routine and discipline of a convent". Lay sisters had no say in the running of the convent or in any convent elections while their recreation and meals were always taken separately. Maria Luddy contends that "lay sisters may have seen convent life as an escape from dependence and economic instability in society."

Records show the names of all the sisters who entered Cahir convent over the years. Many led happy, fulfilled lives. Those who left the order are not listed but should also be remembered because it took great courage to "scale the convent walls" and return to their families, who were often shamed by society for their daughters' departures. Some members were remembered for being harsh, for focussing their attention on pupils from wealthier backgrounds or those who were academically bright, while many others are remembered for their kindness and encouragement, often giving extra tuition to interested students.

In a society which prioritised second level male education, the Sisters of Mercy provided important primary and secondary education for the women of Cahir and beyond. Of course, they were not the first to do so, as laywomen had established or taught in Cahir schools before the arrival of Mercy Nuns. Although the Vocational Education System also provided girls with second level education in Cahir at the technical school from the 1930s onwards, the nuns unquestionably made a very significant contribution to the prospects of many local women.

Final Farewell
In 1997, students left Scoil Chríost Rí for the last time. Seventeen years later, on Sunday, 7 December 2014, the Sisters of Mercy bade a final farewell to Cahir. The hall door of the convent was closed and the lights went out on another chapter of Cahir women's history. The nuns will continue to be remembered for their dedication to the people of Cahir. Their legacy endures; indeed, it has been said that the nuns left their monuments in stone with convents, schools and hospitals dotted around the country.

In 1997, Sister M. Rosarii was asked to suggest a quotation for a plaque at St. Mary's Church, Cahir, to commemorate the sisters in Cahir who worked in the primary and secondary school. She replied, "Beidh a gcuimhne go deo in aigne na ndaoine" ("Their memory will live forever in the minds of the people").

Sources
Edited by Annette Condon, Kilmoyler
http://www.workhouses.org.uk/Clonmel/
Eamonn Lonergan's *St. Joseph's Hospital, Clonmel. A Historical and Social Portrait.*
Bonnie Brennan's *History of the Sisters of Mercy of Ireland.*
Patrick Power's *Parochial History of Waterford and Lismore in the Eighteenth and Nineteenth Century.*
http://stmaryscahir.webs.com/
Denis G. Marnane's *A Lamp Kindled.*
Archives Mercy International, Baggot St., Dublin.
Diocesan Archives of Waterford & Lismore, Waterford.
Interviews with Cahir nuns.
Rosemary Raughter's *Religious Women and their History.*
Catriona Clear's *Nuns in Nineteenth-Century Ireland.*
Maria Luddy, "Presentation Convents in County Tipperary 1801-1900", *Tipperary Historical Journal, 1992*

Mary Dillon's Typical Family

By Breeda Ryan

In an earlier chapter, we learned of a Mary Dillon who had been ordered to Cahir Lodge by the land agent in 1871. At that meeting, she reported that she had been threatened with no Christmas charities and removal from her home if she did not send her children to the National School rather than the Convent School.

Fast forward to 1911 and to Mary's daughter-in-law, also Mary Dillon (nee Grady) and her family which was a typical Irish family. This younger Mary Dillon lived in Cahir with her husband and gave birth to fourteen children. Here are the details of the family:

Dillon Family			
FATHER		JOHN DILLON	
	BORN	23RD. FEBRUARY 1866	
	MARRIED	1888	
	WORK	LABOURER	
MOTHER		MARY GRADY	
	BORN	1869	
		CHILDREN	
1	ELLEN	BORN	1ST. AUGUST 1891
2	MARY	BORN	18TH NOVEMBER 1892
3	MICHEAL 1	BORN	3RD OCTOBER 1894
		DIED	3RD OCTOBER 1894
4	CATHERINE	BORN	21ST. AUGUST 1895
5	BRIDGET 1	BORN	19TH FEBRUARY 1897
		DIED	3RD MARCH 1897

6	Margaret	Born	16th January 1898
7	Micheal II	Born	11th September 1899
8	Bridget Mary II	Born	6th September 1901
9	Elizabeth	Born	19th November 1902
		Died	28th October 1903
10	Twins Daniel	Born	16th October 1905
		Died	27th December 1918 (Clogheen Workhouse Flu)
11	George Gerard	Born	16th October 1905
12	John	Born	18th February 1908
		Died	23rd December 1918 Fractured Neck, Injured while Pumping Engine at Rail Station
13	Patrick	Born	7th January 1910
		Died	9th March 1913 (Meningitis)
14	Thomas	Born	27th February 1912

Each of the above Dillon children was baptized at St. Mary's, Cahir, on the day of birth or the next day or as soon as possible. That was the custom at the time. As the mother was confined to bed for one week following each birth, the midwife attended the baptism to look after the baby.

The family lived in various places in Cahir:
Market Street, 1888-1894
Wellington Street, 1894-1898
Market Street, 1898-1906
Old Church Street, 1906-2000s

The last child, Thomas, was born at Old Church Street in 1912, and that house was still in the family until recently.

According to the censuses, the family paid rent for the Old Church Street house to Lady Margaret Charteris. The house was described as stone with a slate roof, three front windows, five rooms, and outbuildings. In 1901, there was just one outbuilding; but in 1911, there were two - a workshop and a piggery. They would have had a pig or two as most families at that time kept pigs.

More recently, there was a dry toilet, an ash pit, and a shed. At that time, if the shed was stone, like the house, it was sometimes used as a dwelling. The toilet

Number 5 Old Church Street
– Home of the Dillon Family since 1906

and pigsty would have been emptied each day into the ash pit, and the ashes from the fire were thrown in on top. The pit was emptied every year or two and the contents used as fertilizer for gardens and 'plots' (allotments). Where there was no back entry to the yard, everything had to be brought through the house, including the pit contents. Thank God today for flush toilets and wheelie bins!

Mary's husband was a labourer with a large family to support. To supplement the income in 1901, Mary had two lodgers and a boarder – three more people to care for, making a household of ten with the next baby due in months. As Mary's nine surviving children got older, they would have looked for jobs. Her daughter, Bridget, obtained a position with the Irish Command, Queen Mary's Army Auxiliary Corps after the Great War was over. According to records in the UK National Archives, Bridget entered the army at the Receiving Depot in Dublin on 30 January 1919 when she would have been just seventeen years of age. However, her admitting record gives a birth date which makes her a month shy of her nineteenth birthday. She is described with grey eyes and dark brown hair. The next day, she received her "Articles of Uniform": a hat badge, a coat frock, three collars, a pair of gaiters, a greatcoat, a felt hat, two overalls, one pair of shoes, two pairs of stockings, one brassard, and two sets of shoulder titles. Her position was as a messenger. On 18 September 1919, Bridget was transferred to the 2nd Battalion of the Oxfordshire and Buckinghamshire Light Infantry in Cork. She stayed there just five weeks before being transferred to the barracks of the 1st Battalion: "The Buffs" at Fermoy. Her duties were those of "housemaid".

Life was surely hard for Mary Dillon, the mother of this large family. The awful sadness that she must have felt at the loss of six of her young children is beyond comprehension. Bridget's absence from the home must also have been difficult. The hardship and poverty Mary must have endured is unbelievable.

These three generations of Dillon women experienced lives which included struggle. It is due to their courage and resilience, and that of all other women in the same typical circumstances, even our own grandmothers and great grandmothers who lived at that time, that we have a better life. We salute all those women. They truly deserve a mention in the Roll of Honour.

Our Lady of the Laundry
(In Memory of Johanna White, Market Street, Cahir).

Hymns were her shanty songs, her wash-day heave-ho

to keep going with endless pots of sooty water swung from fire irons.

Soul of my saviour sanctify my breast

as I wrestle with the toil-grime of his shirt collars.

Bathe me in waters as I haul bucket after bucket

from the tap in Market Street, my shoes wringing wet.

Guard and defend me from the foe malign

as I take the scrubbing brush to yellowed-in sweat,

the stench of sour towels, the washing board cutting into my chest.

Health of the sick soften the nerve pain in my back

as I stretch for relief.

Comforter of the afflicted soothe the split rawness of my knuckles.

Hail Queen of Heaven distract me with the gleam of stars on the ocean,

the wanderer guided to safety, the surge of life-woe eased.

Inspire me as our poor rags freshen with Rinso and Daz,

my sweat pooling and dripping with the effort.

Protect me

Mystical Rose,

Tower of Ivory,

Mother of Carbolic Soap and Robin Starch,

Queen of Reckitt's Blue

Margaret Galvin.

From Cahir to the USA 1900-1920
By Karol DeFalco

The following fourteen women represent a small portion of the large number of women who emigrated from Cahir to the USA, 1900 – 1920. There are many more who emigrated both before and after this twenty year period.

Mary O'Meara of Cahir also known as Minnie O'Mara, was the sixth child of Michael Mara, a carrier for the railway, and Mary Dwyer. Mary was born 6 January 1885 at Wellington Street and baptised the same day at Cahir. Her sponsors were William Richardson and Johanna Burke. When Minnie was just nine years of age, her father died, leaving his widowed wife with seven children. In the 1901 Census, the mother and four children, including Minnie, were residing at Abbey Street. Minnie, then 16 years of age, was still in school and became a dressmaker.

Mary (Minnie) O'Meara who emigrated to New York on 12 September 1904

In the same year as the census, Minnie's older brother, Michael, emigrated; and in 1904, she followed him. She left Queenstown and arrived in New York on 12 September 1904. Her occupation was listed as dressmaker; but incredibly, she was listed as having no money upon entering the United States. In 1910, Minnie was residing with Michael and his family in rented accommodation at 323, 26th Street, Manhattan, and was a dressmaker.

Five years later and during World War I, Minnie returned to Ireland. She left New York aboard "Cymric" and disembarked in Liverpool on 14 March 1915. Interestingly, her documentation, entering the UK, gives Minnie's address as Cahir and her last permanent residence as England. The document states that her intended residence is also England. However, at some point, Minnie returned to Cahir, resided with her sister, Josie Golden, at Abbey Street, and continued work as a dressmaker. In the 1960s, the Abbey Street house was sold, and Minnie moved to the Reiska Road to live with her niece, Joan O'Neill. Minnie died there in 1975 and is buried at Cahir.

Ellen "Nellie" Lonergan, although born at Scartnaglorane and baptised at Ballylooby, was living in Cahir by 1901. She was born 29 January 1886, the first child of Thomas Lonergan and his wife, Mary Healy. Thomas was from Scartnaglorane and Mary from Tincurry; they married in 1885 at Ballylooby. The couple remained in Scartnaglorane until at least 1898 when their sixth child (Catherine) was born; but by 1901, they were in Cahir for the birth of their last child, Norah.

About 1904, Ellen emigrated to Providence, Rhode Island. By 1910 she was a jeweller for a jewellery manufacturer and resided with her brother, John Patrick Lonergan, at the home of their aunt, Alice Healy, at 22 West Clifford Street, Providence.

Alice Sheehy, born 24 May 1890 at Ballydrehid, was the oldest of five children born to farmer John Sheehy and his wife, Ellen Quinlan, who was from Skeheenarinky. In 1903, Ellen died in the Tipperary Workhouse, leaving her husband with five children aged 8-13, Alice being the oldest. Five years later, nineteen years old Alice boarded "Ivernia" at Queenstown (Cobh) and made the eight day ocean voyage to Boston. She carried $10 and was headed to her uncle, David Quinlan, in Whitman, Massachusetts. Accompanying Alice was her cousin, Alice Quinlan, who was also headed to David Quinlan in Whitman.

Margaret "Gretta" O'Dwyer was the granddaughter of Cahir Quaker Llywelyn Fennell, Gentleman. He resided at Cahir Cottage in Caherabbey Lower until his death in 1897 when his estate was valued at over £13,000!

Llywelyn's daughter, Maria, was residing in Ballydrehid in 1884. In that year, she married farmer Thomas O'Dwyer of Ballydrehid. They were married by T. Heffernan CC at the Bansha Roman Catholic Church. Maria and Thomas O'Dwyer had eleven children, including Gretta (1893), the seventh of the children. The first five children were born at Ballydrehid, the others at Cahir where they were baptised at the Catholic Church.

In Cahir, the O'Dwyer family resided at Tipperary Road. In 1901, the house was stone with a slate roof, two front windows, and two rooms for the family of nine. Thomas was listed as a general labourer.

Within the next five years, Gretta's mother died; and Gretta, aged 15, emigrated to the USA . She and her seven year old brother, John, boarded "Ivernia" at Queenstown on 3 June 1908. Gretta was described as 5'4", dark complexion, black hair, and blue eyes. She listed herself as a domestic and carried $10 into Boston. The two immigrants were headed to their oldest sibling, Catherine O'Dwyer, who was residing at Joslin House in Webster, Massachusetts.

Catherine "Kate" Carmody was the daughter of Michael Carmody, a labourer, and his wife, Johanna Brien, who were both residing at Drangan when they married at Bansha in 1884. Kate and her twin, Timothy, were born on 6 November 1885 at Ballydrehid. The family was still in Ballydrehid in 1887 and 1888 when two more children – Johanna and Hanora – were born. By 1901, however, the family was residing at Tipperary Road, Cahir. In the census of that year, Michael is absent from the family, and Johanna is listed with her four children as a married laundress. By 1907, Kate had married John Leary, a coachman. Their first child, Patrick Francis O'Leary, was born at Cahir on 12 October 1907. On his baptism record, the family's address is given as Mountain Road, and one of the sponsors was Kate's youngest sister, Nora Carmody.

In July 1908, Kate registered the sudden death of her twenty-one years old, younger sister, Johanna Carmody. The death record gives Kate's address as Mountain Road. One month later, 5 '3" Kate - with fair complexion, brown hair, and blue eyes - boarded "Cymric" at Queenstown with her nine months old son. She had $25 and arrived at Boston on 7 September 1908. Her immigration paper reported that her mother, Johanna Carmody, was still residing on Mountain Road and that Kate and her baby were headed to Kate's husband, John O'Leary, at 148 Medford Street in Somerville, Massachusetts. Kate and John had at least four more children and resided in Boston for decades. Kate's mother, who had arrived from Mountain Road, Cahir in 1910 and was widowed by 1920, lived with them.

Hanora "Nora" Carmody was the sister of Catherine "Kate" (Carmody) O'Leary. Nora was born 26 August 1888 at Ballydrehid. She had a fair complexion, brown hair and grey eyes. At the time of the 1901 Census, she resided at Tipperary Road, Cahir, with her mother and siblings. In 1907, Nora was a sponsor at the baptism of Kate's son, Patrick Francis O'Leary.

Nora and her mother, Johanna Carmody, planned to head to America on "Megantic", departing Queenstown on 13 April 1910 and going to Boston, to join Kate and family at 122 Shirley Park, Roxbury, Boston. For some reason, they did not board. Instead, four days later, they boarded "Cedric", leaving behind

Nora's brother, Timothy Carmody, on Mountain Road. The ship was headed to New York, over 200 miles away from Kate in Boston. On 24 April 1910, after a week on the ocean, the two women arrived in New York, each woman in possession of $10 and a ticket to their destination, Boston.

In Boston, Nora was a dressmaker and married Patrick Ridge on 1 February 1914. Their daughter, Mary Louise Ridge, was born in Boston on 14 January 1915. Nora and her family – like her sister, Kate O'Leary, and family - stayed in Boston.

Mary Byrne boarded the ship, "Zeeland", at Queenstown, Co. Cork, on 12 April 1911 and arrived at Boston on 20 April 1911. She gave her age as 25 and her occupation as housemaid. She could read and write. Mary was listed as 5'4" with fresh complexion, brown hair and blue eyes. She was born at Cahir and listed her father, John Byrne, as residing in Cahir in 1911. Mary had $30 and was headed to her cousin Josie Ryan at Church Street, Boston.

Johanna Kenneally, a domestic, aged 33, had resided in Providence, Rhode Island, for nineteen years when she boarded "Franconia" in Boston for a return trip to Ireland, disembarking at Queenstown on 17 December 1911. After a four months stay, Johanna, then listed as 34 years of age, boarded "Celtic" at Queenstown on 12 April 1912 for her return trip to the USA. She reported that she had been born in Cahir and that her closest relative in Cahir was Michael Kenneally of Ballydrehid. Johanna had $50 and, after disembarking in New York on 20 April 1912, was headed to her employer, Charles Briggs, at 364 Thayer Street, Providence, Rhode Island. Charles was a manufacturer of gold and silver jewellery. It is thought that Johanna was a housemaid at his home.

Within the next four months, Johanna was residing at 236 Georges Street, Providence, an impressive house with eleven front windows. She was there in September 1912 when her niece, Bridget Dalton, arrived from Cahir.

Molly Lonergan left Queenstown on 12 April 1912 aboard "Celtic", arriving in New York on 20 April 1912 with $50. She gave her age as 18 and her occupation as housemaid. Her birthplace was Cahir where her mother, Bridget Lonergan, was still residing at Upper Cahir Abbey. Molly paid for her passage herself. She had never been to the USA before and was headed to her brother, James Lonergan, at 48 Roosevelt Street in New York. She was described as 5'6" with light complexion, fair hair, and blue eyes. Traveling with Molly on "Celtic" was Johanna Kenneally, also from Cahir.

Molly was one of eleven children born to farmer Thomas Lonergan and his wife, Bridget Walsh. Molly, the seventh child, was born as Mary Lonergan on 3 January 1891 at Upper Cahir Abbey and was baptised the same day. Her sponsors were John Kelly and Margaret Costello.

Molly's father died in 1910 and by the time of the 1911 Census, five of her siblings were also deceased. In 1911, her mother and the six remaining children, including Molly, were still at Upper Cahir Abbey where Molly's brother, Thomas, had taken over the farm. There was a stable, a cow house, a piggery, a fowl house, a boiling house, a barn, and a shed. The house had five rooms and three front windows. Molly's brother, James, was a chauffeur who moved to Nenagh and married. In February 1912, James and his wife, Mary, emigrated to New York City, and two months later, Molly went out to them.

Jane Murnane emigrated aboard "Cymric" out of Queenstown on 5 June 1912. Her immigration papers in Boston state that she was 5' tall with fair complexion, brown hair, and brown eyes. She was 25 years of age, a servant, had $30, was born at Cahir, and lived there at the time of her departure from Ireland. When asked to give the name of her nearest relative in Cahir, Jane gave the name of her aunt, Mrs. Edmd Whelan, of Toureen, Cahir. When asked for her final destination, Jane replied that she was going to her friend, Sister Catherine Brett, at the Convent of Mercy in Putnam, Connecticut.

Elizabeth Lonergan, sister of Ellen Lonergan (above), was also born at Scartnaglorane. Elizabeth was born 21 August 1890 and baptised at Ballylooby two days later. On 21 August 1912, Elizabeth boarded "Franconia" at Queenstown, giving her last permanent residence as Cahir. The ship arrived at Boston, and her immigration records state that her father, Thomas Lonergan, was residing at Mountain Road, Cahir. Elizabeth carried $25 and a ticket to her destination of Providence, Rhode Island, where she was to meet her brother, John Lonergan, of 222 Power Street. Her records described her as 5'2", fair complexion, brown hair, blue eyes.

Bridget Dalton born 1892, was one of eleven children born to John Dalton and his wife, Bridget Kenneally. John and Bridget were married on 3 July 1881 at Kilmoyler. At the time of their marriage, both were residents of Ballydrehid, and were still living there in 1882 when their first child, Mary, was born. The family relocated to Toureen where at least seven of their children were born. The last child born at Toureen was Honora in 1900.

By the time of the 1901 Census, John and Bridget Dalton had moved to Market Street where they resided with nine of their children, including Bridget. Their rent was paid to Lady M. Charteris. John was described as a general labourer and his son, Michael, was listed as an unemployed footman. The house had two rooms and was made of stone with a slate roof and two front windows.

By 1911, the family had relocated to Tipperary Road. The family included John and Mary with four of their children, including nine year old Ellen who was the last of their children. This house was similar to the one on Market Street: stone with a slate roof, two front windows, two rooms. In addition, there was a piggery. Bridget, who was to emigrate in 1912, is not with the family in 1911. It's possible she is the Bridget Dalton, aged 18, who was working as a domestic that year at Holycross.

Bridget emigrated, boarding the ship, "Franconia", at Queenstown, Co. Cork, on 18 September 1912 and arrived at Boston on 25 September 1912. She listed her age as 19 and her occupation as servant. She could read and write. Bridget was listed as 5'3" with dark complexion, brown hair, and blue eyes. She reported that her father, John Dalton, was residing at Cahir in 1912. Bridget had $20 and was headed to her aunt, Miss Jo Kenneally (above), at 236 Georges Street, Providence, Rhode Island.

Helen Magner was born at Tincurry on 3 October 1893, the second of six children of John Magner and his wife, Margaret Healy. In the 1901 Census, their Tincurry house is listed as stone with a thatched roof, one front window and 1 room. By 1911, the house is described as stone with a thatched roof, two front windows, and three rooms. There was also a fowl house and a shed.

Helen was born as Ellen, and on some documents she is referred to as Nellie. Sometime after the 1911 Census of April 2nd, her older brother, John, emigrated to Providence, Rhode Island, and was residing at 82 West Clifford Street in that city when Helen arrived on 3 October 1912. She had boarded "Cymric" at Queenstown on 20 September and arrived at Boston thirteen days later.

Nellie remained at Providence for years and was residing at 253 Elmwood Avenue in that city on 5 January 1920. At that time, she was a cook for the Russell family. Mr. Russell was the treasurer for a jewellery manufacturer, and one wonders if that manufacturer was Charles Briggs, the gold and silver jewellery manufacturer for whom Cahir native, Johanna Kenneally, was working in 1912.

In 1925, after thirteen years in the USA, Nellie appears to have been in Rhode Island still. In that year, she made a trip home to Ireland aboard "Celtic", arriving at Liverpool on 14 November. On her UK incoming document, it is stated that Nellie intended her future residence to be in Ireland. However, after five months, Nellie boarded "Celtic" again – this time at Queenstown - for her journey back to the USA. She had $35, listed her occupation as domestic, and her destination as 44 East 79th Street in Manhattan, the home of her friend, Mrs. Berry.

Two years later, Nellie came home again, still listing herself as a domestic. This time she returned to New York aboard "Adriatic", arriving on 23 September 1928 with $50 and listed her destination as "home – 2788 Broadway, NY, NY." In the 1930 Census of Manhattan on 21 April, Nellie is listed at 114 East 90th Street, the home of the Roberts family for whom Nellie is a servant.

In 1934, Nellie made her next trip back to Tincurry which she listed as the residence of her mother, Mrs. M. Magner. She returned to the USA aboard "Georgic", arriving in New York on 11 September and carrying $35. She was destined for an address on the west side of Manhattan.

It appears that Nellie's last trip back to Ireland occurred in 1938 when she departed New York on 28 May. She gave her father's address as Tincurry and still listed herself as a domestic. She returned to the USA from Cobh aboard "Georgic", arriving at New York on 11 September with $35. She was described as 5'5", fair complexion, brown hair, blue eyes. Her destination was 115 East 90th Street in New York City, the home of her employer, Baldwin.

At the time of the 1940 Census (April 15th), Nellie was living at 38 West 52nd Street, Manhattan, the home of Thomas J Rhinelarder, a retired trustee of a real estate corporation, for whom she was the cook. She reported having worked 48 weeks in 1939, earning $750. In addition, she reported as having "other income".

Nellie's last residence is given as Pawtucket, Providence, Rhode Island 02860. She died there on 31 December 1966 and was buried at that town in Saint Mary's Cemetery. Eleven years later, her brother, John Magner, was buried at the same cemetery.

Margaret O'Neill lived on a farm at Lissava with her parents and siblings. The farm had a stable, cow house, piggery, fowl house, barn, and shed. Her parents, John O'Neill and Margaret Toohill had thirteen children, three of whom died young, including Hugh who died in 1908, aged eleven. Margaret was the eleventh born, having been baptised at Cahir on 19 March 1893.

In 1901, the Lissava house was listed as stone with a slate roof, three front windows, and four rooms for the family of ten. By the time of the 1911 Census, only two of the children were residing with their parents at Lissava.

In 1914, daughter Margaret was in Queenstown from where she departed on "Franconia" on 27 May. Eight days later, she arrived at Boston, Massachusetts. Her immigration records state that she was 5'1", fair complexion, fair hair, and blue eyes. She gave her age as 19 and her occupation as dressmaker. Her brother had paid for her passage and her mother was noted as residing at Lissava. Margaret had $5 and was headed to her sister at 301 W 51st Street in New York City. The document also indicates that in addition to her sister, Margaret had five brothers residing in the USA. Four of the five brothers have been identified as Michael, Daniel, Jeremiah, and William.

Sources:
United States Immigration Records, Census Records

Ireland: Census Records, Birth Records, Baptism Records, Marriage Records, Death Records, Probate Records, communication with family members

UK: Incoming Passenger Lists

Women's Occupations a Century Ago
By Mary Caulfield

The main source of information for women's occupations in Cahir a century ago is the 1911 Census of Ireland. Female occupations then were very different from those of the present time. Women, apart from the better off, did more work of a physical nature, had larger families and fewer luxuries. Labour saving devices were few and the age of technology was a long way off. In spite of a life of drudgery, women were resilient and resourceful, seeking out a living in whatever way possible. Some worked at home as dressmakers, while others took in lodgers, as well as having large families of their own to look after.

Quite a few occupations no longer exist, like laundresses and sack menders, while some are less common, like priests' housekeepers. In some cases, the job descriptions have changed. The shop assistant has become the sales person, servants are now referred to as staff and the boarding house has become the guest house. Married women must have worried about what would happen to them if their husbands died, as there were no widows' or orphans' pensions then. A surprisingly large number of females in Cahir, quite a few of whom were widows, owned or ran their own businesses. It may be that these widows took over their husbands' premises. Another feature of the time was the number of female workers in the town who had come from the neighbouring counties of Waterford and Kilkenny with fewer from Cork or Limerick. Also interesting was the amount of people who spoke both Irish and English, particularly those who hailed from Co. Waterford.

Servants

At the turn of the century, Cahir had an abundance of large residences. For those houses to function efficiently, many servants were needed. Servants were mainly female, coming from large families where money and food were scarce, living on the premises where they worked, receiving poor wages and working long hours. In most cases this was the only employment available to them, coming from large families where money and food were scarce. Business premises usually had one or more domestic servants while the larger houses had a retinue of servants. The owners of these houses would have been familiar with a book, first published in 1861, *Mrs Beeton's Household Management*.

This large tome, as well as hundreds of recipes, gives very pertinent advice on the treatment of servants. "On the day that mistresses and maids realize their common humanity, their mutual dependence and their mutual interest, the servant difficulty will disappear." Looking back from a twenty first century perspective, it is difficult to imagine the gulf that existed between servant and master. A booklet, written about one hundred years ago lays down the *correct* code of conduct expected of a gentleman. For example, "...a gentleman should raise his hat when meeting a lady on the street, but should he meet his parlour maid, the strict rules of etiquette prescribe a nod."

In her chronicle of rural life in the English Midlands towards the end of the 19th century, Flora Thompson describes the work of the servant: "The maid in a tradesman's family was then always known as *the girl,* irrespective of age." Even though the term "girl" does not appear in the 1911 census in relation to servants, the term was used when only one servant was employed, for example in a small business premises. Referring to one particular "girl" as being overworked, Thompson adds "but if so, it appeared to agree with her, for she was rosy and round as a tub...She kept the whole of the fair-sized house cleaned and polished and whitestoned, helped the washerwoman on Mondays, cooked the meals, and mended the stockings, and all for £12 a year."

Servants had their own hierarchy and a class consciousness existed among them as elsewhere at that time. The lady's maid looked down on the cook and the parlour maid considered herself to be a step above the scullery maid. Mrs Beeton details the duties of these different ranks. The lady's maid looked after her mistress as regards wardrobe and attire. The parlour maid's job was to show visitors into the drawing room, serve afternoon tea and look after table linen etc. The upper housemaid supervised the lower order maids "reserving the lighter and more important tasks for her own share." The job of the laundry maid was self explanatory. According to Mrs. Beeton, "The cook is queen of the kitchen." The cook was assisted by the kitchen maid and scullery maid, the latter doing the "coarser work of the kitchen." At the lowest end of this scale came the charwoman, but she is not on Mrs. Beeton's list. The charwoman lived in her own house, visiting people's homes to perform the most menial of tasks. One such was Ellen Farrell who lived in Abbey Street with Catherine Crowley, a boarder who was also a charwoman. Both were in their fifties and single.

Cahir Park Lodge circa 1925. Household Staff. The Big House. Cahir Park Lodge was the residence of Lt. Col. Richard Butler Charteris. Sadly with the passing of time, the names of those in the photos have been lost to us. Nonetheless, it gives an insight into the number of household staff that were employed at such houses. Women's roles included housekeeper, cook and maids. The house ceased to be a residence on the death of Col Charteris in 1961. (Photo courtesy - Paul Buckley)

An example of the different ranks of servants can be found in Cahir Abbey Lower in one of two adjoining residences. This building would later become known as St. Joseph's College.

1. BUTLER — James Stuart 28 - Born in Co. Cork
2. FOOTMAN — John Streepe 18 - Born in Co. Limerick
3. UPPERHOUSEMAID — Brigid Connor 38 - Born in Queen's Co. (Co. Offaly)
4. SECOND HOUSEMAID — Margaret Lame 22 - Born in Co. Louth
5. COOK — Mary Moulton 28 - Born in Co. Carlow
6. KITCHEN MAID — Alice Carbery 22 - Born in Co. Waterford

All were single and Church of Ireland adherents except Alice Carbery. James Stuart is listed as "Head of Family" and also as "Butler, Domestic Servant." These servants came from different parts of the country, often recommended by the owners of other big houses. All of the above presumably worked in the adjoining residence owned by Grace Sargint, a widow of 32. She had a daughter, Jane, aged 7, and a son Newry, 9. They shared the house with her 60 year old widowed mother, Jane Sadlier. Grace's 30 year old sister, Kathleen Fadley and her 34 year old brother-in-law, George Sargint, a solicitor, also lived there.

Another example of the different ranks of servants is to be found in Bengurrah House, Cahir Abbey Upper. Richard Smith, Director of a Corn Milling Company, lived here with his wife and three young sons. They were looked after by six female servants. Constance Straker was a nurse, while Annie Wheeler, who was English and Church of Ireland, was a nursemaid. The cook, Annie Scelly, was a native of Carlow, and she had the help of a kitchen maid, Norah Carbury from Co. Waterford. The housemaid was Margaret Ryan, and the parlour maid was Sarah Curran from Co. Armagh.

A "useful maid" was employed by William Bell, Captain of the Royal Field Artillery who also employed a nurse, a cook and a parlour maid. William, who lived in Castle Street, was only 35 and single. Quite an eligible gentleman! Another gentleman of means was Alexander English, a member of the Church of Ireland, who looked after his three grandchildren, aged 11, 8 and 2. He employed a governess, Mary Allen, as well as a nurse, a cook, two general servants and a "soldier servant". They all lived on Wellington Street.

Resident on Abbey Street was William Gorry, a Corn Merchant, who lived with his wife and two daughters. William's servants outnumbered his family members. He employed a governess, a cook, a lady's maid, who was Swiss, a parlour maid from Westmeath and an English housemaid! On the Square, Mary Hutchinson, 63 and single, lived with her widowed aunt, Elizabeth Bowen, who was 90. Both ladies were Church of Ireland and came from Co. Dublin. They were very well looked after, having a Tipperary born cook, Lily O'Brien, 48, and a serving maid, 26 year old Nora Roche as well as a housemaid, 25 year old Brigid Roche. The Roches came from Co. Waterford and were possibly sisters. This elegant building operates as Cahir House Hotel at present.

On Wellington Street, Mary Blake, a single lady of 63, worked as a serving maid. She kept a lodger, 74 year old John Cardell who was a messenger and illiterate. Also resident on Wellington Street was Robert Cousens, of the Royal

Margaret O'Sullivan c.1890   Mary Ann O'Sullivan

Margaret O'Sullivan worked in Cahir Military Barracks and later went to London as a Lady's Maid for one of the officers from the barracks. She returned to Ireland and married Mr. Buckley and they resided at 23 Market Street, Cahir, where they are listed in the 1911 census. Her sister, Mary Ann, also worked at the barracks before she too went to London to work. She also returned to Ireland. (Photos: Courtesy of Maria Waters)

Field Artillery who could afford to employ a cook and a parlour maid as well as a governess. In contrast, Catherine Brown, an illiterate widow of 60, lived on Church Street with her four children, two of whom were servants (female), living at home but working elsewhere.

Boarding House Keepers

The practice of keeping boarders or lodgers in the early years of the century brought in some welcome income. These boarders often shared a small space with a large family. There was a distinction between boarders and lodgers; boarders were provided with accommodation and meals whereas lodgers were given accommodation only.

Bridget O' Brien, a single lady of 58, and living on Castle Street, kept an entire family, the McDuffs, consisting of a mother and father in their early thirties and their two children. A 76 year old Church of Ireland lady, Mary Leslie, lived as a boarder there as well. Maria Crowley, a 56 year old widow, had a busy household on Castle Street. Together with her two sons, she housed six male boarders, two were railway porters, another, a labourer in a mill. Others included a gardener and a hairdresser. Spare a thought for her sole servant, Nora Slattery, who looked after the lot! This handsome building is now the private residence of the Ryan family.

Some owners of boarding houses had other occupations, such as Mary Donnelly of Abbey Street, a widow in her early forties who was illiterate. She worked as a domestic servant as did her two daughters. Mary kept two boarders, both in their 70s, one of whom was Mary White from Kerry. Mary Hennessy, mother of two boys, worked as a housekeeper but also kept two boarders, one a gardener and the other a coachman. They lived on Old Church Street.

Some larger shops had resident staffs and these shopkeepers also kept boarders who usually came from outside the town. On Abbey Street, two sisters, Mary and Ellen Roche, both in their thirties, ran a grocery business. They employed a shop assistant, 27 year old Edmund Lonergan, who was also described as a boarder. A single lady living on Wellington Street, Bridget English, kept a female boarder who was a widow. Both were in their 70s and both illiterate. Mary Cummins, 35 years old, single and living on Bridge Street, is listed as a boarder housekeeper but she had no boarders at the time the census was taken.

Hoteliers

Mulcahy's Hotel, on the Square, was one of the largest in the town. Its owner, Patrick Mulcahy, was a native of Co. Waterford, as was the Manageress, Minnie Deasy. The cook was 41 year old Mary Keating, while Jane Conry worked as a waitress and Ellen Quinlan was a servant. The hotel also employed a book-keeper, Margaret Hyland. This building later became the short-lived Glengall Supermarket.

On Barrack Sreet, Catherine Kenny, a 54 year old widow with four children, was recorded as having the occupation of hotelkeeper. She had no employees, and Michael Keating was listed as a boarder and retired hotel keeper.

Grocers, Publicans, Bakers, Drapers

Another source from which we can derive an insight into some women's occupations is commercial directories. One such example is the Slater's Directory (1856). It lists Grocers, Public Houses, Spirit Dealers, Wine and Spirit Merchants under those headings. In 1856, out of twenty three public houses in Cahir, seven were owned by women, one of whom was Margaret Elliott of Abbey Street. Maria Dillon, an enterprising lady of the time, was listed as a Baker, Grocer and Public House owner. In 1911, in Barrack Street alone, six out of eight shopkeepers/publicans were women, three of whom were widows, probably carrying on the business after the death of a husband. One of those was Carlow born Anne McCarthy, a 70 year old widow. She lived with her 39 year old daughter, Mary, who was single and 17 year old grandson Charles McCarthy, born in England. Mary and Catherine Gleeson, both in their 30s and single, were publicans who also kept boarders, including 26 year old Daniel Fitzgibbons who was a harness maker.

Family and Staff at Bradshaws, Barrack Street. These business premises were noted in a trade directory in 1889. (Image and information courtesy of Paul Buckley)

Elizabeth Crosse, 85, a Church of Ireland widow, owned a bakery at number 1, The Square, where she lived with her 40 year old daughter and a maid. Also on the Square, Lizzie Ryan, 54, ran a drapery shop with her husband, a Justice of the Peace. They had no children but they had four draper's assistants, all male. Also on the Square, was Catherine Boles, 63, listed as the owner of a shop which she ran with her sister and brother.

Hannah Condon, a widow of 66, and living on Church Street, was the owner of a public house, her son, Philip, an undertaker. Hannah shared the house with her daughter, Elsie, who lived there with her two children and a boarder. Also on Church Street, a 73 year old widow, Alice Burke, owned a grocery shop. Her daughter, Nora, 35 and son, James, lived with her. Another widow, Catherine Mockler, 45, owned a small grocery shop on Wellington Street. She was the mother of three children, one of whom was a Sailor's Apprentice at the tender age of 14 years. Unusually, Annie Bradshaw, 29, and single, owned a public house on Castle Street. She employed a manager, 20 year old James Maher and a 16 year old apprentice shop assistant, Lizzie Cooke from Kilkenny.

Dressmakers
In the days before ready-made clothes, dressmaking was a popular occupation for women and girls. The days of less expensive, mass produced clothes were a long way off. Most females were skilled at sewing and knitting. Mothers of large families had to be able to knit and sew in order to clothe their children. For special occasions and for those who could afford it, the services of a dressmaker were used. Nearly every street in Cahir had one or more dressmakers, some of whom lived at home, while others resided at the town's many drapery shops.

> "The ladies came there in all colours and shades,
> There were fat buxom lassies and
> Kiln dried old maids,
> Married and single, the truth I declare,
> Attended the races that were held in Cahir...
> I think that those dresses were made for a ball
> That was held down that evening in the Town Hall."
> (*The Races of Cahir* by Tim Dooley.)

In the early years of the last century, Abbey Street had six dressmakers. One of those was Mary Heaton 29, whose husband, Peter, was an Army Sergeant. Sometimes more than one member of a family worked at dressmaking as in the case of the sisters, Bridie and Lillie Bergin who lived with their widowed mother. Additionally, Bridget Burke 50, and her 40 year old sister Johanna, together with a cousin Mary Prendergast, also 40, were all dressmakers, residing at Bridge Street. They kept one boarder, 24 year old Michael Flanagan who was described as a National School teacher, originally from Oldcastle, Co. Meath. Dressmakers were also categorised as seamstresses and needleworkers. Living on the Mountain Road, 47 year old Ellen Pedley, a widow, was listed as a seamstress. On Chapel Road, the Richardson family were all in the business of tailoring, William and his two sons worked at this business and his daughter, 20 year old Josie, was a seamstress. While most streets had dressmakers or seamstresses, Church Street went one better as Mary Mason 24, was a tailoress. She lived with her widowed mother and her brother who was a carpenter.

Milliners and Straw Bonnet Makers

Hats were made in Cahir as far back as the mid 19th century and possibly before. Slater's Directory 1846 lists Mary O'Connor of Church Street and Bridget Sheady, the Square, as having this occupation. These women were referred to as milliners. Some women managed to combine hat making and dress making, like Eliza Black, Castle Street, and Johanna Keating, Abbey Street, who were milliners and dressmakers. Local shops listed as "Linen and Woolen Drapers and Haberdashers" stocked the necessary fabrics and sewing materials. In 1846, Cahir had five such shops including those of Mary Condell, Abbey Street, and Sarah Wilson, Castle Street. By 1856, seven of the town's drapery shops were owned by women like Judith Burke and Hanoria Stapleton, both on Barrack Street. According to the 1901 census, Margaret Forde and Minnie Fahy, both milliners, worked for Patrick Clarke who, with his wife, Catherine, owned a Drapery, Millinery and Mantle Warehouse on Castle Street. In 1911 on Church Street, Catherine O'Neill, a 74 year old widow, was a dressmaker while her daughter, Bridget, was a milliner. Come to think of it, Cahir is still a good place to get a hat!

Teachers

According to the 1911 Census, Cahir had a number of female teachers and monitoresses. The latter were older pupils who taught the younger students before going on to Teacher Training Colleges. Nineteen year old Catherine Cleary, the daughter of a shopkeeper from Old Church Street, is listed as an exmonitoress and scholar. Her brother, 17, was described as being a monitor. John Casey, a cooper, lived on Barrack St with his five children, one of whom, Johanna, 22, was described as a King's Scholar. In those days, the King's Scholarship was an entrance exam to a Teacher Training College, usually taken by monitors.

25 year old Annie Quinn, was a National School Teacher, one of ten children of Michael, a carpenter, and Bridget Quinn who lived on Chapel Road. Three members of the Ryan family, Old Church Street, were teachers: Mary, the eldest, her sister Julia, a music teacher, and Kate, who taught in Cahir Convent National School. Margaret Lonergan, 27, was a National Teacher living in Townparks, while Mary Egan, 58, lived on Church Street with her 23 year old niece and a servant, Mary Hoban, 16. All three hailed from Kilkenny. Mary Keith from Abbey Street, whose husband, John, was a constable with the Royal Irish Constabulary, was also listed as a National Teacher. Both were 32 and came from Co. Limerick.

There were also Church of Ireland female teachers such as Emma Griffiths, 22, who lived with her elderly parents in Townparks. They were originally from Wales and her father was described as a Naval Pensioner. Matilda Ferrit, 33, a resident of Abbey Street, was described as being a Governor. This most likely should have been written as Governess, as some of the wealthier families in the town would have employed such women to teach their children.

Nurses

The term nurse was used loosely to describe servants who worked as domestics and looked after children or older adults. Twenty-eight year old Sarah Carroll, from Co. Cork and illiterate, was a nurse/servant working for Timothy Lynch, a chemist, on Church Street. He had four children under four, including twins. Timothy also employed a general servant 21 year old Johanna McGrath. Hannah Burke, 49, a widow with seven children, employed a nurse, 52 year old Annie Austin, also a widow. They lived on The Square where Hannah ran a hardware shop. Also on The Square, Margaret Murphy was described as a children's nurse. She was 22 and worked for the O'Loughnan family who were described as being shopkeepers and farmers.

Cahir, as elsewhere, had a number of midwives in the past. One example was Margaret Morrissey, 31, who lived on Castle Street, where her husband owned a chemist shop. Also on Castle Street, 23 year old Nora London, had the occupation of Hospital Nurse, which would suggest that she was a trained nurse. She was single and employed a servant, 20 year old Brigid O 'Brien.

Unusual Occupations

Quite a number of Cahir women had unusual occupations a hundred years ago. One such was Bridget O'Loughnan, a 74 year old Irish speaking widow who was listed as an earthenware dealer. Her business was doing well, seemingly, as she employed a 17 year old servant, Margaret Moloney. They resided in Church Street. On the same street, Sarah Jane Hosford, 39, from Co. Waterford, lived on her own. She worked as a Sextoness in the 'Irish Church', presumably St. Pauls which was nearby. On Old Church Street, 18 year old Julia Ryan was listed as an organist. She lived with her father, Daniel, who was a publican.

Unusually for a woman at that time, Catherine Ahearn, 48, was a Post Mistress, while her husband, John, was a sorting clerk and telegraphist. Both lived on the Square with their six children and their servant, 16 year old Bridget Lonergan. Catherine came from Kilkenny. Also from Kilkenny and living on Wellington Street, was a GPO clerk, Maria Murphy, 32, a lodger with a family named Cooke.

On Wellington Street, now Pearse Street, Margaret Peters, a widow, was a cycle trader. Her 17 year old son was a cycle mechanic and there were three younger children in the household. Mary O' Gorman, 37 and single, was a dispensary caretaker on Wellington Street, and a Medical Centre still exists at that same location. Nearby, on the same street, Margaret Ryan lived with her widowed father of 70, who was *receiving a weekly gratuity from Lady Margaret,* the only example of such found. Elizabeth Gaule, 67, originally from Co. Carlow, owned a stationery shop on Castle Street. Her son, John, 27, was described as a stationer. Bridget O'Connor and her sister, Margaret, both single and illiterate, were laundresses who lived on the Mountain Road. To supplement their income, they kept two lodgers, May Murray, 65, and Catherine Phillips. Another laundress, Martha Hastings, lived on the same street.

Mary O'Connor, a widow, was a laundress who lived on Abbey Street, with her two sons, one

Jude the Two - A street fruit seller on Church Street in Cahir (Courtesy of Paul Buckley)

of whom was a tailor. On Barrack Street, Ellen Houlihan, also a laundress, had two children living with her. Still on Barrack Street, Bridget Keating, 24, from Waterford, was a ware room keeper who lived with relatives, also called Keating.

Another unusual occupation was that of sack mender. Sacks were used in the local mills and were made from jute, an expensive commodity, hence it was important to prolong the life of the sack. Older people in town still remember seeing sacks with patches on them. There were two sack menders on the Mountain Road, one of whom was 49 year old Johanna Sullivan, who lived with her husband, Patrick, a gardener. The other was Margaret Myers, 25 and single. She lived with her two nephews, one of whom was a labourer.

While Clonmel in the early part of the last century had one woman whose permanent occupation was knitting, no such woman was recorded in Cahir. Unusually, 31 year old Michael Kelly from the Mountain Road was listed as a knitter!

Surely, the most unusual occupation listed in the 1911 census had to be that of baby, Mary Moynihan. Her father, Malachy, a National School teacher from Kerry, with a touch of Kerry wit, described her occupation as "making noise"! Church Street, where they lived, must have been a noisy place as she had two brothers of 3 and 4 years who were recorded as having the same occupation.

Priests' Housekeepers

It's a terrible come down from the purple to the black and white!

These are the words spoken by Moll, the priest's housekeeper immortalised by John B. Keane in his play of the same name. Moll was confident in her role, looking after her charges as befitted their rank. The job of priest's housekeeper was respected, and like Moll, some of these women had a certain amount of influence in the presbytery and in the parish beyond. Accommodation was warm and comfortable, food was adequate and they were paid and often given tips at weddings and christenings. The kitchen was their preserve and the priest didn't usually interfere. Priests' housekeepers were allowed visitors, in the kitchen of course. Even though the hours were long, the work was easier than farm work. The Very Reverend Thomas Kyne, Parish Priest of Spiddal, Co. Galway, in an interview in *The Irish Times* some years ago, pointed out that the hard pressed wives of small farmers, working seven days a week, would often envy the lot of the priests' housekeeper. "At least she hasn't got cows to look after." On the other hand, some of these women were exploited, underpaid, and had no security. When the priest died, they were left with no home and no money. While Moll thought she had a certain amount of influence in the presbytery, she felt she had little real power, complaining that an altar boy was higher up in the church than she was.

One hundred years ago, the Catholic Church's Code of Canon Law (1917) was short on specifics in relation to priests' housekeepers, requiring priests to employ only women who were of "irreproachable character and of advanced age". More recently, in 1983, Canon Law gave even fewer guidelines in relation to the employment of housekeepers other than that they "observe perfect and perpetual continence for the sake of the kingdom of heaven"

The occupation of priest's housekeeper is quite rare now, but in Cahir, as elsewhere throughout the last century, every priest had a housekeeper. Parish Priest, Fr. Robert Power was no exception. In the early years of the last century, he lived in the Parochial House in Church Street. This building is still standing; its fine brick chimneys and upper story can be seen behind a later extension built when it became the Galtee Hotel. Fr. Power hailed from Co. Waterford as did his housekeeper, Margaret Shanahan, who was 36. He employed a gardener, William Shanahan, 62. Fr. Power's niece, Alice aged 18 and still at school, resided there also. William and Alice were also from Waterford and all spoke Irish.

In Townparks, two adjoining buildings, still occupied by priests to the present day, housed two curates in the early part of the last century: Fathers Everard and Burke. Both employed housekeepers. Fr. Everard's housekeeper was twenty five year old Margaret Murphy from Co. Kilkenny and Fr. Burke's was fifty three year old Margaret O Callaghan from Co Waterford, an Irish speaker. It is interesting that neither of these housekeepers came from Cahir.

SOURCES

Census of Ireland -1901

Census of Ireland -1911

Slater's Directory -1846.

Slater's Directory - 1856.

Bassett's Directory -1889.

Mrs. Beeton's Household Management, 1861.

Cahir – Faces in Places, Paul Buckley.

The Nationalist Centenary Newspaper, 1890 -1990.

Lark Rise to Candleford, Flora Thompson

Correct Conduct: M. Woodman.

[474]

Great Book of Lecan from which the frontispiece of this book was taken. MS. 23 P 2, f.237v
of the Royal Irish Academy)

Back row, l-r: Jimmy Harris, Agnes Keating, Josie Millea, Tess Lonergan, Mary Grady, Eileen Boardman, Nancy Bingley, Bridie Buckley, Maggie Griffin.

Middle row, l-r: J. Walsh (proprietor), May Hanrahan, May Leahy, Chatty Bell, Kathleen Griffin, Josie Roche, Kathleen Dowling, Daisy Holland, Kathleen Hayes, Mary Kerton, Theresa Fogarty, Paddy Walsh.

Front row, l-r: Mary Hall, Mary White, Joan Cullen, Joan Griffin, Isobel Walsh, Madge Lonergan, Bridie Nagee, Nora Gallagher.

Galtee Manufacturing Company

In the autumn of 1933, the Nationalist reported on the opening of the textile firm, the Galtee Manufacturing Company, located on what is now the site of Market Yard. At the time of its founding the company obtained land from the Electricity Supply Board (ESB), the site having been the location of the Cahir Electricity Company. The founder and managing director of the company was Jim Walsh, The Square, his son Paddy Walsh being the manager. The business was somewhat unique in an age when employment opportunities were scarce, for virtually all the employees were female. Initially eight females were employed but this number later increased. The opening of the factory was marked by a meal at which those at the factory opening attended. One of those in attendance, Mr R.T. Hearne of the firm of Hearne and Cahill Boot Manufacturers from Waterford, spoke and said he sincerely hoped that the public would support individual enterprise in order to give employment in the local area and that in a few years they would have all the local boys and girls working. About 1969, the Walsh family sold the business, which carried on for a few years thereafter before closing its doors.

(Image, names and text courtesy of Paul Buckley)

The Golden girls from Abbey Street 1923: Kit, Joan and Esther

Bridget M. Sullivan

Bridget (Bridie) M. Sullivan S.R.N. of Lisava, Cahir was the Theatre Sister of St John's and St Elizabeth's Hospital, St John's Wood, London from 1931 to 1952, years which included World War II and the 'Blitz' of 1940/41. She described it as both a terrifying and thrilling period of huge change. On Bridie's return to Cahir, she married farmer John Walsh of Cahir Abbey. Her surgical instruments were put to use sewing up many a local child or adult in a proxy A&E on the Tipperary Rd. She set up a farm guesthouse business in 1960 and encouraged other women to do the same, championing Cahir tourism. An early member of the ICA and a keen bridge player, Bridie died aged 77 in 1991. Among other Cahir nurses who served in London during the war years were Joan Golden of Abbey Street and Mary Burke of Mountain Road.

(Photo and text courtesy of Bridie's daughter Maria.)

Bradshaws Public House – Castle Street

This public house on Castle Street was established by Annie Bradshaw, daughter of the Bradshaws who had the pub on Barrack Street. Pubs were always good employers of women in rural towns, and Bradshaws was no exception. The inclusion of the Barrack Street pub in Bassetts Directory of 1889, and Annie being at the Castle Street pub until her death in 1946, demonstrates the contribution to Cahir women's employment made by the family over several decades. (Photo and information courtesy of Paul Buckley)

Cahir Women and the Titanic

By Josephine O'Neill

On the 11th of April 1912, Kate McCarthy was one of four friends who boarded the *Titanic* at Queenstown (Cobh). All four had bought their tickets at Castle Street, Cahir, in the premises now occupied by The Black Bee craft shop.

Aged 24, Kate was the daughter of Patrick McCarthy, a farmer from Ballygorteen, near Bansha and his wife Mary Boyce. Planning to live with her sister in Guttenberg, New Jersey, she paid £7 and 15 shillings for a third-class ticket. Travelling with her was Katie Peters from Ballydrehid, Roger Tobin from Ballycarron and Catherine Connolly from Tipperary.

Katie Peters was the daughter of William Peters and Mary Crowley and was one of 12 children. She had emigrated to New York in 1906 aboard the *Oceanic* and returned home for a visit in late 1911. She was returning to America on the maiden voyage of the *Titanic*. On the 15th April, the *Titanic* collided with an iceberg and sank with the loss of 1,503 lives. Katie was among those who were drowned that night and her body was never recovered. The Titanic Relief Fund sent her brother in New York $50 of the money paid by Katie for the passage,

Postcard of the Titanic sent by Katie Peters to her family from Cobh before setting sail on the Titanic. (Courtesy: Brian Costigan)

which he subsequently sent to their father. The English Committee also gave £45 in damages to the family.

Kate McCarthy was the only one of the group to survive the sinking of the *Titanic*. She recalled hearing, "Nearer my God to thee" being played and the horrible cries of those struggling in the water. A month later, her account of the tragedy appeared in *The Cork Examiner* on May 11th, 1912.

> About twelve o'clock on Sunday night, Roger Tobin called us to get up, but told us not to be frightened as there was no danger. To make sure, however, of our safety, he told us to get lifebelts. There was three of us in the room, Katie Peters, Katie Connolly and myself. When Roger Tobin called us, I wanted them to come up on deck but they would not. They appeared to think there was no danger. That was the last I saw of them. I left the room and on going out I met a man from Dungarvan, who took me up to the second class boat deck, where they were putting out the boats. I was put into one boat, but was taken out of it again as it was too full. I was in the last boat to leave the ship and was the second last person put into it. This was a short time before the ship went down. We were only just out of the way when the ship split in two and sank. We remained in the boat all night until near eight o'clock next morning, when we were rescued by the Carpathia. Our boat was so full I thought it would go down every moment and one of the boats capsized when we were leaving the ship. I did not however feel at all frightened and did not fully realise the danger and full nature of the awful tragedy until I was safe on board the Carpathia. When we were put on board the Carpathia, we were immediately given restoratives and put to bed. I slept for an hour and then got up feeling alright. When we landed in New York on Thursday night we were met by a number of Sisters of Charity nurses, who took us up to St. Vincent's Hospital where we were treated with the greatest kindness.

In the aftermath of the tragedy, she remained in the United States, marrying John Croke. In 1921, they returned to Ireland and settled in Dundrum, Co. Tipperary.

Kate McCarthy on her wedding day with her husband John Croke
Photo Courtesy Paul Buckley

Sources
Cahir: *A Photographic Introduction* by Paul Buckley
http://www.encyclopedia-titanica.org/

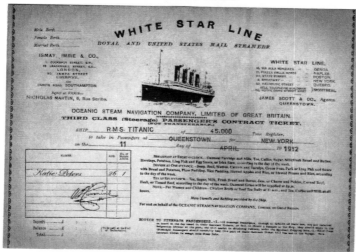

Reproduction Ticket for Katie Peters who was lost when the Titanic sank on 15 April 1912, and a bookmark remembering Kate (Katie) McCarthy who was rescued by the Carpathia. (Courtesy of the Titanic Experience, Cobh.)

Women Who Spoke Irish in Cahir a Century Ago
Beatha Teangan í a Labhairt
By Mary Caulfield

Wexford born Eibhlín Uí Mheachair has the distinction of being the only female Irish speaker in Cahir whose name is listed in Irish in the 1911 Census. Her husband Tomás also spoke Irish as did their son, Seaghan, who could also read at the age of two! Completing the census form 'as Gaeilge' was unusual for the time as people were reluctant to write their names in Irish or even to admit that they spoke the language. A random trawl of the census shows that in Gaeltacht areas of the West very few names of Irish speakers were actually written in Irish. At the time there was a general antipathy towards the language and cases were reported of the Royal Irish Constabulary refusing to accept forms completed in Irish. This happened in spite of the Registrar General agreeing to accept forms filled in the Irish language. On the National Archives website, the modern transcription of the original 1911 census form for the Ó Meachair family has the Irish names but none of the other important details.

Above: Section of Original 1911 Census form from the Ó Meachair Household.
Below: The modern transcribed census form showing the information has been omitted.

175

At the time of the 1911 Census, the Irish language was perceived as the language of poverty and peasantry and its slow decline from the 18th century on was due in some measure to that perception. Dr. Douglas Hyde, first President of the Gaelic League and later Uachtarán na hÉireann, described how in the 19th century the Irish language and literature had been cast aside by the people. There was also opposition to the language from official circles. Railway companies refused to display the names of stations in Irish, while the Postmaster General issued a rule that even if the clerk behind the counter could translate the Irish address into English he was not to do so. The National Bank, founded by Daniel O'Connell, refused to honour cheques written in Irish. The Gaelic League had its account with the bank, but in 1906, it transferred this account to an English bank, which had no objections to the Irish language!

The Irish Literary Revival and the Gaelic League, founded in 1893, sought to give a sense of Irish identity back to the people. The growth of Irish Nationalism in the early 20th century led to a renewal of interest in Irish literature, folklore and our native games. The GAA, one of the largest organisations in the country a century ago had, since its foundation in 1884, shown a strong affiliation with the Irish language and culture. In spite of these efforts, by the beginning of the 20th century, Gaelic as a spoken language had died out except for remote areas along the West coast and a few pockets elsewhere. The Newcastle area of Tipperary had an Irish speaking population up to the 1940s, and was officially recognised as a "Breac-Ghaeltacht" (mixed Irish and English speaking) up until 1966. One of the last Irish speakers there, Séamus Ó Maolcatha, wrote "An Gleann agus a Raibh Ann" in 1963, describing the life of Irish speakers in the area in the early part of the century.

Eibhlín Uí Mheachair, known as Eleanor, and her family lived on Lower Abbey Street, Cahir. Her husband, Tomás, from Co. Kerry, was a National School Teacher who was committed to the Irish language even though at the time of the census, Irish was not a requirement for teaching in schools.

Out of 614 teachers who left teacher training colleges that year, only 32 had a certificate to teach Irish. At this time, the question of teaching the Irish language was a major issue for members of the Gaelic League. Some schools were more sympathetic towards the language than others; in 1899 the Mother General of the Loreto Order directed that Irish should be taught in all the schools of the Order while at the time, the President of Rockwell College was on the Council of the Gaelic League. Local committees of the League employed "múinteóirí taistil", travelling teachers, who journeyed long distances on bikes and were badly paid. Rev. Arthur Carter, late of the Vocational School, Cahir, recalls that some were paid expenses of as little as two pence a mile. One such was Cahir man Seán Hoibéard (Hubbard) from the Mountain Road who cycled on bad roads from Cahir to teach Irish in places like Fethard and Newcastle.

Out of a total of 346 households surveyed in the 1911 Census, approximately 12% had one or more Irish speakers. Sometimes one child in a family spoke the language while in other cases one parent only spoke Irish. In other cases, the females in a family spoke the language while the males did not. The wife and daughter of John Cleary of Barrack Street did not speak Irish while the father and three sons did. None of the three daughters of William O'Loughlin, a shopkeeper on The Square, spoke Irish even though he himself did. Out of ten households on Chapel Road, not one had an Irish speaker, including 25 year old Annie Quinn, a National Teacher. On Market Street, 15 year old Johanna Halpin, whose father was a flour mill worker, was the only Irish speaker in a family of four. Alice Doheny, also from Market Street, spoke Irish while her husband and her three sons did not.

Wellington Street
On Wellington Street, Brigid O'Neill, aged 30, and her husband, John, a tailor, spoke Irish as did Mary, their 9 year old daughter. Brigid was born in Co. Galway. Margaret Neary, 36, born in Co. Limerick and her husband Thomas, a coachman, were both Irish speakers. Mary Natin, 18, a scholar, daughter of John, ex Sergeant of the Royal Irish Constabulary, spoke Irish. Elizabeth Britten, 77, a widow, spoke Irish. She lived with her daughter, Mary, a nurse and domestic. Catherine Cooke, a 65 year old widow and a Catholic spoke Irish but her 44 year old son, John, listed as Church of Ireland, did not. Eileen O'Donnell, 18, a scholar, was the only one of 5 children, of James, a bootmaker, and Eileen, a dressmaker, to speak Irish. Ester Dee, 15, a scholar whose father, John, was a groom, was the only one in her household to speak Irish. Catherine Lonergan , 74, a widow living on her own was an Irish speaker. On the Mountain Road, two households had Irish speakers. Brigid O'Brien was a laundress who spoke Irish as did her lodger, 60 year old Mary Murray. Eleven year old Anne Hayes from Co. Waterford was an Irish speaker who stayed with her uncle, James Conway, a widower who was a baker.

Church Street

On Church Street, Hanoria O'Halloran, 62, a publican, spoke Irish as did her 78 year old husband, Edmund. Their son John did not. Brigid O'Loughnan, a 77 year old widow and an earthenware dealer, spoke Irish as did her servant, 17 year old Margaret Moloney. Brigid Gearon, 54, and her 68 year old husband, Edward, a retired weigh master, were both Irish speakers. They had no family. Alice Power, 18, born in Co. Waterford, and her uncle, Robert Power, P.P. both spoke Irish. Mary Clancy, 51, was the mother of 3 children only one of which survived. She spoke Irish as did 80 year old Ellen O'Gorman, a widow who lived nearby. Strangely, Marian Griffith, 22, spoke Irish while her father, James, 44, who was a National Teacher, did not. On Old Church Street, four households spoke Irish, including 73 year old widow Mary O'Neill, and her 36 year old daughter, Catherine. Two widows, Mary Dillon, 79, and Catherine Williams, 71, a boarder, also spoke Irish. Catherine McNamara, a single lady of 29 and her 17 year old niece, a scholar, both spoke Irish. Catherine's brother, Patrick, a cattle dealer who lived in the same house was also an Irish speaker. Only one of the seven children of shopkeeper John Cleary spoke Irish, 19 year old Catherine, described as an ex-monitress and scholar.

Abbey Street

On Abbey Street, two sisters, Brigid Ladrigan, aged 16, and Catherine, aged 15, daughters of Simon Ladrigan, a retired jarvey, spoke Irish. Kathleen Conway, 9, the daughter of a Royal Irish Constable, was an Irish speaker, while on Barrack Street, Johanna Casey, 22, a King's Scholar, was the only one in a family of five to speak Irish. Her father, John, a widower, worked as a cooper. On Castle Street, Nora London, 23 and single, was a hospital nurse from Co. Limerick who spoke Irish. Twelve year old Brigid Nolan, daughter of John, a painter, spoke Irish as did Anna Grant, a 20 year old shop assistant. Another Irish speaker on the same street was Ellen Teahen, 26, from Co. Kerry who worked as a parlour maid for William Bell, Captain of the Royal Field Artillery, while on nearby Bridge Street, 35 year old Mary Cummin, a boarding house keeper, was the sole Irish speaker on the street.

Townparks

In Townparks, the location of the Convent of Mercy, not much Irish was spoken by the Sisters. Out of 20 nuns, 14 being teachers, only 3 spoke Irish. One of those was 49 year old Florence Robinson, from Co. Limerick, listed as 'Head of Family' which meant that she was probably the Reverend Mother. Listed also were 26 female students ranging in age from 18 to 23, possibly doing a Commercial Course. They came from 12 different counties and 16 of them spoke Irish. Their lay teacher, Lily Cooper from Kerry, did not speak Irish.

Eibhlín Uí Mheachair inherited Kedra Castle, Cahir, in the 1920s and moved there with Tomás and their five children. Her son, Patrick, known as P.I. Meagher, inherited the property and reared a family of nine children, the eldest of which was named Eleanor after her grandmother, Eibhlín.

Eibhlín Uí Mheachair and her daughter Mairéad (Courtesy of Eleanor Phelan)

Sources:

Census of Ireland. 1901.

Census of Ireland. 1911.

The Story of Conradh na Gaeilge: Pádraig Ó Fearaíl. (1975)

Ireland's Own: Centenary Souvenir Edition (1918-2018)

An Gleann agus a Raibh Ann: Séamus Ó Maolchathaigh. (1963)

Interview with Eleanor Phelan (née Meagher), Ballinurra, Carrick-on-Suir, Co. Tipperary.

Bridget Ryan
A Nurse of the Great War
By Paul Buckley

The Great War of 1914-18 was a catastrophe, in its duration, its scale, its enormous loss of life, inconceivable to most at its outbreak. Such was the enormity of casualties, medical services greatly expanded in the course of the war. Within this area, nurses were required on a scale never experienced in previous conflicts. A number of women from Cahir and the surrounding district served in this capacity in the course of the war. Some served at home stations whilst others served in proximity to the battlefields of the various theatres of war.

To cite some examples, Lena McEniry, from Lisava, a qualified nurse, served during the Great War as a nurse in a military hospital in Birmingham. Hanora Burke, from Clogheen was reported in the local press as 'Mentioned In Despatches' for her work as a staff nurse in Harrogate Hospital, Yorkshire. She had previously been acknowledged for her services while serving with the Mediterranean Expeditionary Force. In this capacity, whilst in Alexandria, Egypt, she contracted enteric fever.

It was not uncommon for more than one member of a family to have served in the war. Hanora Burke lost her brother James, killed in Flanders, Belgium in August 1917. Also from Clogheen was Margaret Prendergast who served as a Red Cross nurse in England during the war. Likewise she lost a brother, Maurice, also killed in Flanders, Belgium in 1917.

Another nurse from Cahir was Bridget Ryan, Old Church Street. She was the daughter of Daniel Ryan, originally from Fethard and Ellen Ryan (nee Barrett) from Kilcoran. Ryan described himself in 1889 as a publican; a tea, wine and spirit merchant, cooper and supplier of hay and oats. Bridget was one of nine children, born to Daniel and Ellen, three boys and six girls. Three of her sisters became teachers; Mary, Julia, a music teacher and for many years the organist in Cahir Catholic Church and Kate, who taught in Cahir Convent School. Her other sisters were,

Nurse Bridget Ryan
(Courtesy of Gerry Sheehan)

Annie, Molly and Greta. About 1907 Bridget left for London where she trained as a nurse, and where she spent much of her adult life.

Outbreak of War

When war broke out, it brought casualties on a scale never imagined. The trenches of the Western Front were but a short distance from England. It was a short journey from the battlefields of Flanders, Belgium and Northern France to London, via the Channel Ports of Northern France to Southern England, where on arrival trains would bring the wounded to hospitals, in amongst other places, London. A soldier wounded on the battlefield was treated firstly at a Regimental Aid Post (RAP) in the trenches by the Battalion Medical Officer, his orderlies and stretcher bearers, then moved to an Advance Dressing Station (ADS) close to the Front Line manned by members of The Field Ambulance of the Royal Army Medical Corps (RAMC). If further treatment was required, he was moved to a Casualty Clearing Station (CCS), a tented camp behind the lines, then if required, moved to one of the base hospitals usually by train. The seriously wounded were taken back to Britain by Hospital Ship and thereafter to the relevant hospital for further treatment.

The nature of the fighting during the Great War led to a huge number of injured soldiers and the existing Military medical facilities in Britain were overwhelmed. A solution was found with civilian hospitals turned over to military use, a large number of asylums were also converted to military hospitals, with the asylum patients being sent home, often to unprepared families. As demand for beds grew, buildings such as universities and hotels were transformed into hospitals; wooden huts were erected in hospital grounds and at army camps to cope with the influx. Additional nursing staff were needed, a need met by a combination of qualified nurses and volunteers. Such was the environment Sister Bridget Ryan worked in as a member of the Queen Alexandra's Imperial Military Nursing Service (QAIMNS).

Royal Red Cross Award

Her work in 1917 was acknowledged in an award she received. The *Nationalist* in May that year reported Bridget Ryan, Church Street, Cahir, was recently at Buckingham Palace where she was decorated by King George V with the Royal Red Cross for meritous work in English Red Cross hospitals. The Royal Red Cross is a military decoration awarded for exceptional services in military nursing, the award established in 1883 by Queen Victoria and made to a fully trained nurse of an officially recognised nursing service, military or civilian, who has shown exceptional devotion and competence in the performance of actual nursing duties over a continuous and long period, or who has performed some very exceptional act of bravery and devotion at his or her post of duty. It was first awarded to the founder of modern nursing, Florence Nightingale.

Order of St Stanislaus

Later, she received The Order of Saint Stanislaus, for her military service in Northern Russia. The award is a Russian dynastic order of knighthood founded as the *Order of the Knights of Saint Stanislaus,* a Bishop and Martyr, in 1765 by King Stanisław II Augustus of the Polish-Lithuanian Commonwealth. In 1831 after the downfall of the November Uprising, the order was incorporated into the Chapter of Russian Orders as part of the honours system of the Russian Empire by Emperor Nicholas I of Russia. In regard to her involvement in Northern Russia, she served in the port of Archangel as a nurse on a hospital ship for some eight months.

The North Russia Intervention, also known as the Northern Russian Expedition, the Archangel Campaign, and the Murman Deployment, was part of an Allied Intervention in Russia after the 1917 October Revolution. The Allied intervention was launched during the Russian Civil War in 1918. The Bolsheviks (communists), led by Vladimir Lenin, came to power in October 1917 and established the Russian Soviet Federative Socialist Republic. Five months later, they signed the Treaty of Brest-Litovsk with Germany which formally ended the war on the Eastern Front. This allowed the German army to begin redeploying troops to the Western Front, where the depleted British and French armies had not yet been bolstered by the American Expeditionary Force. After the Bolshevik government withdrew from World War I, the Allied Powers militarily backed the White (anti-communist) Army in Russia. The stated goals were to help the Czechoslovak Legion, to secure supplies of munitions and armaments in Russian ports to prevent Allied war material stockpiles in Archangel from falling into German or Bolshevik hands, and to re-establish the Eastern Front. Also of concern to the Allied Powers was the fact that in April 1918, German troops had landed in Finland, creating fears they might try to capture the Murmansk–Petrograd railroad, the strategic port of Murmansk and possibly even Archangel.

The British Campaign in the Baltic 1918–19 was part of the Allied intervention in this Civil War. The codename of the Royal Navy campaign was "Operation Red Trek". Allied efforts were hindered by divided objectives, war-weariness and a lack of domestic support. These factors, together with the evacuation of the Czechoslovak Legion, led to the Allied Powers withdrawing from Northern Russia and Siberia in 1920. Bridget Ryan was part of the British Expeditionary Force to Northern Russia, in her capacity as a nurse aboard the hospital ship, Kalyan.

Hospital Ship, Kalyan 1918-19. Taken on the ice on the River Dvina, Archangel. It is recorded as being of the ship's captain with the medical and nursing staff. Nurse Bridget Ryan is in the middle row, fifth from right.

The *Kalyan* was a ship operated by the P&O (Peninnsular & Oriental Steam Navigation Co.) shipping line between 1915 and 1932. It was built by the Cammell Laird firm of Birkenhead, near Liverpool. Originally to have been called Khorassan, it was named Kalyan after a town near Bombay, India, and launched in 1915. In April 1915, utilized as a troop ship it took part in the Gallipoli campaign. As a troop ship, it came to be used to transport troops between England, Egypt and Salonika until 1918. In October that year, it was detailed for duty as a hospital ship in North Russia, but first it had to be adapted to suit the climatic conditions of an Arctic Winter. This work was still being undertaken when fourteen nursing staff boarded at Cardiff. A special Arctic kit was issued to those on board, the nurses wearing clothing similar to the men. Leather jerkins, windproof linen coats lined with sheepskin, cloth caps with fur peaks and earpieces, and serge gloves were distributed. Boots were later supplied to the sisters, high felt boots to the knee, similar to those worn by the Russian peasants, warm and proof against frost bite, even with temperatures of 35° below zero. As the ship sailed north, each day grew shorter, the Northern Lights were witnessed. After a twelve day voyage, the Kalyan arrived in Archangel, a city in the north of European Russia, close to the Arctic Circle. Archangel takes its name from the Archangel Michael. The arms of the city display the Archangel Michael in the act of defeating the Devil. Legend states that this victory took place near where the city stands, hence its name, and that Michael still stands watch over the city to prevent the Devil's return.

River Dvina Mooring

The ship moored by the quay on the River Dvina, remaining there for some eight months under the protection of a French cruiser moored in the river. There she acted as a temporary base hospital for British, Canadian, French, Italian, American, Chinese and Russian sick and wounded, capable of accommodating approximately 750 on board. For most of their stay, the ship was ice-bound, with ice having to be broken each day to prevent damage through "pinching".

A first-hand account of a nurse's experience on the Kaylan survives. Helena Hartigan, a farmer's daughter form Crean, County Limerick was on the expedition. Educated in Chester, she trained as a nurse at Saint Bartholomew's Hospital, London from 1901 to 1904, joining the Queen Alexandra's Imperial Nursing Service in 1905. She recalled her experiences in an article entitled, *To North Russia on the Hospital Ship Kalyan 1918-19*. Her experiences were no doubt similar to those of Bridget Ryan. In her recollections she writes:-

> A British Stationary hospital was fully occupied ashore when we arrived and a new Russian building was being adapted for a General hospital, while a casualty clearing station was busy on the other side of the river Dwina. There were several medical units up the line on both the river front and the railway front... ... Sick and wounded were brought to the Kalyan by barge. After weeks in billets and blockhouses the sick found the ship luxurious. Hot water, electric

light and clean linen was a joy after the evil-smelling and dark billets with no mails, no literature, and no cigarettes. Beside British officers and men of the Navy and Army we had Americans, French, Italians, Chinese and a few Russians... ... Archangel was a couple of hundred miles from the fighting line. Transport difficulties were many, particularly the transport of sick, the different seasons requiring different methods of transport. With the severe frost the whole scene changed, the Dwina River became frozen in a night. Snow fell... ... Within a week trains and railway lines were laid on the now solid river, and sleighs drawn by shaggy ponies brought the merchandise across the river, where previously the boats had been busy. Patients arrived by sleigh in what they themselves called coffins. Wrapped in fur-lined sleeping bags, and halting for food and change of horses at medical aid posts, the men found the open sleigh, well padded with hay, fairly comfortable... ...In addition to the Commodore and General Officer Commanding, the ship had many distinguished visitors of various nationalities, including the French Ambassador, the Russian General Officer Commanding and Sir Ernest Shackleton. The arrival of a mail was a great event, we were sometimes six weeks without one, the mail came by dog sleigh across the White Sea.[1]

Not all treated on board survived. In Archangel is the Archangel Allied Cemetery, a cemetery which was begun immediately after the occupation of the town in August 1918 by the Allied Forces and used by onshore military hospitals and the Kalyan. The cemetery contains 224 burials and commemorations of the First World War, including special memorials to 140 officers and men with known burials in cemeteries elsewhere in northern Russia. Within is the Archangel Memorial, which commemorates 219 British officers and men who died during the north Russian campaign and whose graves are not known. One casualty of the expedition was twenty-seven year old infantry soldier, Lance-Corporal Cecil Sidwell who is recorded as dying on the Kalyon in late January 1919 of sickness.

As the winter months passed Helena Hartigan recalled the coming of spring and her departure from Archangel:-

---

1   *To North Russia on the Hospital Ship Kalyan* 1918-19, Helena Hartigan.

About March the days commenced to lengthen and by May there was practically no night, the skies were beautiful just then and the snow reflected the same wonderful colouring. By degrees perpetual sun melted the snow and very quickly forced the silver birches into full leaf... ...Icebreakers cut a way through the ice for the troopships bringing reliefs to enter Archangel. Within a week, part of the original North Russian Force sailed for England. The Kalyan well laden returned at the same time and arrived at Leith early in June, 1919.[2]

Last Resting Place
On departure from Archangel, the Kalyan arrived at Leith Docks near Edinburgh on 3rd June. A number of accounts, albeit brief ones, appear in the press of the ship's return to Leith Docks. The majority returning on the ship were British troops with some Americans, French and Serbians. In 1946, Bridget Ryan, having worked as a nurse in the course of the Second World War, retired and returned to Cahir. Bridget passed away in August 1979 and was laid to rest in the cemetery adjoining Saint Mary's Church, Cahir.

2   *To North Russia on the Hospital Ship Kalyan* 1918-19, Helena Hartigan.
     The Murmansk Venture, Major-General Sir C. Maynard, Naval & Military Press, 2010.

Regret to Inform You
Telegrams from the Trenches
By Paul Buckley

In the course of the Great War (1914-18), next of kin were informed of a family member being wounded, killed, missing in action or a prisoner of war by letter or telegram. The letter, was more a form, with the casualty's details filled in, cold and soulless in its presentation. A telegram was brief in its written content, nonetheless, for something so brief in content, heartbreaking for its recipient. A memorial, adorned by a Celtic cross, to those from Cahir and the surrounding district who lost their lives in the Great War stands on Castle Street. At its unveiling in November 1930, it was recorded widows of ex-servicemen were accorded a special place at the ceremony and women who lost relatives in the war wore the war decorations of their respective relatives. It is reasonable to assume all whose names are inscribed upon the memorial had family members, mothers, wives, sisters, fathers, brothers who received a letter or telegram bearing news, more often than not, tragic in its content. Such were the numbers from the district serving in the various arms of the forces, to see a person, such as the telegram boy, approach your street, your house, filled one with dread.

Mary Walsh – Mother of Joseph

Women were the recipients of such communications. Mothers, wives, sisters, received telegrams usually bearing the opening line, *regret to inform you*. Confirmation of death was not always contained within the telegram. Sometimes it was notification he was a prisoner of war. The pain, no doubt, to a degree was eased, knowing the soldier, though incarcerated, was now far from the battlefield. Sometimes it was notification a family member had been wounded. Some degree of relief must have ensued in this regard, for wounding was not death. Sometimes it was notification someone was missing in action. This gave some hope, it was not final, but in truth such wording meant death. The passing of time eventually brought the realisation that death was the reality. But for many, a telegram carrying the words *regret to inform you... ...died of wounds,* was received. Such telegrams were received by Thomas and Mary Walsh and Mary Boles in the final year of the war (1918) informing them of their respective sons' Joseph Walsh (Royal Engineers) and Robert Boles (Royal Dublin Fusiliers), wounding and death.

Care of Souls

In the aftermath of the family receiving official notification of the death of a loved one, a letter often followed, from an army chaplain, an officer, or a fellow soldier to the deceased family, sympathetic in its content. Each battalion in the British Army had a chaplain, who had 'the care of souls' of the men, ministering to their spiritual needs, and burial of the dead. They would also write letters to the next of kin of the soldiers who had been killed. An officer or comrade of a wounded or dead soldier often did likewise. The words they wrote may have been some consolation to a bereaved family, but simultaneously they were words written many times by chaplains and officers, almost a formula, the structure remaining constant, only the name changing, *he did not suffer, he was killed instantly, he was a joy to the men, he was most popular with his fellow soldiers* and so forth, were expressions contained within such a letter.

Major Offensive

In regard to Walsh and Boles, both died in April and May, respectively, of 1918. In late 1917, Russia had signed a treaty with Germany, thus ending three years of warfare on the Eastern Front. Subsequently German troops transferred en-masse to the Western Front of Flanders, Belgium and Northern France. On 21st March the Germans launched a major offensive against the British and French on the Western Front, its enormity and rate of advance almost beyond the Allies' comprehension. However the Allied defences, though pushed back, did not break. By late April, the German advance halted. In the course of this offensive Walsh and Boles received the wounds from which they died.

Joseph Gerald Walsh

Joseph Gerald Walsh was the son of Thomas, a merchant, publican, farmer and County Councillor, and Mary Walsh, Abbey Street. Their family was large, twelve children survived of fifteen born to them, of whom six were girls. Joseph attended Rockwell College and had an aptitude for languages. Further studies were undertaken, and he developed a knowledge of French and German. In the period before his death, he was a Lance-Corporal in the Royal Engineers. More specifically he was in a signal corps, seemingly a wireless operator, his knowledge of German being utilised. In France, on 18th April he was the victim of gas inhalation, having been exposed to the effects of a gas shell. Death was not immediate, he was transported to a hospital in the French city of Rouen, Normandy, a significant hospital centre in the course of the war. Here, he died on 26th of that month. In the aftermath of his death, he was laid to rest in a military cemetery containing over 8,000 casualties of the war. A telegram was subsequently received by his family bearing the words, *Regret to inform you*. It came from the officer commanding the 12th General Hospital in Rouen, stating Joseph Walsh of the Royal Engineers had died as a result of the effects of a gas shell, the incident having happened a week or so previously. It was probably of little consolation to his family that, at the time he was gassed, he had carried out an act of bravery that saw him posthumously awarded the Military Medal, presented to his family some months later.

Robert Stephen Boles

Robert Stephen Boles was born in 1896, the son of Stephen, a builder, and Mary Boles. They had married in Cashel in 1895 and resided in Cahir, where Robert was born, the eldest of five children. Robert enlisted in the Royal Irish Regiment, Clonmel, in March 1915. On enlisting he gave his age, his height as 5'7, his eyes as blue and his hair fair. In addition, he gave his occupation as a draper's clerk and his mother as his next of kin. A Private in his unit, he became a Lance-Corporal in 1917, becoming an officer, holding the rank of 2nd Lieutenant in the Royal Dublin Fusiliers.

One of the actions fought within the overall German Offensive was the Battle of Lys (9th-29th April), so called after a river in northern France that also formed part of the French-Belgian border. In late April/early May, in the course of this action he was wounded. He was taken to the French village of Ebblinghem, west of the French city of Lille. On a hill adjoining the village was the location of the 2nd and 15th Casualty Clearing Stations, which were established at this location in April. Here he died of wounds, age twenty-two, the officer commanding the 15th Casualty Clearing Station recording he died of wounds received in action, more specifically a gunshot wound to chest. Here, also, he was buried, in Ebblinghem Military Cemetery, a cemetery adjacent to the casualty clearing stations. His death was recorded in *Irish Times* in mid-

May, an obituary also carried in the local press. Within weeks of his death, his personal effects were sent to his mother. Included were letters, photographs, a religious medal, a rosary beads in a case, a wrist watch, and a bullet. Initially, almost in the immediate aftermath of her son being wounded, his mother, then residing in Killenaule, received a telegram, dated ironically, the day her son died, that her son was wounded. It read,

Regret to inform you that 2nd Lieut. R.S. Boles, Dublin Fusiliers, reported sixth May, admitted fifteenth Casualty Clearing Station, France, wounded, dangerously ill.

Despite reading her son was wounded and dangerously ill, there was some hope, it was brief, the following day, she received a telegram. It read,

Deeply regret to inform you 2nd Lieut. R.S. Boles, Dublin Fusiliers, died of wounds, sixth May. The Army Council expresses sympathy.

Cahir Cumann na mBan
By Josephine O'Neill

Feisty Kate Scolds a Minister

In 1940, Kate O'Dwyer, Secretary of the Bansha branch of Cumann na mBan, wrote to Oscar Traynor, the then minister of defence, about pensions for local Cumann na mBan women. Kate drew the minister's attention to the "splendid service" volunteered by these women during the Anglo-Irish War and the Civil War. She did not hold back with her opinion, saying that many of those women "are now in needy circumstances" and some in "poor health" and that "it is a crying shame that they receive such scant consideration from a government, which they helped to establish and have always been loyal to". Kate was obviously acutely aware of the contribution of local Cumann women to the revolutionary era.

Advancing Irish Liberty

Formed in 1914, Cumann na mBan was an Irish Republican women's paramilitary organisation. In 1916, it became an auxiliary of the Irish Volunteers with the primary aims of "advancing the course of Irish Liberty" and organising Irish women in "the furtherance of this object". Another stated aim was "to assist in arming and equipping a body of Irishmen for the defence of Ireland" and to "form a fund for these purposes". The organisation gave women the opportunity to express their nationalism. Although the political role of these women seems to have been limited to providing support, historian Eileen Casey observes that "it [Cumann na mBan] placed equality for women on the political agenda and demonstrated that women could be as politically active and capable as men".

South Tipperary Joins Up

Within six months of its foundation, Cumann na mBan was operating through 63 branches, including Tipperary. In 1937, Mary Cooney, Secretary of the Third Tipperary Brigade of Cumann na mBan, gave Minister for Defence Frank Aiken an account of the foundation of that brigade. She informed him that although most of her records were destroyed when she was arrested in May 1923, she still retained valuable information on the local area.

Strong Response from Local Women

Seán Treacy, a leader of the Third Tipperary Brigade of the IRA during the War of Independence, had asked Mary Cooney to organise Cumann na mBan branches in South Tipperary, telling her that if she could get "one or two girls in each area it would be sufficient". Mary proudly recounts that "we got more than one or two. We were able to form battalion or district councils in each area". Eight battalions were established, and the fact that Cahir and Tincurry numbered 30 members, Poulmucka 14 and Mortlestown 8 gives us some idea of the strong response among local women. Mary outlined the activities of the women under five headings:

> *Military*:   First aid classes, drilling, scouting, dispatch and intelligence work. Care of flying columns, helping financially with the purchase of arms, carrying ammunition and helping in camps.

> *Political*: Assisting in the election of Republicans, pressing forward women candidates. Helping to defray expenses by the sale of flags, etc.

> *Educational*: Irish language, dancing and history classes.

> *Social*: The running of dances or concerts and sales to develop a Gaelic spirit and to make Cumann na mBan financially strong.

> *White Cross*: Care of wounded, invalid, cooking, the making of first field dressings, burying the dead. Helping to provide funeral expenses, masses, etc.

Cahir's "Roll of Honour"

The Military Archives list some of the members of Cahir Cumann na mBan. There were 96 members of the Cahir District Council, but we do not have all their names. For instance, Bridie Ladrigan, Captain of the Cahir branch, mentions a Molly Hartigan as an active member from Mountain Road, and Alice Butler mentions her own sister, who was a nurse and frequently accompanied Alice on dispatches. Neither woman is recorded in the official records.

Members of Cahir Cumann na mBan (Military Archives)			
Mrs H. Tobin, Knockgraffon	Kate Ryan, Clonmore	Cass Daly	Bridie Ladrigan, Abbey Street
Mrs Joe McGrath, Lower Abbey Street	Mrs Tom McGrath, Lower Abbey Street	Mrs Kate Regan, Lower Abbey Street	Mrs Nora King, Mountain Road
Mrs Mary Kelly, Carrigeen	Mrs O'Donnell, District Nurse	Jo Walsh, Carrigeen	Hanora Sullivan, Upper Abbey Street
Eileen McEniry, Mortlestown (Daughter of Patrick McEniry & Mary Ryan)	Mary Cotter, Whitelands (Formerly Mary Connors, Mountain Road, Cahir)	Cattie Casey, Mortlestown (Daughter of John Casey & Jane Marnane, Toureen)	Eileen Carew, The Square
Mrs Jimmy Moloney	Mrs. Tommy Walsh, Cashel Road	Sue Butler	Mrs M. Tobin
Julia Hanrahan	Brigid O'Donnell	Mrs Wall	Mrs E. Hyland
Ellie Slattery	Maggie Leary	Mrs Agnes Regan	Mrs Nora Mahony
Mrs McGrath	Miss M. Prendergast	Bridget Moloney	Nellie Corbett Outrath
May Corbett Outrath	Mrs. P. Tobin	Mrs. Mary Bourke	Mrs. P. McGrath (Secretary)

Mrs Kate Regan.
Courtesy: Tom Regan

Eileen McEniry, Mortlestown.
Courtesy: Mary Moloney

Cattie Casey
Courtesy: Jenny Kiely

The following women provide us with fascinating insight into some of the activities of Cahir Cumann na mBan women.

Daring Mary Delahunty

Mary Delahunty, Mortlestown, Cahir claimed in 1937 that, "During the troubled periods we did all that was humanly possible for the cause." Mary took part in carrying dispatches, transporting arms and ammunition and allowed her home to be used for billeting men and officers "on active service". Mary organised a barn dance as a fundraiser for the cause, this event led to the arrest of her brothers Michael and William, but she continued, and "carried on while her brothers were in prison". Her involvement  continued during the Civil War. On 10 occasions she obtained ammunition from a free state soldier, who also gave her information on the movement of free state troops. (Mary Delahunty. Photo: Courtesy Breda Delahunty.)

Spirited Bridie Ladrigan

Bridie Ladrigan, the daughter of an Abbey Street shopkeeper, had four brothers in the IRA. Her service spanned the War of Independence and Civil War. She recalled British soldiers putting up a recruitment poster in the family shop. She pulled it down and was told by a patrol of soldiers to put it back. Defiantly she told them "you're being paid to do the dirty work so you can do it yourself". Bridie was not supposed to wear the green Cumann na mBan uniform in public, but did so; and it was confiscated by the local RIC. She claims that on fair days Cahir Cumann na mBan women collected money for prisoners, despite opposition from the parish priest, the RIC and the military. Bridie also tells the story of a daring journey to Clonmel during the Civil War to collect first aid supplies for Tincurry and local IRA brigades. Cahir Cumann na mBan women were driven in a van with "Death or Glory" painted on the side.

Brave Alice Butler

Alice Butler of Millgrove, Cahir, was an extraordinary woman whose dedication to the cause also spanned both wars. Alice joined Cumann na mBan in 1916 and was appointed captain of the Tincurry branch at its formation. During the War of Independence, her home was used for weekly IRA battalion meetings from 1917 onwards and during the Civil War. For 12 months before the Truce, the house was "beset by Tans" and at one stage all male members of her family were arrested, including her father who was over 65. Dan Breen confirmed that Butler's house was a "Field General Headquarters" and asserted that "every senior officer in the IRA used the house from time to time". Alice did a "certain amount of catering" for these officers as the Butler house was used as a dispatch centre with Alice taking dispatches two or three times a week from the time the Tans came until the Truce. She generally used a horse and cart for transporting arms and travelled up to 12 miles each way. Accompanied only by her sister, she moved arms to Rosegreen, Ballylooby and Aherlow and gelignite from Rosegreen to Ballylooby! On at least six occasions, Alice drove armed members of the local IRA column.

As a member of Cahir Cumann na mBan, Alice attended first aid classes, which prepared her for some of the work she would have to do. She dressed wounds for members of the column and at one stage looked after a soldier in the mountains for a two-week period after he contracted pneumonia. During the Garrymore ambush in 1920 (when a local IRA column attacked a party of British soldiers bringing foodstuffs to an outpost at Clogheen), Alice, equipped with first aid supplies, hid in a house a distance away and "got away as quick as she could when the column moved on". During the War of Independence, Alice carried out invaluable intelligence work, keeping an eye on military activity. Building up "friendly sources", she went into Cahir and "brought back to the lads any intelligence in town". Working as a barmaid, she befriended Mr. Hardy who was Forage Master to Cahir Military Barracks. He gave her information on raids "to save fellows". She said that "I often got information from him but it was to save us, not for love of the movement". On at least two occasions, she passed information to the column about raids, which they were subsequently able to avoid.

Somehow, Alice also found time to do the "ordinary routine work of Cumann na mBan, doing collections, organising raffles and fundraising dances as well as sending parcels to prisoners in Mountjoy and Ballykinlar". During the Civil War period, a dispatch rider came very day to the Butler home. Alice claims that the IRA columns now "lived with us" and that as many as 40 men occupied their house at any one time. Due to the intelligence network they had built up, they were rarely raided during the Civil War.

Seán Hogan, one of the leaders of the 3rd Tipperary brigade during the War of Independence, claimed that Alice was the "chief means of saving the lives of Dan Breen and myself when held up and surrounded at Kilbehenny in

1923". Alice describes travelling to warn them so that they could escape. In her application for a military service pension, she confirms that she devoted all her time to helping the Active Service Unit, was never absent, obeyed all orders, collected funds, organised work and dispatches in grave personal danger, kept in touch with the columns and "cared for men on the run." Alice went on to marry Patrick Godfrey in 1945 and lived in Castle Street, Cahir.

Conclusion

Records reveal that Cahir women were aware of national issues as early as 1840. Some decades later, during the Land League, Cahir women became active participants in national politics. During the War of Independence and Civil War, active political participation called for militancy and bravery – which Cahir women amply demonstrated.

In 1937, a local Cumann na mBan woman sent a list of members for consideration by the Military Services Pensions committee. She warned, "You are advised to adhere strictly to the enclosed list in considering claims, otherwise you will be imposed on by unscrupulous people." These were the words of a former combatant who obviously remained a force to be reckoned with!

The contribution of these women and their comrades across the country was surmised in the 1919 statement of the Executive of Cumann na mBan: "They have regained for the women of Ireland, the rights that belonged to them under old Gaelic civilisation, where sex was no bar to citizenship and where women were free to devote to the service of their country every talent and capacity with which they were endowed". When Kate O'Dwyer wrote to the Minister of Defence in 1940 about the "splendid service of Cumann na mBan women", she was no doubt referring to the extraordinary dedication of Cahir women like Alice Butler, Bridie Ladrigan, Mary Delahunty and the Cahir Cumann na mBan members.

Sources:

Military Archives, Cathal Brugha Barracks
Eileen Casey's "Cumann na mBan" *Ireland's Own*, May 2014.
Joe Walsh - Interview with Bridie Ladrigan, 1984.
Cumann na mBan Papers, National Library of Ireland.

Votes for Women - A Cahir Link

By Pauline Martin

In 1908, ten years before Irish and British women over 30 achieved the right to vote, Laura McCraith, born 1870 in Loughloher, Cahir, urged Irish women to face the fact that they "need the vote, though they do not ask for it". Believing many Irishwomen to be curiously apathetic about Women's Suffrage, by comparison with their sisters across the channel, she wrote in the *New*  *Ireland Review* of that year, "One reason for this apathy lies in the truism that we're the most conservative people left in Europe. There is though a deeper reason. In this country of paradoxes, in which the subservience of women is a matter of custom, religion and inclination alike, it is the women who rule." The same holds true in India, she says. "There, the women, the old women, rule also unseen, with what can be loosely described as womanly influence."

McCraith continues, "the position of women in Ireland is peculiar, and instructive. Woman may be a drudge, but she is seldom a mere chattel or toy." The reason for this reverence, in McCraith's view, is interestingly historical. "The woman of Celtic Eirinn followed her husband to battle with her infant slung over one shoulder, a bag of bread and meat upon the other." The stories were handed down of great Queens ruling nobly: Maeve of Connacht; Macha of Armagh; Emer, wife of Cuchulain' Bride of Cill-Dara; and the great Granuaile (Grace O'Malley) who held unquestioned sway over her tribal possessions. These historic legends left their mark, resulting in a deep reverence for the woman - the mother, above all. (That much caricatured image of The Irish Mammy in sitcoms 100 years on, continues to be a force to be reckoned with by all politicians come election time!)

Women's Activism

Laura McCraith, although born in Loughloher, Cahir and having travelled extensively, lived in England. She may have been at one remove from a more modern subterranean undercurrent running through the minds of Irish women.

A recent article in Dublin city.ie has this to say' "A lot of suffrage and activism was undertaken by women seeking the right to vote, especially in the first two decades of the twentieth century. Nationalist and women's organizations were formed including Inghínidhe na hÉireann founded by Maud Gonne in 1900, the Irishwomen's Franchise League founded by Hanna Sheehy Skeffington and Margaret Cousins in 1908". This coincided with the year McCraith's review appeared in *The New Ireland Review*.

Two years later on February 1st 1910, according to an article in the *Daily Express* newspaper, a well-attended meeting of the Irish Women's Suffrage and Local Government Association was held in the Mansion House Dublin. One of the letters of apology for non-attendance at that meeting was tendered by Laura McCraith Blakeney, Cahir. In 1911, the Irish Women's Suffrage Federation was formed by Louie Bennett and Helen Chevenix, the Irish Women's Reform League by Louie Bennett, and the Irish Women Worker's Union with Delia Larkin as its first secretary.

It's also of significance that Laura McCraith doesn't refer to the existence of a flourishing Land League & Ladies Land League organization in Cahir in 1880 as evidenced by some 12,000 people massed on the Square in Cahir. Her age (she was just 10 years old at the time), coupled with her background, a daughter of the ruling class, may offer explanation.

"In Ireland women work", says McCraith, "and bear their full share of the economic burden, but they bear it to a very large extent within a circle of home, poor and narrow though it may be, protected and surrounded by that circle." The flaw with this particular scenario is that "not all women are happily placed or protected, not all women have husbands more honourable and generous than the law expects or hearth fires that it's their duty and privilege to tend." However, women who worked outside their homes were being legislated for at every hand's turn, and "Legislation without representation is dangerous". McCraith makes the point that increasing numbers of women contributed directly or indirectly to the home and as such both directly and indirectly paid taxes. Interestingly, she adds that prior to the Reform Act, voters were designated by the word 'persons' without distinction of sex. The exclusion of women taxpayers wasn't directly contemplated until, in that Act, the words 'male' persons were substituted.

Finally, towards the end of the review, she makes a direct appeal to the reader' "Of the expediency and of the methods of giving votes to women, many may have grave doubts, but the justice and logic of their claim, few who have carefully, honestly considered the subject can deny. These women have the duties, but not the rights of citizenship."

In 1918, propertied women were given the vote through the Representation of the People Act. That year also saw the Parliament (Qualification of Women) Act which made women eligible to be elected to, and sit and vote in the House of Commons. Eleven women stood in the 1918 elections with Countess Markievicz being the only woman elected to parliament. It wasn't until 1922 that all Irish women over 21 achieved the right to vote.

Laura Mary McCraith returned to Ireland after the War. She is buried in Loughloher graveyard.

Marian Tobin and the War of Independence
By Annette Condon

Marian Tobin (nee Carew), 1870-1955.
(Source: Kevin Tobin-Dougan, Marian's great- grandson)

Colourful Exploits

My brother Philip, my sister Mary and I grew up in Church Street, Cahir, listening to the colourful exploits of our revolutionary grand-aunt, Marian Tobin, who sheltered Dan Breen and Seán Treacy at her home, Tincurry House, after the incident at Soloheadbeg, in January 1919, which triggered the War of Independence. We heard from our Dad, Marian's nephew, Gerry Condon, how on the 14th of May 1921, the Black and Tans had ransacked and blown up Tincurry House (now owned by Michael and Alice McCarthy). As children we were in awe when we heard that Marian, in a show of defiance, had pulled out the piano – secretly packed with guns and ammunition – onto the lawn and played *God Save Ireland,* accompanied by her 13-year old daughter, Evangelista (Eva). This revolutionary tale was all the more amazing as our Dad had served in the British Army during World War II. I wondered about people in the same family choosing different but equally principled paths.

A Woman Ahead of her Time

Marian Tobin went on to make history in 1920 as the first female county councillor in Tipperary and one of just 43 across Ireland. This was ground-breaking stuff. Only two years earlier, in 1918, women aged 30 and over were granted the right to vote through the Representation of the People Act. Even in 2014, just four years ago, women accounted for just one in five local councillors.[1]

A former editor of *The Nationalist* newspaper, Brendan Long, wrote a history of the Council to mark the centenary of its existence in 1999, saying that the 1920s saw major electoral change and citing Marian Tobin's appearance on the scene as "remarkable".[2]

Service Medal

In 1950, Marian was awarded a Service Medal (1917-1921) from the Irish Government and has rightfully earned a place in all the history books of that period, including Dan Breen's *My Fight for Irish Freedom* and Ernie O'Malley's *On Another Man's Wound*. In this year, as we mark the centenary of the emancipation of women in Ireland, it seems an appropriate time to remember her contribution to the formation of the Irish Republic.

New Information Released in 2017

What firm evidence do we have that Marian Tobin was actively engaged in the War of Independence? The latest batch of documents from the Military Service Pensions Collection, released just a few months ago in October 2017, reveal her hidden role at the very start of the War of Independence.

In a letter written in 1950, in support of Marian's application for a pension, Dan Breen (who was apparently a close relative of John Burke and his wife, who owned the *Railway Bar* in Church Street, now known as the *Granary*) wrote in her praise, saying it was she who sheltered him and the others involved in the ambush for several days "while the area was very hot". Breen praised Mrs Tobin and described her as "one of the best workers we had from 1917 to 1923. There are few woman and not many men who gave more help than Mrs Tobin." He also mentioned her in his bestselling memoir *My Fight for Irish Freedom*, published in 1924, in which he thanked her for sheltering them while they were on the run. "I shall never forget her kindness to us that night. Her house was ever open for the 'boys'," he wrote.

---

1   *http://www.irishexaminer.com, Viewpoints, 270376*
2   Brendan Long, *A Century of Local Democracy South Tipperary County Council*, 1st edition 1999, page 43

A Safe House for Seamus Robinson

Corroborating information was provided too by Robinson, the commanding officer of the Third Tipperary Brigade, who was also at Soloheadbeg. He said that Mrs Tobin had been the first person to receive with "open arms and encouragement" the men who carried out the Soloheadbeg ambush. He went on to state that her home was in constant use by the IRA from 1919 until 1923 and she was a "de facto" member of the organisation. It is important to note that cases of women having official roles in the IRA during this time are rare, and it was more common for people like Mrs Tobin to take up a role without being a member of an organisation to avoid detection.

Mud bombs galore

Family stories recount that Tincurry was constantly used by Treacy and Co. to practice drills and to bury gelignite in the rose beds for the later destruction of bridges in the area, including Ballydrehid by Matt Barlow and brigade. The 96 acres at Tincurry were also used by Treacy to experiment with different types of explosives, especially mud bombs to be stuck on the roofs of police barracks. This is confirmed by Ernie O'Malley, who details in his letter how Tobin's home was used several times as a safehouse, to hide arms, and to mix explosives. It also becomes apparent that it was used for high-level meetings.

> At times, Robinson, Treacy, Breen and I used her house when we were experimenting with incendiary mixtures and with explosives. It was from her house we set off the night in which we were to burn Rehill Rifle Range, and it was there later, when we had avoided the British round-up, that Sean Treacy and I came back, though at different times. Here, in Tincurry, I trained a second group of officers and men, sometime in August of 1920. Sean Treacy was there with them. I had intended them to be the core of a Flying Column for South Tipperary. I had come back from East Limerick to train this nucleus. We trained there all day for nearly a week.

> Mrs. Tobin had arms to dump from time to time, and to look after, Whenever I, or anyone who meant to fight if surrounded, stayed in her house, she knew of our preparedness to fight and she assisted us.

> (Source: Military Service (1916-1923) Pensions Project.)

A Warm Welcome for Ernie O'Malley

In his book *Another Man's Wound*, Ernie O'Malley recounts visiting Tincurry House with Seán Treacy and Seamus Robinson, having been refused beds in two other houses. "Mrs Tobin came out when I shouted from beyond the stream. "Glory be to God, it's you," she said. "Well..well..well! Come in and warm yourself; you must be perished with the hunger. I'll ready the breakfast."[3]

After an attack at Hollyford, Ernie O'Malley, Treacy and Robinson received burns on the roof of the police station before being forced to retreat. They turned up at Tincurry and were met by Marian. "How is every bit of you, you're heartily welcome but glory be to God, what happened to your faces?"[4]

The Gift of Intuition

Marian certainly seems to have been gifted with intuition, once telling O'Malley, "You had best sleep up the hill to-night. I feel that something is going to happen and I'm all nerves."[5] and at another time about a dream she had. "You were all covered in blood," she said, "so here's a dash of holy water for you and be more careful." She also described the frequent raids on her house. "They lie around the house 'til the dawn and then, in they come... It's Mr O'Malley the officers ask for. Oh, he'll be glad enough to meet you, I tell them, but why don't you raid during the night?"[6]

Fuzzy-haired Eva Tobin

Despite being only twelve years of age, Marian's daughter, Eva, played her part in supporting the rebels and is referenced in O'Malley's book along with her sister May. Kevin, Eva's grandson, told me that Eva was a password-holder for the local IRA Brigade and helped in the surveillance efforts. I quote from O'Malley's book, "Twelve-year old fuzzy-haired Eva, who had often scouted the neighbouring roads on her bicycle came down stairs. She had to hear the story too. Her speckled grey eyes lit up with joy: 'Oh show me your revolver,' she begged. She tramped around the house in my Sam Brown and imitated the accents of the raiding officers from the barracks."[7]

---

3   Ernie O'Malley; *On Another Man's Wound*, pages 150 and 151. Published December 21st 2001 by Roberts Rinehart Publishers (first published 1936)
4   O'Malley, op. cit., p.149
5   O'Malley, op. cit., p.298
6   O'Malley, op. cit., p.307
7   O'Malley, op. cit., pp.150,151

O'Malley also describes Eva as a "little girl in a black and white print frock", who was assigned the job of tending tulip slips, which would be planted on the rebels' graves once they were killed.[8]

Eva's grandson recalls that as an adult, Eva always placed English stamps with the Queen's head upside down on letters as a symbolic gesture of defiance.

A Case of the Measles and the Ambush of Knocklong

In 1985, Willy McGrath of Tincurry and the Mountain Road (born 1904) recounted to Joe Walsh that he remembered the Tobin children well. One day he was coming around to play with John when he met Mrs Tobin at the stile and she told him he could not come to Tincurry House as the children all had measles, and "it wouldn't do to spread it all over Garryclogher National School." A few days later, he asked John about the measles only to be told that was the first John knew of it but he remembered the day well as his mother had woken them up early and brought them to their cousins in Ballinard, near Tipperary Town. This was also the night of the Knocklong Ambush (13th May 1919), one of the most dramatic events of the War of Independence when Marian Tobin was sheltering Breen, Treacy and the rescued Seán Hogan.

The Local Look-out Man

Some of you may remember Tom O'Mahony, who had a drapery shop in the Square near the bank. Listed as a member of the 6th Battalion of the 3rd Tipperary Bridge, Tom operated as one of the of the lookouts for Tincurry House at night. The IRA had scouts on the look-out within a two-mile radius to see if the British were coming. According to Tom, the British soldiers used to wear hob-nailed boots and you would hear them coming a mile away. Once he heard the Black-and-Tans approach, Tom would then sprint back to the house to warn the IRA rebels to leave Tincurry and retreat to the mountains.

---

8   O'Malley, op.cit., p.297

Marian Tobin in Her Own Words

In a letter written in 1950 in support of her pension application, Marian said that her home at Tincurry was described by the British as the headquarters of the IRA of that time and the birthplace of Sinn Féin. She described how she risked her life by driving Ernie O'Malley, when there was a price on his head, from Tincurry to Kilbehenny, where he would cross the mountains to Araglen. Marion Tobin also names Ned McGrath, Cahir Abbey and Sean Prendergast, Ballylooby as references for her involvement in the armed struggle. She says her home was raided and that she "kept and cleaned guns as well as those who used them, carried despatches for Robinson, Treacy and Breen, and treated O'Malley and Robinson for burns after the attack at Hollyford."

An extract from Marian Tobin's application for a pension.
(Source: Marion Williams, Marian Tobin's great-granddaughter.)

Early Beginnings

So, where and how did it all begin? Marian (christened Mary) was born on the 25th June 1870 in the parish of Tullamaine, outside Cahir in the shadow of the Motte of Knockgraffon as one of fourteen children born to my great-grandparents, Bridget and Jeremiah (Jack) Carew.

Marriage a Major Turning Point

On the 18th of November 1902, at the age of 27, Marian (recorded as Maria) wed James Tobin of Tincurry with my grandmother, Anne, as her witness along with William Morrissey. In the 1911 census, Marian is listed alongside her husband James and their three children, May, aged 7, John aged 6 and Eva aged 5.

Marian Tobin with her children, May, John and Eva circa 1920. The picture was taken in Cahir by her brother-in-law, Philip Condon, my grandfather, who was a well-known photographer. (Source: Marion Williams.)

Marian Tobin's humour

My father along with his brothers, Paddy and Christy and sister Florrie, often visited Tincurry House to visit their Aunt Marian. One room was circular, built like a tower. Fascinated with this, my father asked, "Aunty, why do you have a round room in your house?" Showing her wit and good humour, Marian Tobin replied, "So the cats cannot pee in the corners!"

Love and loss

Tragedy was to strike as James died of cancer at the young age of 51 at Tincurry House in 1918, leaving Marian with three young children. She was well provided for and had two farms, one at Tincurry and one at Ballinard near Tipperary Town, but nothing could have prepared her for the loss of her loving husband, just sixteen years after her marriage.

Tincurry House - IRA Divisional Headquarters

According to records of the time, James Tobin was an active volunteer in the IRA. The bureau of Military History certainly documents the forming of the "Tincurry Company" (Irish Volunteers and Sinn Féin Cumann were formed together), outside Tincurry on the roadside by James Tobin. This was later to become *The Cahir Battalion* after a joining of seven companies. This battalion was later to become the 6th Battalion of the *3rd Tipperary Brigade*. As a result, it is no surprise that Tincurry House was referred to as IRA divisional headquarters on maps.[9]

James Tobin's headstone records that he was a captain of the Irish Volunteers and in Marian's own words, he was the President of Sinn Féin and in frequent correspondence with Arthur Griffith, following the 1916 Rising. On the death of her husband, Marian felt it was her loyal duty to continue his work and support the armed struggle for independence.

The Tobin Family outside Tincurry House c.1920
(Courtesy of Annette Condon)

---

9   www.bureauofmilitaryhistory.ie/reels/bmh/BMH.WS1393.pdf#page=3

The Destruction of Tincurry House

As previously referenced, Tincurry House was raided for the twelfth time in as many months and destroyed in May 1921 by the British forces in retaliation for the kidnap and execution of District Inspector Gilbert Potter, which is a terribly sad story, reflecting the brutality of war and the atrocities committed on both sides. In reprisal for his death, 14 houses were destroyed in Tipperary, according to the orders of Col. Commandant NJG Cameron, "That persons concerned are active supporters of armed rebels and especially the Third Tipperary Brigade of the Irish Republican Army, that they reside in the area, and Third Tipperary Brigade has admitted responsibility for the brutal murder of District Inspector Potter on or about the 20th April 1921."

Westminster Hears About Tincurry

The destruction of Tincurry House was raised with his local MP by Marian Tobin's brother-in-law, Dr James Tobin, a GP and a magistrate in Derbyshire and was subsequently discussed in the House of Commons in London. Interestingly, Dr Tobin seems unaware of the role his sister-in-law was playing or indeed his deceased brother had previously played within the IRA. A short extract follows:

> *"There is resident in Derbyshire a man whom I know very well and whom everyone knows, a Dr Tobin, who has been a magistrate for about 20 years, who is universally respected, and who, for more years than I care to count, has been the foremost medical man in the central part of Derbyshire.*

> *I say all this to show that such a man may be reasonably supposed, and certainly supposed, to tell one nothing but the truth. I will read to the House his account of what took place, and as will be seen it is only one of many similar occurrences on the same day. I know the House will be shocked....*

> *This is what happened. Dr Tobin writes: 'Our old house and home in Ireland was blown up by the military on Saturday last, the 14th May, 1921—Tincurry House, Cahir, Co. Tipperary. It was an old country house, pre-Cromwellian, with additions and alterations from time to time...*

It was in occupation of my brother's widow and her youngest daughter, 13 years of age. My brother died about 3 years ago. My brother's two other children, 15 and 16½ years of age respectively, are away at school, one, a girl, in England, and the boy, 15 years of age, in Dublin. They, of course, go to the old home for school holidays only. No occupants of the house except the widow, Mrs. Marian Tobin, and her daughter, Eva, 13 years of age, and the servants.

The widow writes me that on Saturday last the military arrived and gave her an hour's notice to clear out her family, that the house was to be demolished. No furniture to be removed, only sufficient clothing, etc. No reasons given—nothing incriminating found, nor ever had been, though the house and place had been searched and raided a dozen times or more night and day during the last 12 months or so.

Before placing the bombs, the house and all its rooms were thoroughly searched, and every article of furniture was smashed with picks and hatchets. The beds and bedroom furniture, as well as all the old mahogany chests, were all broken into matchwood. The new bathroom and bath and its basins, etc., were broken to bits.

In fact, everything in the house upstairs and down was broken with picks and hatchets, so that nothing could possibly be saved or restored. Having thoroughly completed this wreckage, then the bombs were placed in the principal rooms and fired, and the dear old house and home blown to the four winds of heaven. Meanwhile, the widow and her little daughter, Eva Tobin, stood on the lawn as grim witnesses, carefully surrounded by the armed forces of the Crown.

Incidentally this was also the home of my two nephews, who were killed in France and Gallipoli during the Great War…. It cannot be alleged that this lady or her daughter were participants in any outrage. It would seem unlikely that the home of two officers who fell fighting for us in the Great War would be the home of participants in outrages. It could not be used for the purposes of an ambush on the roadside, because I understand it is not on the road. What reason can be given for this action I do not know, but whatever reason may be given, I ask this House to say that such proceedings as these are wrong.'"[10]

Tincurry House around 1921 after the attack. (Source; Kevin Tobin-Dougan.)

The Lady was not for Turning

Family accounts discredit the statement that Marian Tobin entertained the soldiers after the entire house was smashed into splinters and believe it to be fake English news. Family stories recount that out of decency, she automatically gave food, tea and a little beer to the hungry and thirsty squadron, but we believe that she would not have provided peeled cucumber sandwiches and scones after they had destroyed her home! Despite this trauma, Marian remained unrepentant and continued to support Sinn Féin and the IRA.

Rebuilding of Tincurry

Part of the house was rebuilt later in 1921 and completed in 1932 but as a single-storied building. This re-construction is referenced in O'Malley's book when Marian Tobin says, "I'm afraid you can't sleep in your new room yet. It'd be too dangerous now." O'Malley goes on to say, "My room had been named when part of the house

Marian Tobin with Matt Barlow, Commandant and Chief Engineer of the Third Tipperary brigade. The photograph can be dated as Matt has a Thompson machine gun, issued in 1923 and Marian rests with an Enfield 303, possibly imported by Erskine Childers, who was a habitual visitor to Tincurry. (Source: Kevin Tobin-Dougan.)

---

10 http://hansard.millbanksystems.com/commons/1921/jun/01/military-operations-ireland-1

was rebuilt. It looked out on the yard and had a stairway, which would have made escape easier." [11]

Councillor Marian Tobin

On the 21st June 1920, Marian made history by entering Council chambers as the first female county councillor in Tipperary, where she served until the elections of 1925. This was the first election held under Proportional Representation, which has been used

(Tincurry House rebuilt after the bombing. Source: Michael and Alice McCarthy)

ever since. It was also the moment when, as Brendan Long said, "the New Guard took over from the old, the occasion of a major Sinn Féin challenge to the old Nationalists, who had from 1899, dominated the County Council scene."[12] Following declaration of acceptance of office and the election of Chairman, Marian was quick to establish her republican credentials, seconding a proposal that no list of rate payers for the information of British agents be drawn up nor any facilities for obtaining extracts from Rate or Valuation books for above purposes.

The Chairman also proposed that the Council acknowledge the authority of Dáil Éireann as the duly elected Government of the Irish people, which was duly passed. Another proposal – passed unanimously – declared that the members of the Council pledge their "whole-hearted support to the organised workers of Ireland in the great battle they are raging against the tyranny of foreign militarism by refusing to handle munitions of war which may be used to exterminate the remnant of our ancient nation." Marian was also elected to the University Scholars' Committee and to the Insurance Committee.

The Sale of Tincurry

In later years, Marian moved first to Ballinard and then to Limerick with Tincurry House being put up for auction by her daughter, May McCarthy, in February 1942, when it was described as a "choice, modern, residential, roadside holding."

---

11   O'Malley, op. cit., p.307
12   Brendan Long, *A Century of Local Democracy South Tipperary County Council*, 1st edition, 1999, page 43

Marian pictured in later years
with her daughter Eva and son-in-law, Cecil Dougan.
(Source: Kevin Tobin-Dougan.)

The End of an Era

In September 1955, Marian Tobin died, aged 84 years, and is buried with her husband in Ballylooby. Her obituary described her passing as a loss to Ireland and her home at Tincurry as "a haven for hunted men" with callers "whose names are history." All that remembered her spoke of her kindness and good humour, saying she had time for everybody. In 2018, we recall this Cahir woman's brave contribution to the establishment of the Irish Republic.

Irish Press 1931-1995, 21.09.1955, page 5

Her house was haven for hunted men

The passing of Mrs. Marian Tobin, Tincurry House, Cahir, writes "One who knew her well," must recall sad memories and also happy ones The name of Tobin's, Tincurry, was known to most old Volunteers who travelled South from 1916 to 1924.

Her house while it stood—it was destroyed by the Black and Tans in 1921—was a welcome haven for all. It was open day and night.

James Tobin, her husband, died in 1918. He was an officer in the Volunteers. and a good one. Mrs. Tobin was left with three young children, a large farm in Tincurry and another at Balinlard, Tipperary, where she died. Mrs. Tobin felt it was her duty to carry on her husband's work and she did it willingly.

It was to her home the boys got to after Soloheadbeg in the cold January of 1919. They knew they were welcome and that fear was no part of Mrs. Tobin's make-up. They stayed in her house for some days and she was sorry when they moved on She had a high regard for Seán Treacy and his wish was to her a command.

Callers whose names are history

It would be hard to name all the men who called at her home— Ernie O'Malley, Dinny Lacey, Paddy McDonagh, Paddy Ruttledge, Erskine Childers, David Robinson, Liam Lynch, "Sharkey" Breen, Jerry Kiely, and many more.

It was from her house and in her pony-trap that Erskine Childers drove to Barton's in 1922. It would be nearly impossible to name all the events that wound round Mrs. Tobin's name.

Now she is gone. She lived to the ripe old age of 86. Her passing leaves Ireland the poorer. We who are left can only now offer to her dear family, our prayers and sincere sympathy. She is laid to rest alongside her husband in the old family burial ground of Ballylooby.

Marian Tobin's obituary from The Irish Press. (Source: Kevin Tobin-Dougan.)

Acknowledgements

This document was a collaborative effort. I am indebted to my cousins, Kevin Tobin-Dougan and Marion Williams, great-grandchildren of Marian Tobin, who provided much of the material. Thank you also to Michael O'Carroll, grand-nephew, and Rolando de Aguiar, great-grandnephew, who researched and shared the Carew family history. A word of appreciation to the McCarthy family for welcoming me to Tincurry House and for sharing their valuable insights. I am grateful to Tipperary County Council who allowed me access its archives and acknowledge with gratitude the Military Service Pensions Collection and the use of its archived material. www.militaryarchives.ie/collections/online-collections/military-service-pensions-collection

Lily Potter - Victim of War
By Liam Roche

Lily Potter resided in Cahir for eight years from 1913, as the new bride of District Inspector (DI) Gilbert Potter, until her sad departure from Cahir in September 1921. Lily was born to Charles Furlong Harding, Esq., JP and his wife, Mary White, in Charleville, Co. Cork and baptised on 13 July 1881 at the Ballyhea Church of Ireland.

At the time of the 1901 Census, Lillian (Lily), aged 19, was residing at The Terrace in Charleville with her father who was a landowner and Justice of the Peace, her stepmother, Dilliana, and two domestic servants. The house, with twenty front windows, thirteen rooms, and six outbuildings was rated 1st Class. The property included three stables, a coach house, a fowl house, and a turf house. When Charles and Dilliana had a daughter, Georgina, born about 1883, Lily became a big sister. Unfortunately, Georgina died at the age of twelve in 1895, leaving Lily an only child. It is said that Lily had a strict upbringing, played the organ at the local Anglican church, and loved the arts and theatre. Lily's upbringing may explain why she loved to visit her uncle in Dublin as he gave her a great time and introduced her to Dublin society.

Lily and Gilbert Potter
It was on one such trip in 1911 that she met Gilbert Potter. Lily's future husband had been born in Co. Leitrim in 1878. When he was twenty-three, he entered the Phoenix Park Training Depot in Dublin. By 1909, he had served in Castlepollard, parts of Cork, and was also involved in policing marches in Portadown. A whirlwind romance ensued, but Lily's father and stepmother were not happy with the relationship at all. Her father, a successful businessman, saw Gilbert as a man with limited prospects. As fate would have it, Lily's father and stepmother both died in 1912; and in February 1913, Lily was left as administrator of his estate valued at thousands of pounds. A few months later, she and Gilbert were married at St. Ann's Church of Ireland in Dublin.

Cahir
About this time, Gilbert took up his post in Cahir as District Inspector for the Cahir area. The Royal Irish Constabulary (RIC) had rented Apsley House in Wellington Street (now Pearse Street) for their new District Inspector and his

young wife. This fine house, as most locals know, is just a short walk from the site of the RIC barracks (now Lava Rock Restaurant). The couple had a great lifestyle in Cahir and made many friends in and around the area. From 1913 to 1917, Lily gave birth to their four children: Georgina, Hilda, Gilbert, and Freddie. Lily and Gilbert's assets and income allowed the family a comfortable life. They had four servants: a nanny, a nursemaid, a cook, and a part-time housemaid.

War of Independence

The Potters' lovely life in Cahir was about to be shattered. The War of Independence was changing, becoming more intense with many more attacks on rural RIC stations. Many constables had been shot in more troubled locations, one hundred tax offices had been burned down; and locally, there had been ambushes in and around the area. It was believed that Thomas McCurtin, Lord Mayor of Cork city, had been shot by RIC plain clothes agents. Most of all, Black and Tans had arrived in greater numbers to support the RIC. Some Irish joined their ranks, but now more Catholics were leaving the RIC. Violence towards civilians and combatants increased. A brutal war of attrition and retribution ensued. In the spring of 1919, with the actions of the Irish Volunteers and the British Forces, the Anglo Irish War was in full swing. In Cahir, as in many towns, life got more difficult, at times, as the British Forces and RIC set about securing their assets.

In Cahir, District Inspector Gilbert Potter was the man in charge of the RIC. On 23 April 1921, Potter set out in his motor car on a regular tour of inspection of Ballyporeen and Clogheen RIC stations. That night, he did not return home.

Five days later, on 28th April, Lily received a letter stating, "Dist. Inspector Gilbert Potter, having been legally tried and convicted, was sentenced to death, which sentence was duly carried out on Wed., 27 April." It was the first confirmation she had that her husband had been killed. He had been kidnapped by the IRA when he came upon their ambush of a supply convoy at Hyland's Cross, Garrymore, Clogheen.

According to the *Irish Independent* of 29 April 1921, the above statement "was the statement contained in a typewritten letter which Mrs. Potter, wife of D.I. Potter, Cahir, received yesterday in a plain envelope unstamped. The note which bore a Cahir postmark, added that during the time of custody the officer was well treated and shown every consideration. The address on the letter was written in Irish, and at the end of the notification was signed 'O.C.' Greatly upset by this intimation, Mrs Potter, who has young children is confined to bed."

For my Wife

During the days DI Potter was held, he had been allowed to keep a diary and write letters. It was that diary, those letters, and other items that were returned to Lily in a box on May 8th, eleven days after Gilbert's execution. Imagine the sorrow and distress she must have felt when going through those items. According to Wikipedia, Potter wrote,

> *Enclosed in box for my wife*
>
> *Wrist watch, Gold ring, Cigarette holder, Silver match box, Set of keys, Cigarette case,*
>
> *Letter for her and the Bishop of Waterford.*

The Nationalist of 11 May 1921, reported that Lily received a diary, signet ring, and watch along with a farewell letter. The newspaper went on to say that Gilbert explained in the letter that he was writing it in the morning because he was to be executed later that day. "He bade farewell to his wife and four little children in affectionate terms." *The Nationalist* said that "Mrs. Potter received a great shock, being kept so long in suspense, and hoping for the best to the last."

Final Letters

As mentioned, the box of letters Lily received contained a letter written by Gilbert three days after his capture and intended for his uncle, the Bishop of Waterford:

> ~~4th 5th~~ *5th Day of Captivity --- With I.R.A.. 26th April 192#*
>
> *Dear Bishop, I hope you can do something to help Lily in this time of distress for her. I have written her a letter and she may have received it as the IRA officer told me it was posted ---Pals in Ireland have regard for my wife who is Irish more so than I am, as regards her family having held land in the country ---I cannot now write my personal feelings to you --- [Illeg.] --- The I.R.A treat me well and are kind hearted --- comfort my dear Lily. How awful that I should have brought her this trouble ---If you see Lily soon tell her that her goodness to me and devoted love are felt by me and are a treasure in my affliction ---I pray for her and the prayers are heard.*
>
> *Yours affect'ly, Gilbert.*

Lilly Potter and her husband Gilbert resided in Cahir from the time of their marriage until his tragic death. It's possible the photos were taken in Cahir.

The next day, Gilbert wrote to Lily:

27 April 1921.

Dearest Wife I hope you had news of me through my letter ---The IRA say you can send me a parcel if you take steps that the method of sending it is not known & kept secret ---Perhaps you could give a parcel to Mrs Cleary which she could keep at Spelmans[?] until it is called for. I want ---

(1) Clean long drawers (2) Clean long cotton vest (3) Clean cotton shirt (4) pair socks (5) big boots [Illeg] inside with insoles --- the K would suit best (6) Waterproof coat (7) Safety razor with two dozen new blades (8) Shaving brush, soap, a small sponge (9) Tooth brush

If you put the lot in cloth haversack like the RIC have I could carry it --- If impossible to send don't be troubled as the people I meet are really kind and could supply everything except a safety razor --- Now darling wife God will help us. My love to you Hilda, Georgie, Charles and Freddie --- Could you send me a pound?

Your husband, Gilbert.

In that letter, Gilbert seemed to feel that he would continue to be held captive; but in his diary entry later that day, he wrote:

"Slept well rose at 8.30a.m. Tea & and egg at 9:15.

About 11a.m. I was told I was to die this evening. The young men guarding me have been kind all through"

WILL -- 27th April 1921

I leave to my darling and devoted wife Lily everything I possess.— Lilias Potter

I wish her to give my wrist watch to our sweet little son Charles---He has worn it often---My wedding ring also to my dearest wife who gave it to me---I have little to leave, Lily, we had everything in common. My bureau that you gave me—to Hilda our dear angel first born. The little travelling clock to Georgie. My polo cup to your dear [illeg.] of a small success I had in life before meeting you. (I had nothing to bring you, you gave all) You did what no one ever did for me before, you gave me a pure and devoted love --- a home and our children--- You tried in every way to help me and save me but we know there is only One who can do that perfectly. He will let us meet again ---- My walking sticks are for you --- one for Charles, Give Freddy something --- Will you write again to [Illeg] Boyle for the cups silver forks and spoons Golf clubs, balls tennis racket to you Lily --- I cannot find out when I am to be released. I am informed the decision rests with the Dal Eirann. I don't know if you can approach any person connected with it --- I was told a question of exchange might be raised, I wonder does the Government care enough about one who has been their servant for over 20 years to make an effort in my direction? Dal Eirann should be able to find out that I never injured an Irishman and lived always on good terms with the Irish, being born & having lived all my life In Ireland. [Illeg] claim to have the right to -My love to all our friends in Cahir --- and to the Bishop and May and their family in [Illeg] My love to Corre? & John and Aunt Sophie? To Percy & Lilias – To Lyndon Mabel and their boys, To Wilkie --- God bless them all --- Remember me to [Illeg] old Bob Live on at Apsley House dear if you can, if it is God's will --- ask him --- Remember me to Mr. Ford & his family --- to [Ileg] --- the Dennys --- To my Hd. Constable & men--- our rector ---

27 April 1921

*I request those in authority with IRA to send to my wife my note
book which contains messages for her and my will.
There are, I am sure, humane leaders who will pity a wife who is
Irish, as I am also. G.N. Potter*

Collecting Gilbert's Body

In addition to the grief Lily must have felt about her husband's death, it is difficult to imagine the additional desperation she must have experienced when she learned that her husband's death could have been prevented had the government been willing to do an exchange of prisoners as the IRA had offered. In late August, she had to act as a hostage for the return of her husband's body. Although the truce had been signed, the IRA did not trust the English. Lily had to go in the dark of night with one RIC official and two other men in an open truck to collect her husband's body on a country road close to the woods at Knockonaffrin near Rathcormack in Co. Waterford.

After the funeral, the children were sent to stay with their uncle, the Bishop, who resided at Old Court outside Waterford city. A few days later, Lily arrived with baby Freddie. On a very dark night, a couple of weeks later, Lily and her children were taken down to the quayside in Waterford where they boarded a cattle ship that would take them to England.

> "Lilias [Lily] and the four children soon after had a stormy crossing of the Irish Sea by cattle boat before settling in Tunbridge Wells, Kent, England. For some time, the sale of the damaged motor car which realized £50, £25 back-pay due her husband, an insurance policy to the value of £300 and some sundry personal effects were all that came to Lily. There was a modest pension on the basis of her husband's death, but the family were in dire financial circumstances."
>
> (Wikipedia: Irish Times, 22 October 1931).

The *Tullow Historian* website says that Lily and her children "lived in dire financial straits until Potter's dependents were awarded £12,000 compensation."

In England, Lily and the children settled with Gilbert's relations until a flat was rented. More sadness soon inflicted itself upon Lily. Daughter Georgina, who was ill, was sent to a nursing home; and a mere few months after the family's arrival in England, five year old Freddie died, apparently of whooping cough. His death is registered in Tonbridge, Kent.

Just five years after her husband's death and her relocation to Kent, the UK Probate Records show that Lilias Marie Potter of Cliffe Combe Nursing Home, Broadstairs, Kent, and of 12 Cedric Road, Westgate-on-Sea, Kent, widow, died 21 June 1926 at the nursing home. Administration of Lily's estate, valued at over £1300, was granted to Gilbert's brothers, Reverend Henry Lyndon Potter and Reverend Joseph Percy Potter. Lily's surviving children would have been about ten to thirteen years of age when they became orphans. The children would be looked after by their father's relations for years. They and their mother were victims of the War of Independence.

Sources:
Bureau of Military History

Birth records

Baptism records

1901 Census

Death records

Newspaper accounts as cited

Correspondence with Lily Potter's granddaughter

Correspondence with Michael Desmond

Mollie Fitzgerald - Irish Republican and Socialist
By Maurice J. Casey

Mollie Fitzgerald of Ballydrehid, Cahir, was a republican, socialist and, throughout the 1930s, the personal secretary of the veteran suffrage campaigner and founder of the Women's Freedom League, Charlotte Despard (nee French) (1844-1939). Mollie's older brother, David Fitzgerald (1897-1933), directed the Tyneside Irish Republican Army during the Irish War of Independence, 1919-21. David later played a crucial role in the IRA's temporary embrace of socialism in the late 1920s. Although few documents survive, relating to Mollie, the actions of her redoubtable feminist employer and militant brother allow us to trace her path through the tumult of early 20th century Irish history.

Ballydrehid
Born 10 June 1899 at Ballydrehid, Mollie was the fourth of eight children of Michael Fitzgerald, a labourer, and his wife, Bridget Burke. For the first few years of Mollie's life, the family remained in Ballydrehid, residing in the home of Mollie's grandmother, Margaret Fitzgerald. Uncle Mathew Fitzgerald, an egg dealer, also lived with them. The 3rd class house was made of stone with a thatched roof, had two front windows and three rooms. The property contained a stable, cow house, and piggery.

Family Stressful Situations
Between 1901 and 1911, four stressful situations struck the Fitzgerald household. First, Grandmother Fitzgerald, with whom Mollie had lived since birth, died in December 1902. Next, within a month of the grandmother's death, Mollie and family had relocated to town and resided at Lower Cahir Abbey where her father had a position as caretaker. Third, when Mollie was just six years of age, her youngest sibling, Ellen, aged 10 months, died at Cahir Cottage. The fourth event, probably the most upsetting of all, was the death of Mollie's mother, leaving Michael with six surviving children.

Although Bridget Fitzgerald had died while Mollie was a child, there was still a mother figure in Mollie's life. The 1911 Census shows that Bridget's sister, Margaret Burke, had moved into a house at Lower Cahir Abbey, joining Michael and his six children. At that time, Mollie's father was a farm labourer. The house was made of stone with a thatched roof. It had three front windows and three rooms. The property contained a cow house, piggery, and fowl house. Although the Fitzgerald family had a cow, pig, and hens, income would have been minimal for a farm labourer.

David Fitzgerald

Certainly, this modest upbringing appears to have instilled in the Fitzgeralds a revolutionary desire to alter their surroundings. In 1914, Mollie's oldest brother, David, travelled to London. Writing to his family back home, David recounted his growing interest in Irish national politics while living and working in the capital of the Empire. He soon joined the increasingly rapid flow of Irish nationalist politics as it streamed towards the insurrectionary moment of Easter 1916. David's letters to the family must have left an impact on teenage Mollie's political leanings. During the War of Independence, Mollies brother, Edmund, died aged eighteen; her brother Matt was in active service with a Flying Column; and David's activities became more subversive, and communication with him stopped. These events must have caused Mollie a great deal of worry and must have influenced her political development. Her father was so troubled by David's lack of contact during the War of Independence years that he wrote

From Russia with Love. Postcard from David FitzGerald in 1930 to his sister, Mollie, at Ballydrehid, Cahir. (Courtesy: Fitzgerald family)

to Michael Collins enquiring to his son's fate. In addition to David's actions, the activities of Mollie's youngest brother, Mathew, must also have had an impact on her. Having been born in 1904, he would have been a teenager when he took up arms during the War of Independence and joined a Flying Column.

The War of Independence ended in a compromise that was unpalatable for the Fitzgeralds and many others who saw the 1921 Anglo-Irish Treaty as a betrayal of the principals for which they had risked their lives. The resultant civil war ended in defeat for the cause that the Fitzgerald family supported. Throughout the 1920s, recalcitrant Irish republicans settled with varying degrees of discomfort into the reality of the Irish Free State. With a war-weary populace more keen on dealing with the daily realities of surviving in a post-independence nation than the lofty goal of national restoration, the republican calls for a return to armed resistance struck a dud note. Individuals such as novelist Peadar O'Donnell and Charlotte Despard proposed a route to salvation. By dedicating itself to the egalitarian project of international socialism, they argued, the IRA and its politically minded collaborators could attract a constituency within Ireland and find a sympathetic hearing in the wider world. This political direction put the republican agenda on steady footing with the 1920s cultural bohemia of Dublin, bringing excitement to the progressive scene that Mollie, now moved to Dublin, within which had placed herself. David took wholeheartedly to the political project. In 1930, he joined Despard on a trip to the Soviet Union where they studied the political project then underway in the world's first self-described socialist state.

Bríd and Mollie Fitzgerald
(Courtesy Fitzgerald family)

Shortly after the journey to see 'the Soviet experiment' in action, Mollie became the personal secretary to Despard. It was likely through her brother's connection to the internationally recognised revolutionary that Mollie secured the role. An octogenarian who had suffered bouts of imprisonment during her suffragette days, Charlotte required someone like Mollie to act as nurse, eyes and ears. One regular task of Mollie, who was secretarially trained, was writing Despard's turgid revolutionary poetry and correspondence as she engaged with her radical contacts across the globe.

In 1933, two events would alter Mollie's life. In the early part of the year, anti-communist mobs, whipped into violence by a Dublin priest, surrounded Despard's properties, burning one building to the ground. Fearing for her life, Despard's friend, Hanna Sheehy Skeffington advised that she relocate – this time to Belfast.

David's Death

At the end of the same year, David Fitzgerald died as a result of Non-Hodgkin lymphoma, believed by many of his comrades to have resulted from the stress of life on the run. He was buried in Ballydrehid at a funeral that featured numerous luminaries of the Irish Republican movement. The celebrated Dublin artist, Harry Kernoff, painted a posthumous portrait of David in his IRA uniform. Mollie is likely the author of a letter, describing a visit to Kernoff's studio after the portrait's completion, which stated that the depiction was so lifelike as to make it appear as though David was in the room.

Mollie, now permanently based in Belfast with Charlotte Despard, found new companionship in the form of Jack Mulvenna (1905-1993), a local member of the left-wing Republican Congress, who joined Despard's Belfast staff. One contemporary of Despard's remembered the pair in an unflattering recollection as flippant youths who spent most of their time riding in the staff car and smoking cigarettes. Despard, for her part, described fondly the young women who surrounded her in those days. "I am very proud of this young generation," she said at a birthday celebration. "I like to see these young girls with their long legs and short skirts. When I was a girl, we were not allowed to show our ankles."

Despard continued to engage in socialist and republican activity in Belfast, assisted by Mollie and Jack. Their actions included support for the unemployed movement and solidarity with the forces fighting against Francisco Franco in the Spanish Civil War. Mollie was pictured in the *Belfast Newsletter* alongside Despard and the rest of the Northern Ireland Joint Committee for Spanish Relief. In January 1938, Mollie was among many Irish republican names to be listed in the *Irish Press* expressing their sympathies following the death of James Connolly's widow, Lillie.

In November 1939, aged 95, Charlotte Despard died in her Belfast home after suffering a fall. Mollie was the last person to see Despard alive and to hear her last words which were spoken in German: 'sweet dreams and silent repose'. In Glasnevin Cemetery, where Despard was buried alongside the most significant figures in the history of Irish nationalism, Mollie laid a wreath for the revolutionary inscribed from "Your own Mollie". Mollie's sister, Brid, accompanied Mollie at the funeral.

Charlotte Despard

Despard's death provides an unfortunate epilogue to what we know of Mollie Fitzgerald's later life. In her will, the wealthy heiress to the French and Despard fortunes, although largely bankrupted by her underwriting of revolutionary agitation, left her estate to Jack and Mollie. The Madame's family, the French dynasty, re-emerged to dispute this inheritance, denouncing Jack and Mollie with the charge of being scurrilous manipulators. The legal dispute over the will drained whatever money was left in the estate. It is unlikely that Jack or Mollie received any of the money which Despard had bequeathed to them.

Mollie's later years remain a mystery. To my knowledge, she did not have any children. The location and date of her death also remains uncertain. Yet, she had played a role in the life of a woman who shaped the history of feminism in Britain and Ireland while also being the sister of someone who was a significant figure in the history of Irish socialist republicanism. Mollie's relationship with extraordinary people has ensured some details of her life have survived. As Irish women's history continues to develop and new sources are digitised, perhaps the historical darkness surrounding Mollie will be illuminated. For now, however, we are left with only brief glimpses into the extraordinary life of a radical Cahir woman.

Sources:
David Fitzgerald Letters (held in private ownership)
Belfast News, The Vote, Evening Herald
Genealogical assistance provided by Karol Defalco

Women's Work – Never Done
By Margaret Galvin

The saying, "women's work is never done," was coined for the women of Cahir who reared us. They were the hewers of wood and the drawers of water, always patiently hauling bags and buckets, coaxing reluctant fires, fretting over pots and kettles hanging from fire irons. Theirs was a ceaseless and largely unchanging "now". Patient, diligent application to repetitive tasks ensured that each day passed in faithful servitude and continuity. Their every hand's turn was crucial for the survival of the family.

A Woman at a farmhouse near Cahir cooking for the family.
Photo: Courtesy of Weber/Cronin Collection

Women were responsible for channelling the two life-giving elements of fire and water into the home. The drawing of water was a never-ending activity throughout the day. Washing days were particularly onerous. Big pots were heated on the open fire, the zinc bath pan was set up between two chairs as the women scrubbed and rinsed and wrung out, their knuckles sore from harsh detergents, Tide or Omo. They watched the weather like hawks. A shower of rain meant the misery of wet towels and sheets steaming in front of the fire, at risk from a stray spark, filling the house with a stale damp smell. Keeping the home fires burning from morning to night was essential from both symbolic and practical viewpoints. The women joined their men folk at the saw-horse to cut timber into logs. They never returned from a walk without a bart of sticks to start the fire in the morning, coaxing the frail flame to life before the man and the children came down, providing a bit of warmth and comfort, a steady heat to bake the bread in the pot oven or boil the swill for the pig or the hens. Saturday nights saw the bath pan filled before the fire as the stain and grime of the week was washed away with Lifebuoy and Loxene, in preparation for the Sabbath.

Our women hauled messages from town in hessian bags, walking or cycling the miles in all weathers. They watched the pennies as the tally was written into "the book" by the shopkeeper who occasionally made them a gift of a quarter of sweets or a slab of Cleeve's toffee. They fed us on lamb's liver and pig's head, chalky processed cheese and fresh eggs. They'd have given us the bite out of their mouths if needed. Some women made several trips to Cahir on a daily basis to stock up on the large bottles their husbands drank with the tragic thirst that couldn't be quenched. Such women knew the humiliation and worry of grinding poverty and often had to look to the priest or doctor for help with their electricity bills.

These women also watched out for the postman with great anticipation, longing for letters from emigrant children or parcels from England or America. The arrival of those parcels, carefully and lovingly assembled in strong ridged brown paper and string, was a break from the humdrum of the daily grind. The packages were delved into with such hope and faith; wellington boots for the children, half empty bottles of Apple Blossom perfume and an unlikely assortment of clothing from jumble sales in London sent by emigrant sisters who knew how vital this contribution was to the family at home. Hems were taken up and let down and buttons were sewed in, toes were squeezed into too-small shoes or newspapers were used to fill the spaces in shoes that slopped about the feet. No catwalk model paraded as proudly as our mothers dressed in hand-me-downs from an English stranger.

The seasons of the year brought specific tasks. Blackberries were picked for the "jam man", the agent who puffed by on a little Honda 50 to collect and weigh the fruit. The hard-earned "few bob" would then be set aside for the Communion or Confirmation outfit at Sheehan's, Walshe's or Tom Mahony's. Branches were shaken to dislodge wild damsons for jam, and mushrooms were gathered from early morning fields. This was hard work, foraging among thorns, briars and nettles, decades before it became a chic and fashionable occupation for those flirting with "recession". Pigs were killed, black pudding was made with the hot blood, and a share was brought to the people in the cottages. Apples were gathered, tarts were delicious and steaming, alluring because of their rarity. Potatoes were picked, and there was poetry in their varieties: Golden Wonders ("Balls of Flour"), Roosters, Aran Banners.

A tidy house near Cahir almost ninety years ago.
Photo: Courtesy of Weber/Cronin Collection.

Rooms were wallpapered in preparation for the occasional American visitor, the paste a home-made concoction of flour and water that rarely held, with strips dislodging and hanging down, forlorn and splodged. School books were covered with wallpaper in September, and pencils were sharpened with a kitchen knife. Christmas saw the washing of the good delft and the gold-dusting of the picture frames, the hanging of paper chains from the ceiling, the gathering of holly from the Crows' wood and the paying off on the toys, a shilling a week, at Sampson's. These rituals provided solace for the women as they looked with pride on their capacity to bring a little shine and sparkle into the home with lavender polish, brightened with cardinal red.

The Drama of Ritual

The sacred cycle of the seasons brought the drama of ritual too. Clothing was left out for Saint Brigid to bless on the eve of February 1st. Many the toothache or sore belly was comforted by a blessed scarf as our mothers became faith healers, keeping away for as long as they could from the dispensary doctor who was often harsh and forbidding. Flowers were gathered for May altars, placed in jam-pots in front of statues of Mary. The Mother of God came among us, presided calmly over the routines of the house, listened as rosaries were recited, mantra-like, watched as our mothers rubbed cut onions into our chilblains, fine combed us for nits, spooned sweet medicine into us for worms, tied bows in our hair. The land was blessed with Easter water to save us from the evil eye, the neighbour who might wish us ill by leaving nests of rotten eggs in the ditches, spiriting away our luck with gluggers.

In Blind Street and Hogan's Square, the houses were bedecked for the Corpus Christi procession as the body of Christ was carried by the priest along the transformed streets of our little town. The women followed in their mantillas, heads bowed, shy to be in public. They assembled on the women's side in the church to recite the Litany of Loreto, saluting the Blessed Virgin in the lofty language of prayer, "Mother most pure, inviolate, undefiled, Mystical Rose, Morning Star, Queen of the Family". Familiar with death, they laid out the corpses, led the prayers at wakes, kept a tight rein on the whiskey bottle from husbands who "could be violent in drink". In November, they circled the church, praying the litanies that would free their people from Purgatory. They confessed and were "churched" following child-birth, stretched hands and hearts to accommodate families of ten or more children, three to a bed. They donned the blue mantle of the Legion of Mary, stood aside to let the nuns pass on the street.

Bread and Circuses

And where did these Maggies, Marys, Nellies, Kits, Bridgeys and Joans find their "bread and circuses"? They sang along with Bridie Gallagher or Slim Whitman on the wireless, listened on Sundays to *The Clithero Kid* and followed the goings on of *The Archers* or *The Kennedys of Castleross.* Those who had the impossible magic box of an early television fell in love with Gay Byrne or Charles Mitchell, solemnly reading the news – posh men from Dublin, inhabitants of another planet. They linked arms on a Sunday afternoon and took a stroll to the Swiss Cottage, sat at one another's fires to puff on a Sweet Afton, enjoy a mug of tea and a Goldgrain biscuit. Managed to get the hair done once in a blue moon at Mary Riordan's, eased their feet into bowls of salty water at night, toughening up the skin for all that lay ahead. They looked forward to a play in the Parochial Hall during Lent, something light about a bossy priest's housekeeper. They saved the pennies for a trip to Duffy's Circus, wondered at the glossy foreigners hanging from the trapeze.

Our brave, generous, hard-working, diligent ancestors must have hoped that we'd experience better as they took us on their knees to pour iodine onto cuts and scrapes, fed us on the best they could provide, washed our hair in rainwater. What, I wonder, would they make of the women we've become or the society that has changed beyond all recognition in a few short decades.

Women in Farming

By Jenny Kiely

Women on the farm had little influence outside the farmhouse, and life for farm women in the early 20th century was not easy. Farm homes usually housed many women as well as men. Households were made up of the farmer and his wife, their own family and possibly his elderly parents and single brothers and sisters. In some cases, the elderly farmer and his wife remained the heads of the home while they lived.

Three generations of Costigan women, Cahir, all of whom worked in farming.
Photo taken 1920 approx. (Courtesy of Jenny Kiely)

Single Girls

Some single girls on the farm may have found work in the nearest town; they would have taken up apprenticeships in shops. Others may have married into another farm in the area. This would have been usual if the girl had a dowry which could be a sum of money or farm stock given by the girl's father. Sometimes this dowry was given to her husband's unmarried sister so she could then marry out of the house. Many of these marriages were "made" matches, arranged by a matchmaker. He was approached or contacted by a man looking for a wife or by a farmer who wished to marry off his daughter so that his son could bring in a wife. The matchmaker would know many people, would suggest likely suitable candidates and would introduce them. Older farmers sometimes would waive the dowry.

Children

Most families had large numbers of children, often up to fifteen. Everybody had their own jobs to do. Boys would work in the farmyard before school. Girls would help younger children to dress and feed them before school.

Schools

Schools were usually in the local area. Everyone walked to school, perhaps a mile or two. Children would meet up on the road and walk together. Most children carried a lunch which consisted of a slice or two of homemade bread and a bottle of milk if available. Wood for the fire was collected on the roadside on the way. This was the only form of heating in the school. Schools didn't have electricity or running water. Electricity came in the mid-1940s. It was marvellous progress, but running water did not come to many areas until years later. When the children returned home from school, a dinner would be ready for them, prepared by their mother or grandmother. This meal would usually consist of potatoes and butter and maybe cabbage or turnips. After dinner, most children would have jobs to do such as bringing in sticks for the fire for the night. They would also go out to the fields and bring in cows for milking, feed calves and feed the pigs. The farm women would milk the cows and do other jobs around the yard along with the older children. The farmer worked in the fields with horses tilling, making hay or keeping hedges trimmed and tidy.

On Saturdays, children were all on hand to do jobs in the fields such as thinning turnips or turning hay. Picking stones was a hated job, but it had to be done. During school holidays, cousins that lived in towns would be sent out "the country" to spend several weeks with aunts and uncles. All the visiting cousins had to help out with the work. School holidays were always looked forward to by the children, but it meant extra work for the mother catering for everybody.

Housing

Farmhouses were single-story thatched houses. Today, this would be called a cottage. Usually, it faced into the farmyard and had one door into a small porch. The parlour was to the right, the kitchen to the left. The parlour had a fireplace, maybe a table and chairs and a china cabinet, where the good delph was stored. Sometimes, a bed had to be put into the parlour. The kitchen was the centre of the house and everything happened here: cooking on an open fire and washing. The table was used for preparing and serving meals, homework and card playing at night. Off the kitchen were two small bedrooms with a loft overhead, accessed by a ladder. A bed in the loft was used when required. New houses were more modern, with two stories built in concrete, with slate roofs. These houses were similar in size to the older houses, but they had an upstairs with two or three bedrooms. It was the late 1950s before running water with bathrooms and toilets became regular installations in rural farmhouses. Before this, water had to be brought in by bucket from a tank in the yard or from a local fresh water source such as a well, stream or a pump.

Light was from a candle or the fire. Some houses had an oil lamp which could be brought from room to room. The arrival of the "Tilly Lamp" was a big improvement as it hung on a pulley from the ceiling and gave great light. This lamp was always installed in the kitchen.

Woman feeding fowl on a farm outside Cahir - 1932. Courtesy Weber/Cronin Collection

Women's Lives

Women were very busy on farms as they had many chores. In addition to having and rearing children, they did the cooking, baking washing, mending, knitting and dressmaking. Women would always help with milking cows and feeding calves, pigs, sheep and lambs. Many women also looked after the kitchen garden, hens, turkeys, geese and eggs. Some farms produced butter, and this was the woman's job.

Often women did almost all the yard work. Granny would keep an eye on the children while mother was out at work. Often two or three workmen worked on farms along with the farmer. All the men would be in for dinner and tea. Some would live on the farm. They might sleep in a house in the yard; this was known as the "Sleeping House". Sometimes at night, card games were played, mostly by men, but if they were short numbers for six or nine, women would be asked to play.

Shopping

Farm women went to town once a week to do shopping. They brought home all the basics for the week: tea, sugar, fresh meat, flour, shop bread, etc. They might also bring eggs with them and sell them to the shop where they bought their groceries. Most families had an account (credit) or a "book", as it was called.

Farm Woman arriving in Town 1932. (Courtesy Weber/Cronin Collection)

The purchases were made on credit and paid for monthly or three monthly. If the woman reared turkeys or geese, she would have regular customers to purchase them for Christmas, and this brought in some extra money.

Social Life
Social life on farms was minimal. Women went to visit their own family on a Sunday, and they would travel by pony and trap and bring the children. They would go after dinner and return in time for the evening work. Should they have to go a long distance, they would leave older children at home with the husband to do the evening work as it would be late when they got home and the work still had to be done.

Irish Country Women's Association
The United Irish Women was founded in 1910 to help women to improve their quality of life through education and by coming together to share their views and support each other. While it had some success, it did not flourish until the mid-1930s, when it changed its name to the Irish Country Women's Association (ICA). Many guilds were founded all over the country. Women and their daughters joined in big numbers. They learned many crafts such as rushwork, basketry, lacemaking and dressmaking, lumra rug work and crochet. They also spent many enjoyable nights doing sketches and small plays, and there were competitions for short stories. This was a good opportunity for women to meet other women and discuss problems and support each other. In the 1940s, electricity came, and later, the ESB sent demonstrators to ICA guilds, who gave cookery demos and promoted the use of electrical appliances. These were very popular. Some women did not join the ICA and were quite sceptical of it all; others didn't join because husbands wouldn't agree to it.

An ICA guild was formed in Cahir in 1944 in the Parochial Hall, where members from Fethard guild came to advise and help in the formation of a new guild. They acquired a meeting room known as "The Hut"; and when this was not suitable, they held their meetings in Cahir Vocational School. The members were mainly from the town with just a few farmers' wives because they couldn't travel to town at night.

Kitty O'Brien of Husseystown at the controls of a tractor c.1940
(Image: Courtesy Jenny Kiely)

Conclusion

Conditions for female farmers had improved dramatically by the end of the 20th century. In some farmhouses, all modern appliances and conveniences were available. Televisions, radios, computers and phones were in many homes. Families were smaller and houses larger with bathrooms, toilets and showers. There was a car in every yard and women were able to drive, so it became much easier to travel. Education improved, and all children went to the secondary or vocational school in the local town. Many went away to cities for third-level education and to find jobs. Others went into nursing and the civil service; and some trained to be teachers, later returning to teach in the locality. Some joined religious orders.

Many women in rural areas now work outside the home. Some still remain in farming, but automation has reduced the workload, with some farms managed by the farmer on his/her own, with contractors coming in to do the heavy work. These advances can, however, create new problems, including increasing a sense of isolation. Nevertheless, it is to be hoped that women will still be involved in agriculture in the future.

Reopening Cahir Jubilee Nurse Association in 1927

By PJ O'Meara

Many of our older residents will have vivid memories of the contribution made by the "Jubilee Nurse" and the Cahir Jubilee Nurse Association to the health and well-being of the people of the town over several decades. The origins of the term "Jubilee Nurse" can be traced to the 1887 establishment of a community nursing organisation known as "Queen Victoria's Jubilee Institute for Nurses". The organisation was started by private subscription to mark the Golden Jubilee of Queen Victoria's reign. The title was invariably abbreviated to "Jubilee Nurse" in popular conversation. Under this scheme, a local committee – officially known as the District Health Association – provided community support for the nurse who worked in a role similar to that of the modern Public Health Nurse. There was little or no government funding for this service.

Mrs. Pamela Charteris seems to have played a pivotal role, as president, in the revival of the Cahir Jubilee Nurses Association in the late 1920s. Indeed, it appears from the committee's minute book that it was her decision alone to appoint Nurse Knox as Jubilee Nurse, starting work on 2nd February 1927. The other members of the 1927 committee were Rev. Wm. O'Donnell, Rev. Canon Deane, Mrs. Burke, Mrs. Stokes, Ms. Smith, Messrs Going and Ryan, Dr. Stokes and Mrs. Talbot.

Ms. Knox's salary and emoluments were set by the association at £60 for the first year, rising by £2 a year to £68. £10 was granted for uniform, £58 10s for board and laundry, and £26 for fire, light and attendance. The committee decided to insure Nurse Knox under the Employer's Liability Act and for all sicknesses and accidents for which the employer is liable under the Workmen's Compensation Act. Colonel Charteris provided a rent-free furnished house for the Jubilee Nurse, at the rear of Cahir House on St. Mary's Road.

In 1928, the committee minute book records that, in her first year, Nurse Knox paid 2,319 visits to 105 patients and handled 2,259 child welfare cases. The report of Miss Mooney, inspector, in late February 1928 stated that:

> *Very good work was seen on a round of visits with Ms. Knox who carried out her duties in a business-like way and with due regard for her patients' comfort. Judging by the number of cases which Nurse has attended during the short time the District has been re-opened,*

there is no doubt that the Cahir District Nursing Association has supplied a much needed want.

It appears that Pamela Charteris recognised that the working conditions of the Jubilee Nurse would have to be improved if the locality was to retain her services. At a September 1928 meeting, she proposed that the committee should agree new Rules for Nurse's Guidance which provided, inter alia, that:

The Jubilee Nurse shall be allowed one month's holiday each year, but she should hold herself in readiness to be recalled in the event of serious illness in the District, in which event she shall be permitted to go for the unexpired period of her holidays, as soon as conveniently possible afterwards. The Jubilee Nurse shall also be allowed a weekend holiday every three months. Before leaving on holiday, the Jubilee Nurse must notify the Doctor and also leave her address with the Hon. Secretary.

After his wife's premature death in 1932, Colonel Charteris succeeded Pamela Charteris as committee president. The committee seems to have remained quite diligent in attending to the Jubilee Nurse's work requirements, providing her with an auto-bicycle for her rounds in the late 1930s. In addition, the colonel paid for the erection of two bedrooms on the top story and the distempering of the walls of the nurse's house on St. Mary's Road, while a sum of £62 was incurred by the association in refurnishing the property.

To pay off that debt, the committee decided to hold dances and whist drives at an early date. Cahir District Coursing Club responded by holding two successful dances in 1939, which raised over £35 for the funds of the Cahir Jubilee Nursing Association. The band at the second dance performed free of charge, for which they were thanked, in writing, by the committee. These are just two examples of the esteem in which the services provided by the Jubilee Nurse were held by the wider community.

The association's work in support of the town's Jubilee Nurse continued until the early 1970s when Nurse Joyce entered into the employment of the South Eastern Health Board as a Public Health Nurse. Even though this particular model of community-backed public health nursing was made redundant, ultimately, by the expansion of state services, it is important to recall that the attachment of the people of Cahir to the Jubilee Nurse and the Cahir Jubilee Nurse Association crossed all social, economic and religious divides. To paraphrase *Othello,* "They had done our town some service."

Miss Burke and Miss McCoole of Cahir House Hotel
By Sinéad McCoole

In 1974 when Cahir House Hotel was sold as 'an old established licensed hotel on three acres', it was after almost 50 years in family ownership. From 1926 to 1958, Miss Burke was the Proprietress, after her death the hotel was run by her niece Miss McCoole.[1] It was described in the *Irish Independent* sale notice as 'one of the best-known hotels in these islands, indeed in Europe and North America.[2]

Nora Burke

In 1926, four years after the establishment of the Irish Free State, thirty-five year old Miss Nora Burke took the possession of a house that had been occupied by John Rochfort J.P. who managed the Cahir Park Estate. Previously, it had been the home of the Butlers when they ceased to live in the Castle in the 1830s[3] and formed part of the holdings of Richard Butler, the Baron and Viscount of Cahir, second and last Earl of Glengall. It had passed by descendant to the Charteris family, firstly to his eldest daughter Lady Margaret Charteris

Miss Nora Burke
– Founder of Cahir House Hotel

and after her death to her eldest son Lt. Colonel Richard Butler Charteris. Therefore, direct descendants of the Butlers had been in possession of these lands since the time of Cromwell in the seventeenth century. With the opening of *Cahir House Hotel*, it marked a new era for the town of local ownership when the doors opened for the first guests in February 1927.

---

1   The spelling of her name was often given as McCool, but McCoole was used by her father and his branch of the family. McCoole was given on her birth certificate. Some of her direct relatives were registered as McCool, including my father, in his case, in order to formalise his documentation when he was in the U.S. he was required to change his name by deed poll.
2   *The Irish Independent*, August 4 1974.
3   *The Landed Estates Database*, NUI Galway.

Nora had a level of education many women of her era did not attain. She remained in school in Cahir until the summer of 1909, aged seventeen.[4] After her schooling ended, she went to work for Miss Eliza Dwyer who ran the *Commercial and Family Hotel*. An advertisement for that hotel in *Bassett's Book of County Tipperary 1889* described it as providing 'a special conveyance for the use of commercial gentlemen.' It also provided direct access by 'attending all trains' and boasted 'comfort and cleanliness at a moderate rate of charge.'[5]

The purchase of the lease for Cahir House Hotel was made possible by the assistance of the local parish priest Fr. O'Donnell.[6] Miss Burke was described 'as having great standing' with the clergy and they would frequent the Hotel, giving her patronage. Local priests and Bishop, and visiting clergy from across the globe including Boston's Cardinal Cushing, who would later preside at the marriage of John F Kennedy and Jacqueline Beauvais, were also visitors at the hotel.[7]

Miss Burke (as she was known to her staff and her customers) was born Hanora Burke in 1891 to Patrick Burke and his wife Bridget née Carey (1856-1921). The youngest daughter in a family of eleven,[8] she became known as Nora to her friends, but to the family, she was always known as Baby. Miss Burke's father, known as Foxy Burke (1845-1902), had made his money as a 'car' man, driving a horse and cart, between Cahir and Clonmel. By the time of the purchase of the hotel, her brother William[9] was in the business, he had a car hire and hackney business which had been operating from the family's home in Wellington Street. Within months of his sister taking over the hotel, he opened the Cahir House Hotel Garage (from a premises owned by the hotel) along with their nephew, twenty-four year old Pat John McCoole (who had served his apprenticeship with King & Keating in Clonmel).

Nora's Siblings

No member of Nora's family had to leave Ireland in search of work, and she and her siblings remained a close family unit. The Burkes had a small town farm on

---

4 Thank you to Patrick F. McCoole (son of Pat John McCoole) for allowing me access to his family research.
5 Thank you to Mary O'Donnell for providing this reference.
6 Information provided by Paul Buckley.
7 It is said that Jacqueline Kennedy visited Cahir House Hotel. In June 1967, the widow of President Kennedy visited Ireland with her two children. She is recorded as visiting Dublin, Clare and Waterford. The author could not find documentary evidence to substantiate this visit, but it is likely to have taken place at this time given Cahir's location on the route between Limerick and Waterford.
8 Three of the children, Catherine b. 1887, William b. 1888 and Patrick b.1889, died as infants.
9 Willie, aged 34, married Mary Ryan in 1930. Their children were: twins Paddy and Jim in 1932, Cyril born in 1933, and twins - Noel and Christopher, born in December 1933. Christopher died in February 1934 and Noel in December 1934.

Wellington Street, Cahir from the 1870s and also a farm at Farrannagark. Nora's elder brother, James (1878-1934) ran the farm at Farrannagark[10] along with their younger brother Sonny[11] (1893-1950). Another brother John Francis[12] (1880-1958) had served his apprenticeship in Waterford and Dublin and had returned to Cahir and set up in antique dealing and auctioneering in the premises of the old *Commercial and Family Hotel* which also served as an annex to the hotel.

As for Nora's sisters, Mollie had married local publican John Carew in 1904. Julianne married Thomas Maher in 1910 to Castlemoyle North, Armayle, Cashel. Only Bridget Mary Josephine, known as Cis (b.1882), moved away from Tipperary. When she was serving as an apprentice in the drapery trade (a skill which, it should be noted, would have allowed her move home to Cahir and the possibility of opening her own shop), she met Donegal man, Patrick McCoole.[13]

Patrick McCoole

Patrick McCoole was from outside Donegal town, from a farm on the townland of Glenborin. One of ten surviving children five boys and five girls, Patrick was fifth in the family, a sister Ellen died in childhood, Margaret and Bridget married locally and his brother John remained on the farm while Peter, Hannah, Mary, Hugh and Michael left Glenborin.[14] Patrick, by becoming a teacher,[15] was the first of his family to have moved up in the world, beyond the subsistence living on the farm, which meant emigration for many of his siblings.

In Dublin in January 1901, Patrick McCoole, a Donegal man, then aged thirty-six, married Cahir native Bridget (known as Ciss) Burke, a sister of Nora Burke. Bridget was 18 years old. Patrick had begun teaching in November 1888 at the age of 24. The reason he was in Dublin was to get a formal qualification, as at a time when the Department of Education were trying to formalise qualifications in schools throughout the country. Patrick returned to Donegal with his training certificate from St. Patrick's College in Drumcondra. This ensured him an increase in income, making it a good start to married life for the couple.

---

10 James Burke, aged 36, married Mary Bergin in 1914. Their children were Paddy Burke b.1914, Kitty Burke b. 1917, John b.1918 and Willie b.1922.

11 His given name was Patrick. He was born after the death of his brother Patrick b.1889, and he was given the same name. This was a common practice at the time.

12 John F., aged 40, married Julia Hayes in 1920. Pat (Yank) b.1925, Billy, b.1926, Jackb.1928, Jim (Burkeen) b.1929 and Dolores b.1934. Julia, their mother died in 1938 aged 45.

13 Patrick F. McCoole (son of Pat-John McCoole) interviewed, Spanish Point, Co Clare, July 2018.

14 John McCoole remained working on the farm at Glenborin until he died unmarried in 1912. His younger brother Michael, my grandfather, (1874-1948) returned to Glenborin to take over the farm. He married at the age of 50 and had seven children before his sudden death in aged 74.

15 Years later his brother Hugh joined the Royal Irish Constabulary and was stationed in Northern Ireland when partition came he became a member of Royal Ulster Constabulary. He returned to Glenborin and is buried in Killymard, Donegal.

Patrick returned to the Four Masters School in Copany , Co. Donegal. Rural Donegal in 1901 would have been a different place for a young woman who had grown up in the town of Cahir surrounded by family. Patrick and Bridget lived in the rural townland of Meenadreen when their first two children were born, Mary Josephine (known as May) on 24 January 1902 and Pat John on October 19 1903. They moved again, still closer to the school in Copany, where Bridget Eileen McCoole was born on 8 November 1905. (She was known to generations of Cahir people as Aileen).[16] The birth of a fourth child was on 1 December 1907, another son, named Michael.

By 1907 Bridget and her four small children were well-established in Donegal. Patrick became Head Master of the Four Masters School when tragedy befell the family. In 1907, when Bridget Eileen was three, May was just six, Pat John was aged 5 and Michael was one, their father became ill with TB and began to have long absences from school for which he was not paid.

In 1901 he had established one of the first small cooperative credit societies, the Tullnaught Credit Society, a form of Parish bank located in the local school.[17] The Chairman, Patrick himself, soon needed to avail of it in order to pay for a cure for his illness. He took leave in 1907 and asked for an extension of time of six months to full recover but he was refused. Unfit to teach, Patrick had to resign on 30 September 1908. He went to a sanatorium in Wicklow to seek a cure.[18] As he later wrote, he 'exhausted all his means' by doing so and thereafter was penniless and in debt. His wife moved home to her family and his children May, Pat John and Bridget Eileen (now given as Eileen) enrolled in September 1909 in the Cahir convent infant school. It was at the family home in Wellington Street, the following January 1910, where Bridget gave birth to another child who was christened Julia Veronica (always known as Vonnie).

The following year, Patrick, now deemed to be well, was reappointed Master of the school in Copany on 1 April 1911. On the night of the census, on 2 April 1911, Patrick is recorded in the house in Donegal with a domestic servant; his wife and their children are recorded in Cahir. In June of 1911, Bridget herself contracted TB, although she was described as a 'strong healthy woman',[19] she was completed consumed by the disease and died within 9 months of contracting

16   It is unknown when she began to use Aileen instead of Eileen.
17   Patrick F. McCoole (son of Pat-John McCoole) interviewed, Spanish Point, Co Clare, July 2018.
18   Information in the National Archives files relating to Patrick McCoole. Thank you to Patrick F. McCoole for sharing this research.
19   Letter from Patrick McMullin to Board of Education. Thank you to Patrick F. McCoole for sharing his research.

it. Her youngest daughter Vonnie recalled years later, that the journey from Donegal to Cahir took two and a half days, when undertaken by pony and trap.[20] It is unclear when Bridget returned to Donegal but she died there on 29 March 1912.[21] She was twenty-nine years old and was buried in the graveyard at Clar, outside Donegal Town.

McCoole Children

The Burkes of Cahir once again looked after the McCoole children. In the immediate aftermath of his mother's death Pat John McCoole was living with the Mahers (his maternal aunt's home) in Ardmayle, near Cashel. His aunt Julianne was pregnant,[22] so in June he returned to Cahir to live with his grandmother Bridget Burke[23] and his Aunt Mollie, who had been widowed in April, without children and returned to Wellington Street.[24]

A file of correspondence survives that tells the story of the McCoole family in the aftermath of their mother's death. Patrick, with the assistance of the Parish Priest the School Manager Mon. Walker, wrote to the Board of Education on his behalf trying to get his pay re-instated to that which he had enjoyed before he took his leave of absence because of illness. Patrick McCoole was re-appointed Head Master. In October 1912 Pat John McCoole left Cahir National School and returned to Donegal to his father.[25] His brother, Michael, also went back to Donegal some time later. The McCoole girls stayed in Cahir. Vonnie started infant school in Cahir in 1914 when she was four and a half. [26] She never lived for any length of time with her father who now battled expulsion from the school as he was accused by Patrick McMullin of the Board of Management of infecting the pupils at the school with TB. It was a personal quest because McMullin's own daughter, a monitress at the school, had died of the disease. Patrick McCoole pleaded his case to J.M. Starkie who was Resident Commissioner at the Department of Education, expressing the difficulty he would find getting other work at his age. He described teaching as 'the work I love so well' and that he had 'devoted the best years of his life' to his profession. [27] He was not

---

20 Information from Barbara McCoole, who met Vonnie (her husband's first cousin) in the 1970s and 1980s.
21 Her sister-in-law Bridget Cassidy (née McCoole) was the informant.
22 Jamesie Maher was born on 4 July 1912. Thank you to Patrick F. McCoole for this information.
23 Bridget died on 15 November 1921 aged 65. Thank you to Patrick F. McCoole for this information.
24 Patrick F. McCoole (son of Pat-John McCoole) interviewed, Spanish Point, Co Clare, July 2018.
25 Pat John McCoole and his father in the school picture, Copany School, 1913.
26 Records of the Cahir Infant School sourced by Patrick F. McCoole.
27 Information in the National Archives files relating to Patrick McCoole. Thank you to Patrick F. McCoole for sharing this research.

dismissed; but illness overcame him once again, and he retired on a disability pension in March of 1917.

Michael, who had gone to Donegal to be with his father, then returned to Cahir, enrolling in Cahir Boys' School on 1 October 1918. He was sent to boarding school in Rockwell College in 1924 having finished National School in Cahir. In 1926 while Michael was at Rockwell, his father died; so the providers of his on-going education were his late mother's family, the Burkes.

May was twenty three when her father died in 1926, the same year that her aunt established *Cahir House Hotel*. From the start, it was a family run hotel; and it is thought that at that time May and her younger sister, Eileen, started to work there. According to the family, Aileen (as Eileen now styled herself) may have also worked with her aunt in Miss Dwyer's hotel, having left school in 1921 at the age of 15.[28]

May left the hotel to get married to Michael O'Connor on 8 January 1929. After some years when she had no family, she came back to work in the hotel and was in charge of service.[29] After school, Vonnie worked in the hotel, she may have had culinary training as she was a cook in the hotel.[30] In 1939, the hotel was one of a small number of establishments in the country to install an electric kitchen.[31]

Cahir House Hotel Success

During the difficult years of the 1930s, *Cahir House Hotel* became a success. Baby Burke (Nora) worked hard to build up a steady clientele. The newspapers record special lunches and dinners for those travelling back and forth to horse-racing at Powerstown Park Races. Formal dinners included the annual Tipperary and Offaly Bar dinner and the Tipperary Hunt Dance (in 1932 the music was by Major Watt's United Hunt Band). A steady trade came from meetings of organisations such as those of the Waterford & District Curia of the Legion of Mary. In 1939 the Great Southern Railway included lunch at *Cahir House Hotel* for those undertaken railway tours.[32] Among the noted visitors in those early decades were the President of the Irish Free State, W.T. Cosgrave; Eamon de Valera, who remained a frequent visitor; as well as Dan Breen, later a TD for

28 Patrick F. McCoole (son of Pat-John McCoole) interviewed, Spanish Point, Co Clare, July 2018.
29 Ibid.
30 Ibid.
31 *The Irish Press*, May 2 1939.
32 *Irish Independent*, June 12 1935.

the county. Newspapers record the arrival of a delegation from Australia at the hotel in 1937, which included the Prime Minister of South Australia.[33]

The Emergency 1939-1945 with its rations would have been a difficult time for the hotel, but with the end of the war more visitors arrived including Walt Disney, who arrived in Ireland in November 1946.[34] It was Disney's first visit to Ireland. The purpose of his visit was to 'get an intimate sense of land and home life of village and farm' to give authenticity to his film *Darby O'Gill and the Little People* (1959).

After the War, one of Baby Burke's acts of kindness was to welcome several refugees, girls who came from East Germany escaping the Russian invasion. A number of them found work with the Irish tourism industry and others married Irishmen.[35]

The Visitors

The 1950s brought a range of visitors to *Cahir House Hotel* because of its location on the road from Waterford and Limerick and Cork and Dublin. It became a favourite stopping point for patrons on long car journeys which increased in popularity as more people purchased cars. Visitors from oversees came for the fishing on the Suir.

Locals were never overlooked (although barring was enforced). Ballroom Dances attracted many patrons. Mick Delahunty's Band was a regular attraction at the hotel. Vincent O'Brien's race victories were always celebrated in the hotel.

Colonel Brook's room on a nightly basis was used by a select group of local men, merchants, doctors and judges who would come to play poker. Those who attended the Fair once a month had a special speak-easy in the cellar. The carpeting was protected from the dung that was all over the square and surrounding street with hessian mats making a make shift flooring.[36] No access to the lounge or dining area was permitted. The custom of the commercial traveller was valued. A Commercial Travellers' Room was left of main entrance hallway. Upstairs residents had a private sitting room. [37]

---

33 *The Irish Examiner,* June 12 1937.
34 This is vividly recalled by Dolores Murphy nee Burke (daughter of JF Burke). With thanks to Aileen Murphy for this information.
35 Patrick F. McCoole (son of Pat-John McCoole) interviewed, Spanish Point, Co Clare, July 2018.
36 Ibid.
37 ibid.

In 1950 Nora's grand-nephew Patrick Francis McCoole aged-eight years-old stayed at the hotel when his parents Pat John and Shiela (née Neville) went on pilgrimage to Rome. His memory of the hotel was a very pleasant stay with the exception of having to eat parsnips. He had little room for protest as they were served by his Aunt May, prepared by his Aunt Vonnie.[38] In 1952, Vonnie left the hotel to be married, at aged forty-two. She married a retired bank manager Mr. H. Cuthbert on 18 January 1952 and moved to his native Thurles.[39]

In December 1955, the hotel welcomed the European Youth Campaign for a study weekend. The aim of the society, formed in France in 1952, was 'to break down the barriers of hate and suspicion built between nations during two world wars.' Members of organisations from all over the country attended.[40]

The 1950s saw an increase in tourism with the popularity of the motor car. While Willie and his family ran the garage in Cahir, Pat John and Michael opened a garage in Thurles where Michael now lived. Pat John commuted from his home in Cahir. In 1953 after years of persuasion Pat John acquired 1909 Renault AX (the oldest car in Tipperary) from the Cahir Estate, a previous owner had been Mr. Hickley, the Galty Castle Estate agent and Manager of the Skeheenarinky School. [41] The car had pride of place in the Thurles showroom.[42]

Changing of the Guard

In August 1958, Nora Burke died, unwell for a time.[43] She died in Dublin; and her niece, Aileen, who had been managing the hotel for some time, became the owner.[44] Miss McCoole's office (located at the back of reception) was described by her nephew, Pat, as the 'holy of holies';[45] and her library, located in the hotel was also very important. Each book was covered to preserve it, a job given to Pat when he was old enough. He recalls the books were covered by x-rays from the local hospital, which he had to wash clean with a solution and then fold and tape, making durable covers for her books.[46]

The hotel maintained its old world charm, with antiques (located by John F. Burke) and magnificent flower arrangements. The hotel had twelve single

---

38 Ibid.
39 Unable to have children, they adopted two girls. They owned a stationary shop.
40 *Irish Examiner*, November 19 1955.
41 Ed O'Riordan, *Skeheenarinky News*. The car has a registration of HI-77.
42 This 109 year old car is still in family ownership.
43 She had been suffering pachyosteosclerosis and osteosclerois, which caused a hardening of the bones.
44 Nora Burke died in St. Vincent's Nursing Home, Dublin in 20 August 1958.
45 Patrick F. McCoole (son of Pat-John McCoole) interviewed, Spanish Point, Co Clare, July 2018.
46 Ibid.

bedrooms, six twin rooms and six double bedrooms along with six staff bedrooms. The glassed function room known as the ballroom was a favoured location for wedding receptions with access to the ornamental garden. In 1959, Dolores Burke (Miss McCoole's first cousin) had her reception there following her marriage in St. Mary's Church to Dennis Murphy, original of Mallow who had come to Cahir to work in the Munster and Leinster Bank.[47]

Miss McCoole of Cahir House Hotel

Throughout the 1950s, the hotel was a regular location for training of leaders. Members of Macra na Feirme and the Irish Countrywomen's Association gathered there to train Macra na Tuaithe (Macra's junior section).[48] In 1959, the hotel was the location of the National Public Speaking Competition.[49] The importance of these events meant those visiting *Cahir House Hotel* were ,and would be in future, local and national leaders. The hotel continued to attract the custom to those in politics, Seán Lemass (Taoiseach and Leader of Fianna Fáil 1959-1966) visited as well as President Sean T O'Ceallaigh and his wife, Phyllis, who on one occasion stopped at the hotel on the return from a festival in Cobh. There was a wedding reception in progress; and they agreed to be photographed with the couple, which was reported in the *Irish Press* with the headline: 'President pictured with Clonmel newly-weds.'[50]

In the 1960s, Eamon de Valera - now President - continued to visit. One family story recalls on one visit Miss McCoole brought him to Cahir Park House to sign the visitor's book, he had stayed there, but not signed the guest book. The reason, he had stayed there when he was on the run during the Civil War![51]

---

47 *Irish Press*, April 13 1959. This issue contains a photograph of the couple.
48 *Kerryman*, November 9 1959.
49 *Irish Farmer's Journal*, February 28 1959.
50 *Irish Press*, June 7 1959. The couple were Robert Kerr of Kilkee, his bride Moya Reidy of Clonmel.
51 Patrick F. McCoole (Op. cit.)

End of an Era

In March of 1962, with the death of Richard Butler Charteris, the contents of Cahir Park House and the estate were auctioned off. The collection of paintings and property was so substantial, it took place over two days. This event brought people from all over Ireland and Europe.

At the sale, Miss McCoole purchased from the Charteris estate, the estate office building, the Cahir Court House and the Jubilee Nurses residence. Within a decade they would be for sale again when she died suddenly in Colonel Brook's room on 2 May 1974. Her death notice described her as a person of 'great dignity and intelligence'. Her kindnesses to the people of the local community, like her Aunt Nora before her, were described as acts of 'secret charity'.[52] While her grand ways are remembered, they were mere affectations; the circumstances of her own childhood were never quite forgotten. She was childless, but her affection to her nephews and nieces and later her grand-nephews and grand-nieces and her cousins showed the importance of the extended family. As her aunt had before her, the Burke and McCoole families were welcomed to *Cahir House Hotel*. It was not only a hotel but a home from home.

Personal Note

My father, Michael McCoole (1933-1986) was a first cousin of the McCooles of Cahir. He spent time in Cahir in the 1950s. With the help of Pat-John McCoole he was trained in the Ford Motor Company in Cork. Originally it was planned that his younger brother Hugh would avail of the opportunity, but when Hugh was home sick for Donegal, my father went in his place. My father was welcomed by the McCooles and the Burkes. When he became engaged to my mother Barbara Folan, he brought her to Cahir. She recalls being 'interviewed' by Miss McCoole. She must have done well, as she was presented with a silver toast rack which adorned our table when we had visitors. The hotel was sold when I was five years-old, I always knew we had a familial link with Cahir House Hotel, if only through the decorative piece of silverware that survived from yesteryear.

---

52   *Irish Examiner*, May 9 1974.

Sarah Rummel – Cahir Lady of Note
By Mary Caulfield

Nous aurons pour nous l'eternity

Dans le blue de toute l'immensite,

Dans le ciel plus de problemes,

Dieu reunite ceux qui s'aiment.[1]

Edith Piaf

The above are words written on the headstone in St. Mary's Churchyard, Cahir, of Sarah Rummel, now largely forgotten in her native town, words redolent of her time in Switzerland and her love for that country. For those who remember her, she stands out as a slight figure, elegant and eccentric, with a penchant for coloured scarves!

Sarah Rummel – taken in 1960s when she was a member of Cahir Dramatic Society (Courtesy of Liam Roche)

Born in Cahir Abbey Lower, on July 1st 1900, to John Hetherington, a plasterer and Cahir Estate worker, and Elizabeth Guinan, Sarah was the youngest of fourteen children, four of whom died in infancy.[2] There was no indication in her early upbringing that she was destined to go on to live a colourful life in England and the Continent. Her schooldays were spent in Cahir, and by 1921 she was living in Islington, London. Her life up to this point seems to have been uneventful, but things were about to change when, in 1925, she married Walter Rummel in Marylebone, London. Although they were divorced by 1930, those few years turned out to be eventful for Sarah by all accounts.

---

1   Hymne a l'Amour, Edith Piaf.
2   Census of Ireland - 1901

Walter Rummel

So who was this Walter Rummel? He was a musician, one of the great pianists of the 20th century. In 1913, one critic wrote of him that Rummel was first and foremost an artist who aimed to put us directly in contact with the composers as if we were hearing them express themselves. His name is not generally known today because he left so few recordings. Amongst those recordings, one of his finest works from the 1940s is the *Ave Maria* by the Hungarian composer, Franz Liszt. Rummel also left recordings of waltzes by Polish composer, Frédéric Chopin.

Walter Morse Rummel was born in 1887 and came from a long line of musicians. He first studied with his father in Berlin, but his father died when Walter was fourteen. His mother was Cornelia Morse, daughter of Samuel Morse of Morse code fame, hence the name Morse as Walter's middle name. In 1906, Rummel visited the composer, Edvard Grieg, in Norway and in 1909 moved to Paris where he became friendly with the French composer Claude Debussy whose works he performed. By this time, Walter was married to his first wife, Thérése, but by 1918, Thérése was in a lunatic asylum.

Around this time, he became a friend of the American poet Ezra Pound and collaborated with him on several works. Simultaneously, Rummel and the dancer, Isadora Duncan, she of the coloured scarves, became lovers, touring together and giving joint recitals. But Walter seemed to grow tired of his women rather quickly, for in 1925, the handsome Walter married Sarah Hetherington, probably having met her during his tour of England. He, for some reason, called her *Patricia*. Such was his love for her that in 1923, Walter penned music to the poetry of William Blake with the following dedication... *For John Mac Cormac to sing; For Patricia to dream; For the Irish mothers to remember...*

Two years after he married Sarah, he fell in love again, this time with a Russian poetess, Francesca Eric. He married her in 1932, having divorced Sarah in 1930. The 1930s were his most successful years, during which he toured Europe and North America. He and Francesca ended up living in France where he died in 1953.[3]

O'Casey and Yeats

While Walter was married to Sarah, they visited William Butler Yeats and his wife George, in Dublin, Walter having become enamoured of Ireland sometime before. His friendship with Ezra Pound is likely to have led him to the Yeats's.

---

3   Prince of Virtuosos: A life of Walter Rummel, American Pianist – Charles Timbrell.

Ann Saddlemyer in her excellent book – *Becoming George* – gives an account of the Rummels' visit to Dublin in 1926. According to this, Walter shared Yeats' interest in the occult and séances. Rummel's visit coincided with the Abbey row over Sean O'Casey's play, "The Plough and the Stars." George Yeats brought Walter to the play and he performed backstage for the actors to help relieve the tension caused by the row.

When Rummel visited the Yeats's, his reputation as a womaniser became the subject of much gossip according to George Yeats. During the Rummels' three day stay, the other female guests complained about Walter that they were afraid of him as he was "such a chaser of women" but agreeing *that... anyway at the moment he is very happily married and no one has ever existed before.* George Yeats, at one point, seems to have found the Rummels' visit a little tiresome. She said she could cope with Walter; *I've known him long enough to tell him to run away and play. But Patricia???* Obviously there was no love lost between those two ladies. George expressed a wish that Lennox (Robinson) would be an angel and would ask them out to his home in Dalkey.[4]

Home to Cahir

This 'happy ever after' situation between Walter and Sarah did not last long. Walter Rummel moved on to his next conquest. Sarah did not return to live permanently in Cahir until the 1960s, even though she did visit her relatives in the town in the intervening years. She lived for some years in Switzerland before coming back to settle in Abbey Street once again where she spent the remainder of her life.[5] Her house was divided into three apartments, while she herself lived downstairs on the premises. Her tenants remember her as a strict landlady insisting on low noise levels and early bedtimes, but she showed a compassionate side if they were sick - often sharing her lovely honey and almond biscuits sent to her from Switzerland. She became a familiar figure in the town, with her cultured manner and flamboyant attire. Sarah Rummel became involved with Cahir Dramatic Society and co-authored a play "The Dream of Analon" (1976) with the late Ernest V. Alton. She also acted with this very successful local drama group, but spoke little about her own dramatic life.

---

4   Becoming George: The Life of Mrs W.B.Yeats – Ann Saddlemyer.   Pp: 345, 346.
5   Interview with Liam Roche, The Square, Cahir.

Sarah Rummel died on the 6th January, 1977. The lines on her headstone are taken from *Hymne a l'Amour*, written and sung by the great French singer, Edith Piaf. These lyrics were of special significance to Piaf, written in the tragic aftermath of the death of her lover in a plane crash. Are the words on a headstone in a quiet corner of a Cahir churchyard Sarah's own *Hymne* to her one time husband and lover, Walter Rummel?

We will have for our eternity,
In the blue of all immensity,
In the sky no more problems.
God reunites those who love Him.[6]

Thanks to Joe Walsh for his contribution to this article.

---

6   Hymne a l'Amour.

I was an Upper Housemaid
By Kathleen O'Neill Carroll

Kathleen O'Neill

Cahir Park Lodge was built in the 1860s as a residence for Cahir landlords, the Butler family, in an idyllic location on the riverbank with a view of Cahir Castle. On the death of Lady Margaret Charteris in 1915, it was inherited by her son Lieutenant-Colonel Richard Charteris. On his death in August 1961, it was sold and shortly before it was due to open as a hotel, it was lost in a devastating fire. Mrs Kathleen Carroll, (née O'Neill) who lives on the Mountain Road, Cahir, has vivid memories of her days as an upper housemaid in Cahir Park Lodge in the 1940s. This is her story.

I was sixteen years old when I started to work for Colonel Charteris. I was one of two upper housemaids. The Colonel had a large staff, some of whom worked in the house, others worked on the farm, and there were gardeners and bailiffs also. Mrs Moray, an English lady, was in charge of the household staff that included a cook, a kitchen maid, as well as other workers. Both the cook, Kathleen O'Reilly, and the kitchen maid, Helen Ryan, came from Co. Limerick. Paddy Dalton, who lived on the estate, spent most of his life working for the Colonel as his butler and chauffeur. His son worked under him for a time as a footman. As well as other duties, Paddy looked after the silver, aided by the regular footman, George

O'Meara, who also polished shoes and looked after the Colonel's wardrobe. One of the more unusual duties was the winding of the many clocks in the house and this was done by Mattie Woolfe, a clockmaker, who lived in Pearse Street.

I had a lovely comfortable bedroom, one of twelve, in the main house. My day started early, usually at half-seven, as there was lots to be done. My work was varied; I was responsible for the front hall, drawing room, dining room and bedrooms. In the morning, I had to light fires, dress beds, open windows and clean floors. All bedrooms were carpeted. Bed linen was inspected regularly by the housekeeper, and when necessary, mending was done. A seamstress was employed to help with this work, and sheets were sent regularly to the laundry in Clonmel.

My working week was long, with one half day and every second Sunday off. Most of the household staff lived on the premises. Estate workers swept the Mall every Saturday night because the Colonel attended service in St. Paul's on Sunday mornings. As the majority of the workers were Catholic, we were allowed time off to attend Mass on Sundays. We would take a shortcut over a suspension bridge – "the swing bridge"- that spanned the river Suir. This bridge still hangs forlornly over the river but is no longer safe to use. I remember Gus Gibbons, who worked in the garden, carrying vegetables over this bridge for use in the kitchen. The head gardener, Mr. Kirk, lived in the walled garden, in a house still inhabited to the present day. I looked forward to Sunday, when I would cycle the few miles home to Clogheen to visit my family. At Xmas, all staff had one week's holiday as Colonel Charteris went away at this time of year.

Like a lot of other women of the time, I was a member of the Women's Confraternity; and as was usual then, I went to Confession once a month. While the working hours were long, there were some highlights – we went to dances in the Parochial Hall and in the Castle, where Kevin Flynn's Band frequently played. This band later became known as the Tipperary Express, touring all over the country as well as playing in England during Lent when dances were forbidden in Ireland. All the staff wore smart uniforms. Mine was a dark red frock with a white apron. Even though the wages were low and were paid monthly, the Colonel was quite nice to us and treated us well. I have fond memories of my days in Cahir Park.

Banished Women

'Magdalene'

This drawing is dedicated to my aunt, Mary-Jo Maher of Kilmoyler, Cahir and to all the unwed mothers of Ireland who were banished from their homes, cast into lifelong servitude, their children taken from them, and their identities erased.

'Magdalene'   Alice Maher   Charcoal on paper   170 X 370 cm.   1997

267

Agnes Sullivan: Show-woman Extraordinaire!
By Kevin Sullivan

Agnes Sullivan settled in Cahir where her descendants still reside. The following is an account of Agnes' life as part of a circus/fit-ups family.

Growing up on the fit-ups in Ireland in the 30s/40s was a life less ordinary. To say my mother, Agnes Sullivan, was the head of our household would not be an understatement. That is not to say she was overbearing or controlling, quite the opposite; but she was accepted as the single person from whom we all took direction. She was a charismatic, generous, caring woman with an appreciation of learning and knowledge. This was self-evident throughout her life as you will see later on.

I believe we need to put her life into perspective by providing some background into what made her the woman she turned out to be. By doing this, I will refer to another Tipperary woman, her mother Susan.

Agnes' Mother

Agnes' mother was Susan McCormack née Hudson. She was born into a circus family in the village of Newcastle, just outside Cahir in 1899, born from a Scots-German lineage into a long line of entertainers stretching back many generations. She was a tall woman for her time (approx. 5'11"), bearing in mind her husband James McCormack was 5'1"! Susan, as I mentioned, married into the McCormack family. These were Irish royalty in showbiz circles back in those times and the marriage was pre-arranged, as was the tradition of the day.

Susan McCormack with her two daughters, Agnes (left) and Vera (right)

Susan had nine children, with Agnes being the seventh to arrive and the first girl. It was said that when Susan had her ninth, she proclaimed she had "fulfilled her duty" and from that day onwards slept in a separate bed to her husband!

Women in Charge

Susan was a strong woman and managed raising nine children while simultaneously working on the fit-ups show every evening. Her role entailed making the costumes, learning and performing songs/plays, and collecting the money at the door. Doing this allowed her to have a large stake in the family business and was very important to the whole running of the show. However, it was plainly clear, for even back then, that Susan was also the "Boss"! Although the family business might have had "James McCormack & Sons" over the door, it was clearly understood by all that should know that it was run by "Mrs. McCormack"!

To clarify, it is not in any way unusual for the woman to be the manager, or family head, in show-business. Regardless of the time, even before women had the vote, they ran circuses, and fit-ups all across Ireland. Most people have heard of Ireland's national circus, the great "John Duffy & Sons". However, the great John Duffy himself had the great "Mrs. Duffy" at his back...and she ran that circus. Even though John Duffy was a charismatic leader who had seven sons, it was "old Mrs. Duffy" that was recognised as the boss! There was never a question and all freely recognised that fact!

There was also the world famous "Vic Loving's flash parade", in which another Irish lady managed a large troop of performers that travelled the world! So it was not uncommon to have a matriarch in showbusiness.

Agnes' Childhood

As said earlier, Agnes was born into a showbiz family. She was born on the town green in Carrick-on-Suir in a "wagon" in 1929. This wagon was hand built by her father using walnut and mahogany and drawn by 2 Irish draught horses. Although Agnes eventually settled in Cahir, she spent a great deal of her life travelling the country with her family, entertaining the people of Ireland.

In the 1930s, her family operated a variety show, playing 2-3 nights in towns and villages across Ireland. A variety show consisted of various singing and dancing acts, with a raffle in the middle, followed by the main feature, the drama of the night. Interspersed with these would be novelty acts, short sketches involving two or three actors, some tricks and magic, and someone telling jokes! In 1937, just before her eight birthday, Agnes made her debut in the green tent! She performed a song called "Did Your Mother Come From Ireland?" by Bing Crosby. From that day to her last, she always loved entertaining people.

Agnes was blessed with a phenomenal memory, right up till the day she died. She could clearly recall events from her childhood such as when WWII broke out. She recalls her mother telling her to go to the local shop to buy the Irish Press and it proclaiming "War has started". She was in a little village called Knock in County Clare, and remembers her brothers and her being excited to hear this. They had heard their parents speak of the Great War and the "troubles" and were thrilled that a real war would be fought in their time.

While the war was on, and for some time after it ended, there was rationing. This meant you were allocated a ration book from which you were allowed a particular portion of sugar/flour/cigarettes etc per week. Of course, these rations were totally inadequate for most people, but people had to make the best of what they had.

She remembers "black bread". This was bread made with flour and added bran to make it go further. A directive from the government at the time made it illegal to make bread with flour alone. Agnes could particularly recall the generosity of simple people back in those times. There was always someone who would drop up a couple of dozen eggs, or whatever they had, to share with you. And likewise, her mother would share what she had with people. I think this is the picture of Ireland the people in the tourist board nowadays would like to project to the outside world. Such a pity it no longer exists.

Throughout her childhood days, she travelled the Irish countryside meeting, playing with and learning with Irish children. It was commonplace for showbusiness children to spend just 3-4 days in a local primary school, then move along to the next one. Agnes enjoyed school so much, she let on to be younger than she actually was to allow her stay in school longer than the requisite age eleven (6th class). It was virtually impossible for the vast majority of people get second level education, never mind show-people!

The West of Ireland

On her travels as a young child, she and her family moved up along the west coast from Clare, to Galway, to Mayo, up to Donegal. She recalls in particular an incident in a Gaeltacht area in Connemara. She was about eight or nine at the time and was out picking flowers with her younger sister. After a while they noticed some boys staring at them. Now these boys were dressed in the attire of the day for that region with red and white petticoats, bare feet and shaven heads. At first, the boys did nothing but peek around hedgerows at them, but then made a dash to grab the girls! Both Agnes and her sister ran for dear life home to their wagon and family, terrified that they would be kidnapped or hurt! On seeing this, the local PP called to the show and explained that the boys chasing them thought the girls were fairies and wanted to catch them! The boys had never seen girls dressed up like Agnes and her sister and thought the sisters were spirits.

Agnes' Parents 1918
- James and Susan McCormack

During those times in the west of Ireland, the national electricity grid had not reached many outlying parts of the community. When her parents put on the shows they had a little generator for the electricity. This in itself was a cause of amazement to the locals, and many thought it was magic! This might be hard to accept, it being only 80 or so years ago; but these are facts, and she did experience it.

Then another time she recalls bringing the first "Talkies" to the west of Ireland. As mentioned earlier, the west was a neglected part of the country and particularly in the 1930s. People were amazed and confounded by this new invention and thronged to the tents to see them. The talkies were part of the overall variety show but still the main draw.

Agnes also remembered the poverty of the 1930s in that region with the UK blockade still in place. It had a terrible effect on the people of the west. Emigration was common with only the very young or the very old remaining. However, her childhood was a glorious time and one fondly remembered.

The North

Agnes particularly remembered growing up in the border counties between Donegal and Derry. As a child, depending on the children of the locality, she would sing "King Billy" songs or "pro-Pope" songs! This was not uncommon as they were children and did not have any interest in any part of domestic politics. Their interests were just playing with the local children. At this point I should point out, show people were always considered very neutral to all sides of the conflict.

That being said, there was no tolerance for bigotry, regardless of the side you took. Agnes recalled her aunt telling a story of back in the troubles when a young boy came rushing into the tent being chased by the Black & Tans. She quickly sat him down at the dinner table and when the soldiers came in to investigate, she told them there was no one there except her "four" sons, after which they left. She probably saved that young man's life.

However, back to Agnes' early years, she recalls a beautiful story of the kindness and generosity of the people, in particular those of Killybegs. The storms of her childhood were a constant frightening threat. And due to this instinctive fear, she would always fill with dread when a storm was on its way. Please bear in mind, showpeople lived in handmade caravans (wagons) which were obviously susceptible to climate conditions. Therefore, any disturbed weather had a massive impact to the lives of those within. One day in Killybegs, a nasty Atlantic storm was brewing out to sea. The locals were very well attuned to weather in coastal areas as their lives depend on it. They could see the threat it posed to the show-people and offered to cast their fishing nets over the wagons and anchor them to the ground. Duly, the storm arrived and my mother swears only for the diligence and kindness of the local fisher-families, they would have lost everything.

Wartime Plane Crash

There were certainly plenty of incidents throughout the country that made Agnes' life less ordinary. At one point during WW II while the show was set up in Lahinch Co. Clare, a huge B17 flying fortress crash landed on Lahinch strand! These were the famous bombers from the US and exceptionally large. This one had gotten lost and rather than bail out at sea, they found the only flat surface they could see on which to land their airplane. When it landed, its axels dug into the fine sand on the beach and the plane was immobilised. Of course, the crew were escorted to the local Garda station to be later evacuated to the now famous Curragh camp where allied and axis forces were to live together until the war ended. When the crew were removed, of course all the local people, including the show people, went to view this attraction. However, the plane itself, of course had "scandalous" nude pictures painted on the walls. Immediately, the local parish priest went into it and painted over them all with black paint! But this didn't stop people from taking little souvenirs and mementos. Agnes had a treasured little door handle with her for many years after, as a reminder of that day. Of course, the Irish government didn't have the capabilities to extract the plane from the beach, so it remained there. Every year for the following few years, the show would return to Lahinch; and every year the plane had sunk a little more under the sand until eventually it was gone. Today there is a brass plaque erected on the sea wall in Lahinch from the US airmen, thanking the locals for their help and stating the plane remains, to this day, under Lahinch beach.

Wife - Mother - Writer

Agnes met her husband, Paddy Sullivan, and married after a short engagement. Paddy left Carrick-on-Suir to be a singer on Duffy's circus, when he was only 10 years of age. So although not born to the show business life, he started very young! However, Paddy himself was very well known throughout the show business fraternity and was an exceptional trapeze artist, trick horse rider and juggler, not to mention a famously well-known baritone singer. Together, they raised a family of 5 children, who have extended family now in the Cahir area.

As previously mentioned, Agnes had a thirst for knowledge and writing. She had numerous forays into the literary world, but her love of poetry, especially, started from a very tender age. When she was pre-teen, she would write little poetry notes to herself but destroy them immediately, before someone found one, to avoid embarrassment! This "process" carried on throughout her teenage years until finally she gathered the courage, many years later, to send some into the Irish peoples magazine, *Ireland's Own*. They were published to great reception by the public. This success gave her the confidence to pursue a grander ambition, and she applied to be the Irish correspondent for the British show business paper, *"The World's Fair"*; and to her delight, she was hired!

Agnes' life was an exceptionally different life to most people, and she had the intelligence to appreciate this. She had a very keen interest in

Agnes and Paddy at the
Annual Showman's Dance

the history and tradition of show people in Ireland. She wrote down a lot of this history and in a very personal way, writing about her experiences growing up on a family variety show and circuses in the 1930s and 1940s. This book was never published but will be in the near future.

In line with her love of education and knowledge, at the age of 65, she undertook the exams for the Leaving Certificate in English and History in which she was very successful and received an honours "A" and "B" respectively in both subjects! In fact, she took the exams at the same time as two of her grandchildren, Joanne Whitney and Suzanne Sullivan.

Closing

Although Agnes was born in Carrick-on-Suir, she loved living in Cahir; and her legacy is still there to be seen with many children, grandchildren and even now great grandchildren, living in the town and surrounds. Both she and her husband, Paddy, are buried alongside each other in St. Mary's cemetery.

Agnes, who experienced Ireland as only few can, was a pioneering woman of her day, going to every town and village in the country and entertaining the people in a simpler more uncomplicated time. She was a leader and matriarch to whom so many looked up. She had a keen appreciation of literature and the arts, as well as an understanding of a way of life all but gone now. She has documented it, lived it, and will be lovingly remembered as a true patron of Irish show business. Agnes Sullivan née McCormack - the last of the strolling variety players.

Flying Pigs

Townie girls got work when the circus camped
in Butler's field. Glittery pencils appeared
on the desks of young ones who hitched
up their uniforms, spat into dried-out pots of rouge,
ran messages for fire eaters and jugglers,
pints of milk for the strong man,
aspirins for the knife-throwers.

They fell for the glib talk
of the ringmaster in swallow-tails and sequins,
accepted his invitation to pucker-up in the kissing booth.
Applied make-up for tattooed ladies and tumbling dwarfs.
Spent mornings helping the tricksters to balance
on unicycles, while the snake charmer roped
his torso with pythons from Burma.

And why wouldn't they succumb
to the outlandish and bizarre, those townie girls sick
of sweet-rot damp cottages, half- washed clothes
mouldering on hedges, the slug-fat fingers
and bad breath of junior clerks, groping behind the dancehall?

They were quiet when the menagerie moved
on, skipped school to wave the stripy wagons
into the distance. Scrawled their addresses on pages
ripped from copy-books.
They cogged the homework of sensible girls
who bedded down with malted milk and plain biscuits.
Toughened themselves
for snide remarks about rabbits drawn from top-hats,
flying pigs spotted over Cuckoo Hill.

Margaret Galvin.

Cahir Woman at Navajo Pow Wow
By Mary Beston

Sister Katherine Barrett (Sister Miguel) was the eldest daughter of eleven children of Daniel and Mary Barrett of Rafane, Cahir. She had grown up on a farm with her siblings and loved animals, and she was a keen horse rider. Having completed her education in Cahir Apostolic School, she was professed in the Order of the Blessed Sacrament.

Katherine attended Cahir Apostolic School and left to join the Order of the Blessed Sacrament, Pennsylvania. Her immigration record reveals that she was 16, "of fair complexion, black hair and brown eyes". Her passage had been paid by Mother Drexel, who was the foundress of the order. When asked, "if in possession of $50?" Her answer was "No". The 1935 census lists her residing in rural Bucks County,

Katherine Barrett – Sister Miguel

Pennsylvania and the 1940 census shows her living in New Orleans, Louisiana. It is noted that she had submitted forms for citizenship.

Native Americans

Katherine spent her life working among Native Americans and young black people in Arizona, serving as teacher, principal or director in all of the schools affiliated with her order. She was passionate about her work and one of her great joys was watching her students graduate from college. Katherine had the distinction of becoming the first white woman to attend a Navajo Pow Wow, receiving special permission from her convent to attend.

When asked later in life if she ever regretted her decision to enter the convent, she said that as the oldest of eleven children that she would most likely have been married off to a much older man. She died, aged 90 in 2004 and is buried in Pennsylvania. Her obituary appeared in the newspaper "Navajo Nation".

Sr. Katherine Barrett fifth from left in Back Row with members of her Community in the USA.

The Colonel and the Nurse
Recollections of Days in Cahir Park Lodge
By Mary Caulfield

Over 60 years ago, a young nurse took up employment in Cahir Park Lodge that would have positive repercussions on the life of her employer. The employer in question was Lieutenant-Colonel Richard Butler-Charteris, then approaching his 90th year and the nurse, Wexford born Lily Fielding now, in 2018, approaching her own 90th birthday. Richard was born in 1866. As the eldest of two sons, he inherited the Cahir Estate on the death of his mother Lady Margaret Charteris in 1915. The large house built c.1864, was further extended by Richard with the addition of a billiard room and library. What follows is the story of a young nurse as she recalls the dying days of life in the 'Big House'.

Lily Fielding as a young nurse
(Courtesy of Lily Carew)

On arrival in Cahir Park Lodge Lily found that the Colonel, as he was known to most, was unable to walk and confined to an upstairs bedroom. The first act of this spirited young nurse, much to the Colonel's delight, was to release him from the confines of his upstairs prison. She managed to get him to the top of the stairs and sitting beside him, they came down step by step. His loyal, long serving butler, Paddy Dalton, had a wheelchair waiting at the bottom.

In Cahir Park Lodge, in a world reminiscent of *Upstairs Downstairs*, Lily was witnessing the end of an era. She recalls with fondness her days there, painting a vivid picture of life in the 'Big House'. These were days of elaborate entertaining, when friends came for the shoot and guests dressed up for dinner. Lily occupied a room on the top floor, next to that of the Colonel. Her sleep was often broken by the clanging of bells throughout the house when the Colonel called for assistance during the night. The building was lavishly furnished. One room on the ground floor had a very large Sheraton cabinet filled with Waterford glass. Yet, all that glittered was not gold! The Colonel had a commode fashioned in the style of Sheraton, by his own carpenter at a cost of £20. This veneered item was sold at auction, in 1962, for a much larger sum. The large entrance hall, with its big copper flower container and dinner gong, led to an elaborate dining room beside which was a room referred to as "The Boudoir". This room, filled with furniture specially imported from France, had a wash basin and the aforementioned commode. The purpose of the room was to facilitate guests to freshen up and dress before dinner.

Dining at the Lodge

Up to nine household staff were employed in Cahir Park Lodge at the time. Lily demanded and got £50 per week, much to the annoyance of George Robinson who looked after the Estate's finances. She became very friendly with Miss O'Reilly, the cook, who had come to Cahir with a very good reputation, having previously worked for President Sean T. O'Kelly. Miss O'Reilly lived up to this reputation as she was an excellent cook, even baking special scones which the Colonel, with his new found freedom, fed to the peacocks that graced his lawn. Because of the ingenuity of his young nurse, Colonel Dick, as she called him, could now join his guests at mealtimes in the large, flower filled dining room. Lily recalls up to twenty vases of fresh flowers from the walled garden, being produced by Mr. Kirk, the gardener, each week. Lunch, at 12.30pm, was substantial, with pheasant in season or trout from the river Suir. Often, after a shoot, other gentry from the area, Mr. Alexander "Alec" Smith from Duneske, Cahir, Major Paddy Pole-Carew from Shanbally, Clogheen and Mr Baker from Lismacue, Bansha, would join the Colonel for lunch. Afternoon tea was served at 4.30pm in the drawing room, where sandwiches and Miss O'Reilly's legendary cakes were the order of the day.

Colonel Charteris in spite of his age was fastidious in his dress. A local barber, Mr Patsy Gregg, came regularly to shave him and cut his hair. For dinner, aided by the ever diligent Lily, he dressed in his tails and large bow tie. At 7.00pm, cocktails were served in the Lounge and at 7.30pm, the gong would sound ten strokes for dinner. Dressed in evening wear, Lily sat next to the Colonel at the dinner table where she discreetly controlled his food intake.

The meal consisted of many courses. A hostess trolley was used to convey the main course of beef, lamb, fish, all served with vegetables from the garden. Red wine was always served with the main course. Dessert usually consisted of strawberries and cream, soufflés, trifles or jellies, all prepared under the watchful eye of Miss O'Reilly. The cheese course, usually Stilton, was served with port. Guests then took their port to the lounge where the affairs of the day were discussed. On special occasions, of which there were many, the Colonel would produce champagne from his well stocked cellar.

Walks by the River

The Colonel loved the riverbank according to Lily. Together, the old gentleman and the young nurse travelled the path by the river, stopping along the way to talk to the bailiff about fishing, or calling into Eugene Hevey in the Swiss Cottage, a cottage ornée by the river to discuss fishing flies. Mr Hevey was an expert at tying flies, some of which he exported to England. Then, aided by Paddy Dalton, they travelled further up the hill where the Colonel would visit the Estate farm to admire his prize cattle. However, these outings were not without incident. On one occasion, having taken a woodland path, Lily noticed a man sitting against a tree, his dogs standing guard by his side. On closer inspection, she realized that the man, the Colonel's friend and neighbour, Major Wise, was dead. The Major lived in Rochestown, further along the river. Undaunted, she summoned help, and later she was asked to lay out the body, at the Major's home, Rochestown House. She still has the silk scarf given to her on the occasion by Mrs. Wise.

Sometimes these walks would take them by Cahir Castle, where Mrs Silcock, who lived in a cottage in the grounds, would call out, in her shrill voice, "Now Dick Darling, we must go together down the river fishing". It never happened! Yet, she often joined him for lunch on Sundays.

Often, this brave nurse and her charge ventured further afield. As the Colonel liked going to the races, she would dress him in his tweeds, and with chauffeur, Paddy Dalton, at the wheel, they would head off to Limerick Junction or Gowran Park. At one time, the Colonel owned several racehorses one of which, Ballyheron Wood, won the Irish Derby in 1921. There was one memorable occasion that outshone all others for this young nurse. The Colonel and Lily were invited to the wedding of his friend, Lord Waterford, in Adare Manor, the stylish home of the Earl of Dunraven. The friendship between the latter and the Colonel was long standing. In 1936, the British magazine, *The*

Tatler, published photographs of Colonel Charteris's shoot in Cahir Park. Lord Adare was included in these photographs with other gentry, Major McCalmont, Lord Rossmore and others. In 1957, John de la Poer Beresford, 8th Marquess of Waterford, married Caroline Wyndham-Quin, daughter of the 6th Earl of Dunraven. As one would expect, this wedding turned out to be a lavish affair, with dinner for over one hundred guests. Because Lily accompanied the Colonel, such occasions demanded that she be suitably dressed. Consequently, she had the added expense of a large wardrobe.

Mutual Regard

Lily recalls many acts of kindness by the Colonel. She remembers accompanying him to Clinton's Drapery, in Clonmel, where he had suits made for members of his male household staff, the material bought from Ardfinnan Mill. In winter, he bought warm underwear for workmen and at Christmas, on instructions from the Colonel, Paddy Dalton would fill the car boot with bags of coal, turf and wood for the retired estate workers. Others were given food and bottles of wine.

Lily's days in Cahir Park came to an end when she met and married Fred Carew, going to live in Clonmel. With her first child due, she was no longer able to look after the Colonel's needs. Such was the value he placed on her work and companionship that he offered to fit out a nursery for her forthcoming baby in an upstairs bedroom. Lily declined the offer, but the Colonel continued to write to her after she left. These letters, still in her possession, show how much the Colonel missed his "guardian angel" with phrases like, "you were so angelic to come and look after me". Colonel Richard Charteris lived but a few short years after his young nurse left his employment. He died 1961 and was laid to rest by his wife Pamela's side in Kilcommon cemetery not too far from his beloved riverbank. The mutual regard and respect between the old gentleman and his caring companion is evident from Lily's story. There was a great rapport between the two, and secrets were shared which will remain forever so.

Ellen Conway – Single Mother

By Karol DeFalco

Records indicate that Ellen Conway was born and grew up at Barrack Street, Cahir, and had a childhood similar to other girls. She was raised with brothers and sisters, mourned the death of her father, sponsored her nephew at his baptism, worked as a servant, had a sister who married an English soldier, and experienced the loss of brothers who apparently emigrated. Then her ordinary life changed.

In 1895 at about age twenty-seven, Ellen was unmarried and pregnant. Unlike others, this mother-to-be did not marry. She did not emigrate to England or the U.S.A with her baby bump, neither did she give birth to her baby to have it taken away never to be seen again. She was not placed in a Magdalene Laundry. She went the road less travelled in that time and became a single parent.

Ellen gave birth to her son on 7 July 1896 at the Clogheen Workhouse which serviced the town of Cahir. On his birth certificate, she is listed as a servant; and the informant was Michael Burke, Master of the Workhouse. Ellen named her son John; he was baptised the following day. No father's name is listed on either the birth or baptism record.

Similarly, on 3 December 1899, Ellen gave birth to her second son, also at the workhouse. He was named Christopher and baptised the same day. Again, no father's name appears on either document.

Residents of the workhouse did not warrant names on Irish censuses. Instead, they were listed by their initials -- listing surnames first. The 1901 Census of Clogheen Workhouse shows the following two consecutive entries:

C.E., 33, female, Roman Catholic, single, servant, reads & writes,
born Tipperary, from Cahir
C.C., 1, male, Roman Catholic, born Tipperary, from Cahir

It is thought that these two entries refer to Ellen Conway and Christopher.

Apparently, Christopher resided at the workhouse for some years, beginning his education at the workhouse school. It's possible that Ellen was at the workhouse during those years also.

Research indicates that Ellen's father died in 1888 and her mother in 1902. Her older sister married and moved to Co. Waterford; her younger sister married a soldier and moved back and forth to England, and her brothers appear to have emigrated. There wouldn't have been much family support for Ellen and her sons.

Christopher Conway

On 20 July 1908, Christopher enrolled at the National School at Skeheenarinky, Cahir. The school register reports that Christopher was a transfer student from Clogheen workhouse school. The register also shows that in that year, Christopher was residing at Coolagarranroe with a farmer and the farmer's family.

All three Conways – mother and sons – are recorded in Coolagarranroe in the 1911 Census. In that census, Ellen, unmarried, and John are listed as 40 and 15 years of age, respectively, and are farm servants with the Sheely family, while Christopher was a farm servant with the English family.

The Sheely house, in which Ellen Conway was residing while working as a farm servant, was made of stone with a slate roof. It had five front windows and seven rooms. The outbuildings included a stable, two cow houses, a dairy, two piggeries, a fowl house, and a barn.

The Conways appear to have stayed in Coolagarranroe a few more years. The sons left in the 1910s, but local people have said that Ellen remained in Coolagarranroe until at least 1936. She may even have stayed there years longer, before relocating to Co. Cork; but what became of her sons?

Christopher's Military Career

According to Sean Ua Cearnaigh, whose father resided at Coolagarranroe and was a childhood friend of 'Christy's', Christopher joined the British Army in 1915. Sean has written:

> Whether it was a desire to escape from his unrewarding life as a farm labourer, a wish to see foreign countries, or a belief that a war effort by Irishmen would hasten Home Rule, the reasons for his enlisting are not clear. In any event, he regretted his decision almost immediately and soon parted company with the army.

Ua Cearnaigh reports that Conway feigned insanity in order to get discharged from the military station at Kilworth.

According to an account at Ireland's Bureau of Military History, Chris – while on leave from the British Army - deserted the army and became a Republican in Ireland's War of Independence, being a regular member of the No. 2 Flying Column of the 3rd Tipperary Brigade. After the War of Independence, Chris joined the Free State Army and is listed in the military census of 1922:

> *Tubbercurry (Co. Sligo), 3rd Western Division*
> *Christopher Conway, 22, single, Roman Catholic*
> *Address: Coolagarranroe, Burncourt, Clogheen*
> *Next of kin: Mrs Conway, Coolagarranroe*

The reference to his mother as 'Mrs' Conway is puzzling. It's possible that Ellen Conway married a Mr Conway sometime after the 1911 Census, in which she is listed as unmarried, and before the 1922 military census; but no such marriage record has been found. It's also possible that Christopher referred to his mother as Mrs to cover the details of his birth.

Again according to Sean Ua Cearnaigh, Christopher ...

> ...joined the Free State army and served at the Curragh and later in Clonmel and Cahir Barracks. At this time nearly all his old comrades were on the anti-Treaty side. Joining the Free State army was a decision Kit soon ruefully regretted. He found himself utterly out of sympathy with his Treatyite associates. All his friends were on the other side and his heart was very much with their cause. ... Finally, however, Kit deserted. Finding it impossible to continue to remain

a member of an army he opposed he deserted in the late autumn of 1922. Aided by my father and other republican friends he managed to escape to Dublin. Soon after his arrival there he made contact with the anti-Treaty group and fought on the Republican side during the remaining months of the Civil War.

Having deserted from the Free State Army, Chris would have been 'a wanted man'.   Some say that he fled to the U.S.A. because of activities he may have been engaged in during these difficult times. No immigration record has been found, but this may be because Christopher may have boarded the ship under a different name to escape detection and capture for deserting the army and/or for his role in the Civil War and his activities in the Free State Army.

Nevertheless, Christopher's name is found in the 1930 Census of New York, taken on April 7th:

128 W. 102nd Street, Manhattan
Christopher Conway, boarder, 30, single, born in Ireland, arrived in 1923, has filed papers for citizenship, occupation = cable operative with Manleys

In Ireland in the early 1930s, Eamon de Valera was preparing to take over as head of government. Having an anti-treaty colleague about to become head of government may have made it easier for Christopher to return to Ireland. In the early 1930s, he was in Dublin, often using the name Kit rather than Christy.

Bob Doyle, who shared a room with Conway in Dublin's Capel Street, says he first met Kit in 1931 when Kit recruited the teenage Doyle into the 1st Dublin Battalion of the IRA: "I found lodgings...and learned that Kit was a well known IRA activist who was regarded as a legend in his native Tipperary, he had fought against the Black and Tans and later against the Treaty. In one action, a bullet went through his mouth and left him with a slight lisp. Kit Conway was a model instructor and a strict upholder of military discipline. He recruited me to the 1st Dublin Battalion of the IRA. We used to train in the fields of the Dublin suburb of Cabra West...an expert in handling a machine gun, he was able to disassemble any one of them with his eyes closed."

Spain

In July 1936, the Spanish Civil War broke out, the Republicans against the Nationalists led by General Francisco Franco who was supported by the Catholic Church. At that time, applying for travel from Ireland to Spain was not allowed. Kit, wanting to get to Spain to fight with the Republicans, applied for a passport in October 1936 stating that he would be travelling to Europe and visiting Lourdes.

According to "Irish Socialist Volunteers in the Spanish Civil War" (Wikipedia), the first men left Ireland for Spain in December 1936, travelling through Great Britain and France, becoming part of the International Brigades in Spain. Training took place; then in January 1937, the Irish contingent was moved to the Jara Valley.

In February, the Irish were involved in the Battle of Jarama. From David Convery's publication comes the following:

> No. 1 Company under the command of ex-IRA member Kit Conway from County Tipperary, initially held in reserve, was sent up the line to give much needed experienced assistance. The attack by the Nationalists was unrelenting. Man after man fell, and the companies were decimated. No. 4 Company fell back, as did No. 3. The ridge, now held mostly by No. 1 Company, came under a constant heavy fire, the 'thin grass and weeds on the crest of the hill were being slowly mown down, as if a gigantic scythe was passing and repassing, by bullets from the machine-guns of the Moors and machine-guns of the Germans.' The situation on the hill was frantic, as described by Jim Prendergast: "My rifle is soon burning hot. 'Kit' comes over. I notice his face with lines of sweat running through the dust. He hands me a note. It is from Brigade H.Q. telling us that we must hold out at all costs. . . . I reach the hill-crest where 'Kit' is directing fire. He is using a rifle himself and pausing every while to give instructions. Suddenly, he shouts, his rifle spins out of his hand, and he falls back. . . . His voice is broken with agony. 'Do your best boys, hold on!' Tears glisten in our eyes. . . . 'Kit' is taken away. . . . I see Fascist tanks rolling up the road to the right. The Moors are sweeping us front and flanks. We'll never hold out now. I move to a firing-position. Suddenly, I am lifted off

my feet. Something terrific has hit me in the side. I cannot breathe. . . . In the ambulance I meet 'Kit'. He is in terrible agony, and can talk little. 'How are the rest?' is his constant question . . .

Next morning they told me our great leader was dead.'"

Kit Conway died on 12 February 1937, just weeks after having arrived in Spain. He was thirty-eight years of age. There are monuments to Kit Conway at both Jarama and Burncourt, Cahir, Co. Tipperary. When the Burncourt monument was dedicated in 2005, two of Kit's International Brigades colleagues – Bob Doyle and Michael O'Riordan – were in attendance.

John Conway

The above being the story of Christopher Conway, what became of Ellen's first son, John Conway? We know that he was with his mother, Ellen, in Coolagarranroe in 1911.

By 1919, John was residing in Donnybrook, Dublin and was a labourer. On 23 November 1919, he married Bridget Clinch in Blanchardstown, Dublin. Twelve years later, Bridget, aged thirty-five, died at their home, Mountain View House in Inchicore, a suburb of Dublin. Bridget's death left John with five children, aged 2-9 years. To help care for the children, John took in Bridget Roche, a woman from Mitchelstown, Co. Cork. He married her on 6 December 1931 at Clondalkin, listing his occupation as machine operator. John and Bridget had four children.

Curiously, on both of John Conway's marriage records, he gave his father's name as Michael Conway, a labourer. In an article in a recent edition of the magazine, "Who Do You Think You Are?", the author states that it was not unusual for people born out of wedlock to give made-up names for their fathers to disguise the details about the births. It appears that this is what John did.

A few years later, the news of Kit's 1937 death reached John's home in Inchicore. John's wife, Bridget, formerly from Mitchelstown, wanted to have a mass said for him. However, the priest would not allow the mass. Apparently, this refusal was the result of feeling that those who fought for the Republican cause in Spain were fighting "against the church".

Likewise, similar lore exists in Co. Tipperary. It is said that when the people in Ellen's community learned that Christopher fought "against the church", Ellen was not treated kindly and had to leave the area. Apparently, Kit's Republican colleague, Peadar O'Donnell, who had also fought in Spain, used his influence to find her a home "somewhere in Co. Cork".

Ellen Conway, by this time, had lost one son but gained nine grandchildren via John. John's granddaughter, Ann, who lived next door to him in a house he had built for her parents, states: "My grandad John never talked about his family life…We were never allowed to mention Christopher (Kit) Conway because of his (political activities)."

There could be many reasons why John distanced himself from his brother. According to Ann, John was opposed to Kit's political views. Perhaps they were on opposite sides of the Civil War. Perhaps the reason has something to do with Kit's time in Spain. As indicated above, some Irish felt that if the church was supporting Franco, then those who fought against Franco were fighting against the church.

John Conway was a man of faith. According to Ann, John visited Jerusalem. He also made generous financial donations to the Oblate Church in Inchicore and did much physical labour for the priests there. In return for his generosity, the Oblate Fathers arranged for John to have an audience with the pope. It appears that John was in Rome in 1954. The family is in possession of an authentication certificate for a relic. The certificate was signed by D. Albertus Parenti on 8 December 1954. Parenti was the Postulator General whose responsibility it was to investigate the lives of those being considered for beatification or canonization and to administer the funds collected for the case. Perhaps John made a donation and was given a relic in appreciation. In any case, one can see why the religious John Conway may have distanced himself from Kit, not allowing Kit's name to be mentioned.

Ann continues, "(My grandfather) went by the name of John Joseph Conway. He became a very successful businessman, in Dublin. He opened an Iron Monger foundry and provided manhole covers across Ireland."

Steve Conway, a grandson of John's, states on the Internet that block machines were also made at the foundry from the 1940s-1970s. He describes those machines as "cheap, simple, human-powered technology". According to Steve, those machines were used not only in Ireland but also in Africa.

John's wife cooked for the foundry workers; and John built a shop for his wife to run and in which the workers could shop. It was "the only shop for many a mile", and he told Bridget that any money she made there was hers.

After years running a successful business, John retired. According to Susan, another of John's granddaughters, the Conway foundry was used to film the television programme, *Strumpet City*. In later years, John and his wife resided in Portlaoise. One day after a fall, John was taken ill and brought to hospital. He died there on 15 January 1981, aged 84. His funeral mass was said at Oblate Church in Inchicore. Granddaughter Susan reported that John "had a big send off. No expense was spared. The coffin was the most expensive looking ever, the outside being beautifully carved with flowers. His removal was extremely well attended, the church was packed. He went out like an emperor!" John Conway, son of Cahir's Ellen Conway, was buried at Dean's Grange Cemetery, Dublin.

A farm labourer from Co. Tipperary raised by a single mother had become a foundry owner and the inventor of block machines! Manhole covers inscribed 'JJ Conway & Sons, Inchicore', can still be seen in the streets of Ireland. Keep your eyes open! In 2016, two plaques engraved "JJ Conway & Sons, Inchicore, Dublin" were sold at auction by Purcell Auctioneers in Birr, Co. Offaly.

John's daughter-in-law related that she met Ellen Conway about 1956-57 in Mitchelstown, Co. Cork, "where Ellen resided" and when Ellen would have been at least eighty-seven years of age. To date, Ellen's death certificate has not been found. At this point, she lies in an unknown grave.

For a woman who found herself unmarried and pregnant; delivering her babies in the workhouse; having no family support; sending her younger son off to his first days of primary school - at the workhouse; contracting out to farm families for a place to stay; worrying about her younger son joining the British army, then the Irish War for Independence, then the Civil War, then his emigration to America and returning - only to go off to another war in Spain; suffering the death of that son without having his body returned to her; relocating from her community; experiencing trouble finding housing; and having one son disavow the other, this Cahir woman's life was filled with difficulties.

One wonders if Ellen ever had the opportunity to be proud of John's accomplishments as a businessman and inventor. One wonders how she would feel today, knowing that monuments are dedicated to Kit, not only in Burncourt but also in Spain. These influential men, a revolutionary and an inventor, were sons of Ellen Conway – a single mother from Cahir.

Sources:

Irish birth, baptism, marriage, and death records

Irish Census records

USA Census records

Ann Jadwat; Malaga,Spain; granddaughter of John Conway

Convery, David, *https://thedustbinofhistory.wordpress.com/2013/02/20/ theres-a-valley-in-spain-commemorating-the-battle-of-jarama/*

Corcoran, John, "Memorial to Kit Conway Unveiled", *An Phoblacht,* 23 June 2005

Ua Cearnaigh, Sean, "Barton and Conway", *Ireland's Own Centenary Souvenir Edition,* 2018

Ua Caernaigh, Sean "Kit Conway – Hero of Jarama", *Irish Democrat, February* 1987

Bureau of Military History

Skeheenarinky National School Registers

1922 Military Census of Ireland

Conway, Steve, grandson of John Conway,   *steveconway.wordpress.com*

"Irish Socialist Volunteers in the Spanish Civil War", Wikipedia

Lillian Grubb Metge - Suffragette
By the Editors and Ed O'Riordan

On the night of 31 July 1914, an explosion caused serious damage to Lisburn Cathedral in County Antrim. The chancel window was shattered in the blast and suspicion soon fell on a group of militant suffragettes; suffragette leaflets having been found strewn amongst the rubble.[1] The reverberations caused by the explosion were felt throughout the island of Ireland and rippled through Cahir, Co. Tipperary. Four women were arrested and brought to trial for the offence, one of whom was the daughter of Cahir man, Richard Cambridge Grubb.

Richard C. Grubb, born in 1841, was the son of mill owner Richard Grubb, J.P., and Maria Louisa Garratt of Cahir. They lived at Cahir Abbey. On 7 September 1870, he married Harriet Richardson, youngest daughter of Jonathan Richardson, Esq., J.P., Lambeg House, Lisburn, County Antrim.[2] Following a few days honeymoon in Scotland,[3] the couple travelled to Cahir and their arrival was announced in the 'Fashionable Intelligence' column of the *Tipperary Free Press*

Lillian Grubb Metge
(National Library of Ireland)

on 20 September 1870. Ten days later, Richard Cambridge Grubb and his wife, Harriet, were part of the 'brilliant gathering' at a ball in Clonmel which was held to 'inaugurate the festivities of the season'.[4] The couple made their home in County Antrim where their daughter, Lillian Margaret, was born in June 1871. A brother for Lillian was born in 1873.

It is safe to presume that Lillian occasionally travelled with her parents to Cahir Abbey, Cahir, to visit her grandfather who lived until 1886. In 1880, the *Waterford Standard* reported that Mrs. Richard Cambridge Grubb (Lillian's mother) had caught several salmon at Cahir. The article opened with a rather prophetic sentence - "The ladies are beating us all out everywhere."[5]

---

1   www.navanhistory.ie (The website of Navan Historical Society) and *History Ireland* November-December 2014
2   *Derry Journal*, 10 September 1870
3   *Newry Telegraph* 13 September 1870
4   *Tipperary Free Press*, 30 September 1870
5   *Waterford Standard*, 1 May 1880

In 1893, Lillian Margaret Grubb married Robert Henry Metge of Athlumney House, Navan, County Meath.[6] After just eight years of married life at Athlumney, Lillian was a widow. She returned to Co Antrim where the 1901 census shows her living with her daughters. By "1912 she was an active and able agitator and a leading voice of Irish Suffrage".[7] She was active in two suffrage organisations but later resigned from both because she "intended to play a more militant role". In April 1914, her parting words to the Irish Women's Suffrage Federation were "I have never done a militant act, but whatever the future may hold, the only possible dishonour would be in having seen the vision, yet turned back."[8]

One month later, Lillian "was part of a 200 strong deputation that charged George V as he entered Buckingham Palace. She was arrested and witnessed the police brutally beating the suffragettes with batons. The incident had a strong effect on her: 'I see now how militants are made'."[9]

Women being arrested following the incident at Buckingham Palace. Lillian Metge is the woman (with tall hat) in the middle of the photo. (Courtesy of *History Ireland Magazine*)

And then came the dynamiting of the Lisburn Cathedral on 31 July 1914. While under arrest, Mrs. Metge, like others, went on hunger-strike for which she was later awarded a medal 'for valour' for participating in a 'hunger strike' on 10 August 1914.[10] At the conclusion of the trial for the bombing, during which the defendants caused consternation in the courtroom by their constant interruptions of proceedings, things 'looked bleak for the women' but due to the 'crisis in Europe' it was announced that the "Home Secretary remitted all suffragette sentences and approved the release of

6 *Northern Whig*, 3 August 1893. (Lillian was second wife of Robert Henry Metge who was a son of John Charles Metge and a nephew of Peter Ponsonby Metge, Athlumney House. From Peter Ponsonby Metge who died in 1873, Robert Henry, who was from nearby Sion House, inherited Athlumney. www.dumville.org)

7 Spink auction house, London. *www.spink.com*

8 *History Ireland*, November-December 2014

9 Ciarán Toal, *History Ireland* November-December 2014

10 Wording on Medal. (This medal was recently sold by Spink of London for £8,500)

any prisoners."[11] Lillian Grubb Metge, daughter of a Cahir man, died in Dublin in 1954 and is buried at Deansgrange cemetery in Dublin. According to Ciarán Toal, she was "arguably, Ireland's most militant suffragette".[12]

https://www.antiquestradegazette.com/news/2018/medal-awarded-to-the-militant-irish-suffragette-who-tried-to-blow-up-a-cathedral-comes-to-auction/

Sold by Spink of London in July 2018 for £8,500.
(While the spelling 'Lilian' is used on the medal, all records seem to use 'Lillian'.)

(We are indebted to Jerry Sheehan of Cahir
for drawing our attention to this remarkable suffragette.)

---

11   Ciarán Toal, op. cit
12   Ciarán Toal, op. cit.

Take up your responsibilities and be prepared to go your own way
depending for safety on your own courage,
your own truth, and your own common sense.

Artist: Aislinn O'Keeffe

The drawing, on wallpaper, of Cumann na mBan women marching explores the ways in which women were pushed back into the domestic sphere after independence, their contributions erased from public record.

Front Cover Illustration 'Born Seeing' - Artist Alice Maher

Alice Maher is a visual artist, born in Kilmoyler, Cahir in 1956. Her art spans painting, drawing, photography, sculpture and film. Her work touches on a wide range of subjects often challenging and expanding mythic and vernacular narratives. Over the years, she has sought to reclaim and install images and histories of the female at the centre of her practice. She has exhibited widely in Ireland and internationally and is represented in many public collections including The Museum of Fine Arts Boston, the British Museum, The Hammond Museum L.A., The Georges Pompidou Centre Paris, and the Hugh Lane Municipal Gallery of Modern Art. She represented Ireland at the 22nd Sao Paolo Biennial. In 2012, The Irish Museum of Modern Art presented a retrospective exhibition of the artist's career which included many of her iconic works. She is an elected member of Aosdána, the RHA, and a founder member of the Artist's Campaign to Repeal the Eight Amendment.